The

COMPLETE

IDIOT'S

GUIDE TO

Internet
E-Mail

by Paul McFedries

D1450282

que

A Division of Macmillan Publishing
A Prentice Hall Macmillan Company
201 W. 103rd Street, Indianapolis, IN 46290

This book is dedicated to all those books whose dedications are fourteen words long.

©1995 Que® Corporation

International Standard Book Number: 1-56761-596-1

Library of Congress Catalog Card Number: 94-73198

97 96 95   8 7 6 5 4 3 2 1

Interpretation of the printing code: the rightmost number of the first series of numbers is the year of the book's printing; the rightmost number of the second series of numbers is the number of the book's printing. For example, a printing code of 95-1 shows that the first printing of the book occurred in 1995.

Printed in the United States of America

Publisher
Marie Butler-Knight

Product Development Manager
Faithe Wempen

Acquisitions Manager
Barry Pruett

Managing Editor
Elizabeth Keaffaber

Senior Production Editor
Michelle Shaw

Copy Editor
San Dee Phillips

Cover Designer
Scott Cook

Designer
Barbara Kordesh

Illustrations
Judd Winick

Indexer
Brad Herriman

Production Team
*Brad Chinn, Angela Calvert, Dan Caparo, Kim Cofer,
Jennifer Eberhardt, David Garratt, Joe Millay, Erika Millen,
Kim Mitchell, Beth Rago, Karen Walsh, Robert Wolf*

*Special thanks to Discovery Computing Inc. for ensuring the technical
accuracy of this book.*

Contents at a Glance

Contents

11 Getting Graphical with Eudora 119

12 Taming Pegasus Mail 135

Introduction

It's official: the Internet is now a Big Deal. Television shows by the dozen talk about it; magazines as diverse as *Time*, *Business Week*, and *GQ* gush over it; newspapers from every state in the union send out bemused "technology" reporters to figure out just what the heck is happening out there. Meanwhile, millions of ordinary citizens who wouldn't wear a pocket protector if you paid them, and whose heads are decidedly unpointy, are flocking to the Internet like so many swallows heading for Capistrano.

And what do these people find when they get there? Well, on the positive side, they find truckloads of information on just about every topic under the sun; they find lots of like-minded people hanging around in Usenet newsgroups and Internet Relay Chat forums; and they find files located in the far-flung corners of the world that they can zap onto their hard drives in just a few seconds or minutes.

Unfortunately, they also run smack into the Internet's all-too glaring shortcomings:

➤ The Net (which is the aficionado's hip short form for Internet) has umpteen different services, and it's confusing trying to figure out (and then remember) what they all do. Why, there's FTP, Gopher, the World Wide Web, Telnet, WAIS, and many more. Keeping it all straight is a full-time job.

➤ Once you've figured out which service you want to use, then you face the often-daunting task of learning how to use all the different software packages that let you access the service. Baby, this ain't no Infobahn.

➤ Finally, once you have a handle on the software, you're then faced with the nontrivial job of actually finding the information you need.

In short, the sheer size of the Internet makes most of us feel like complete idiots, but there's a way to overcome these hurdles and knock the Net down to size: just take it one service at a time. Pick out an Internet feature that looks interesting, get comfy with it, and then move on to the next one.

Welcome to The Complete Idiot's Guide to Internet E-Mail!

And that, really, is what we're up to in this book. *The Complete Idiot's Guide to Internet E-Mail* breaks off a single, manageable chunk of the Net—the e-mail system—and holds it up to the light so you can get a good look. Don't sweat it if you've never used e-mail before. We'll begin at the beginning so you'll be comfortable with the basic e-mail concepts and terms, and then we'll build on this knowledge so you'll be able to get exactly what you need out of the e-mail system you use. Later chapters will then show you how to leverage your newfound e-mail know-how to get the most out of the Internet.

Does this mean you'll have to wade through interminable technical treatises, memorize all kinds of minutiae, and learn the ins and outs of networking? Not on your life! My experience has been that most people learn best when they're taught just what they need to know, *not* everything there is to know. So, in that spirit, I'm going to assume right off the bat that you're a busy person who just wants to get up to speed with this e-mail thing and then get on with the rest of your life.

This book, in the interests of simplicity, also makes a couple of other assumptions. First, I'm going to assume that you and your computer are quite familiar with each other by now, and that things like the mouse and keyboard no longer make you break out into a cold sweat. If you're not quite there yet, may I suggest checking out *The Complete Idiot's Guide to PCs* by Joe Kraynak, or *The Complete Idiot's Guide to Windows*, by some geek named Paul McFedries.

Second, I'm going to assume that you've managed to survive the often painful process of setting up an Internet connection and that you're on at least a first-name basis with the major Internet services. Chapter 2, "An Introduction to the Internet," does contain some Internet basics, but it's really only a quick review, not a true tutorial. If the Internet is completely new to you, it may be a good idea to pick up a copy of *The Complete Idiot's Guide to the Internet* by Peter Kent.

What to Expect in This Book

For most of us, time is money when it comes to our Internet connections. So, for most topics, I'd recommend reading the relevant sections *before* you jump online. This way you won't rush through the material and give yourself brain cramps. However, for those times when you *are* reading while connected, I've set up the book so you can get the info you need quickly and then get back to the action. Also, each of the chapters is self-contained, so you can browse around at your leisure. In the few places where you do need some background info from another part of the book, I'll include a note telling you the relevant chapter to head for. Just so you know what to expect, here's a short summary of the book's structure.

Part 1: E-Mail Made Easy

The opening seven chapters of the book give you the basics of e-mail. Chapter 1, "The Least You Need to Know," takes you through a Top 10 List of frequently-asked e-mail questions. Chapter 2, "An Introduction to the Internet," gives you some background info on the Net that will make your e-mail travels easier. Chapter 3, "A Brief E-Mail Primer," gives you the lowdown on e-mail and explains fundamental e-mail concepts, such as addresses and the different parts of a mail message. Chapter 4, "You Send Me: Some Stuff About Sending E-Mail," gives you the skinny on topics such as message etiquette, exchanging mail with other e-mail systems, and how to send nontext files as attachments to your messages. Chapter 5, "Learning the Lingo: E-Mail Jargon and Acronyms," translates some common Internet and e-mail words, acronyms, and symbols into plain English. Chapter 6, "Stopping E-Snoops with E-Mail Security," tells you how to keep your private messages private. Finally, Chapter 7, "Where's Waldo (and Wanda, Too)? Finding an Address," takes you through the sometimes tricky process of finding someone's e-mail address.

Part 2: A Guide to Popular E-Mail Software

To join in the e-mail fun, you'll need some software designed to handle the basic e-mail chores of reading messages, responding to them, and composing your own missives. The chapters in Part 2 take you through eleven of today's most popular e-mail programs: the UNIX mail program, Pine, Elm, Eudora, Pegasus Mail, Chameleon Mail, Air Mail, and the e-mail systems available through America Online, CompuServe, Prodigy, and Delphi.

Part 3: E-Surfing: Accessing the Internet Via E-Mail

The Internet e-mail system is mostly used for sending messages between individuals across town, across the country, or across the International Date Line. However, that's not all e-mail is good for—not by a long shot. The chapters in Part 3 take you through a wealth of other Internet services that are available through the mail. For starters, you'll get the scoop on standard services, such as mailing lists (Chapter 19), finding and retrieving files (Chapter 20), and Usenet (Chapter 21). You'll also learn how to fax documents via e-mail (Chapter 22), play e-mail games (Chapter 23), and access things such as personal ads, a movie database, an online dictionary, and lots more (Chapter 24).

The Complete Idiot's Guide to Internet E-Mail also includes a glossary that translates the arcane jargon of the Internet into plain English, as well as a tear-out reference card that gives you at-a-glance access to some handy e-mail facts.

Features of This Book

The Complete Idiot's Guide to Internet E-mail is designed so you can get the information you need fast and then get on with your life. To that end, I'll use certain conventions throughout the book. For example, if you ever need to type something, it will appear like this:

type this

When I show you what something is supposed to look like on-screen, I'll put it in a "computer font" that looks

`like this`

Some e-mail software packages use particular *key combinations* to access their features. I'll be writing these key combinations by separating the two keys with a plus sign (+). For example, I may say something such as "press **Ctrl+S** to save a message." The "Ctrl+S" part means you hold down the **Ctrl** key, tap the **S** key, and then release **Ctrl**. (Don't worry: you are in no way required to memorize these keyboard contortions to become a competent e-mail user.)

Speaking of keyboards, you should note that I'll often tell you to do a certain thing and then "press **Enter**." If you're using a terminal that doesn't have an **Enter** key, just press the **Return** key instead.

Also, look for the following icons in sidebars that'll help you learn just what you need to know.

 There are always dangerous ways to do things on a computer; when you see this frightened-looking fellow, you'll find out how to avoid them.

 This geeky-looking fellow in fact offers up plain-English translations of e-mail and Internet-speak.

 If you re-arrange the letters in "complete idiot," you end up with "de cool tip time," and that's just what this cool lady gives you. She's full of handy tips that show you easier ways to get things done in e-mail.

 No, this isn't a drawing of me, but when you see this computer-loving guy, you'll also find notes, asides, and technical data about e-mail that you may find interesting, or at least useful. I'll also use these boxes to tell you about Internet sites and locales that contain handy info.

Acknowledgments (Assorted Pats on the Proverbial Back)

The English essayist Joseph Addison once described an editor as someone who "rides in the whirlwind and directs the storm." I don't know if that's true for editors in some of the more sedate publishing nooks (novels and cookbooks and such), but I think it applies perfectly to the rigors of computer book editing. Why? Well, the computer industry (and the Internet in particular) is so fast-paced that any kind of editorial (or authorial) dawdling could mean a book will be obsolete before it even hits the shelves.

The good folks at Que avoid premature book obsolescence by subjecting each manuscript to a barrage of simultaneous edits from a number of specialists (I call it "gang editing"). So a process that normally may take months is knocked down to a few short weeks. This means you get a book that contains timely and relevant information, and a book that has passed muster with some of the sharpest eyes and inner ears in the business. My name may be the only one that appears on the cover, but each of the following people had a big hand in creating what you now hold in your hands:

Barry Pruett—Barry was my Acquisitions Editor, and he's the one who asked me to write this book. (He is, in other words, the one to blame for the whole thing.)

Faithe Wempen—Faithe was my Development Editor for this book, Her job was to make sure the overall structure of the book made sense and to be a sounding board for all my cockamamie ideas.

San Dee Phillips—A writer, as Oscar Wilde said, "can survive everything but a misprint." It was San Dee's job as Copy Editor to ensure that no misprints occur, to clean up my slapdash punctuation, and to rearrange my slipshod sentence structure.

Michelle Shaw—Michelle is the Production Editor and it's her job to get the manuscript ready for the production process where the figures are added in, the little icons and pictures are placed just so, and the whole thing is made to look like a true member of the *Complete Idiot's Guide* family.

Martin Wyatt—Martin was the book's Technical Editor and it was his job to check my facts and to make sure the procedures I tell you to follow won't lead you astray.

Besides the editorial team, there are quite a number of other people to thank. To begin with, a big round of applause to Ted Alspach who provided all the Macintosh information in the book. Also, thanks have to go to e-mail guru Laura Garton for her help gathering e-mail research. Thanks, as well, to my friends Ellen Worling and Paul Jones who let me perform e-mail experiments on them. A huge hug goes out to Karen Hammond for taking me on a post-book trip to beautiful Vancouver. And, last but by no stretch of the imagination least, I'd also like to thank the untold numbers of Net denizens who were only too happy to proffer comments, ideas, advice, and laughs.

Part 1
E-Mail Made Easy

There are two kinds of Net citizens: those who get online and stay there for the long haul, and those who merely poke around for a while, quickly lose interest, and are never heard from again. The problem with the dabbling, dilettantish folks is that they dive in without learning a few basics. Without even a minimal base to stand on, enthusiasm quickly goes down the tube.

Part 1 will help you avoid the ignominy of such a miserable destiny by giving you a solid e-mail education. Chapter 1 answers ten of the most common questions asked by e-mail newcomers. Chapter 2 provides you with an introduction to the Internet as a whole, followed by a primer on the e-mail system (Chapter 3). Chapter 4 gives you some information on sending e-mail—including the all-important e-mail etiquette—and then we get into jargon (Chapter 5) and security (Chapter 6). Finally, Chapter 7 tells you how to find e-mail addresses of the rich, famous, poor, and unknown.

Chapter 1

The Least You Need to Know

I have a friend who insists on telling me the "good parts" of all the movies he sees, thus ruining these scenes for me when *I* get around to seeing the film. I've tried to stop him, but you know how it is: some people are just plain incorrigible. If, like me, you prefer not to know the good bits beforehand, then you may want to skip this chapter.

On the other hand, if you're someone who likes nice, neat summaries that capture the gist of whatever topic you're dealing with, then, hey, have I got a chapter for you! What I'll be doing is running through a Top Ten List of the questions that new e-mail users ask most. Each of these questions is answered in more detail in other parts of the book, but this chapter gives you some snappy answers to satisfy your curiosity.

What Is Electronic Mail?

Electronic mail (or *e-mail*, as it's normally shortened to) is just a message that's composed, sent, and read electronically (hence the name). With regular mail, you write out your message (letter, postcard, whatever) and drop it off at the post office. The postal service then delivers the message and the recipient reads it. E-mail operates basically the same way, except that everything happens electronically. You compose your message using e-mail software, send it over the lines that connect the Internet's networks, and the recipient uses an e-mail program to read the message.

For a more detailed look at e-mail, see Chapter 3, "A Brief E-Mail Primer."

How Does E-Mail Know How to Get Where It's Going?

Everybody who's connected to the Internet is assigned a unique *e-mail address*. In a way, this address is a lot like the address of your house or apartment because it tells everyone else your exact location on the Net. So anyone who wants to send you an e-mail message just tells their e-mail program the appropriate address and runs the Send command. The Internet takes over from there and makes sure the missive arrives safely.

For the lowdown on how Internet addresses work, be sure to read Chapter 3, "A Brief E-Mail Primer."

How Do I Know Which E-Mail Software to Use?

Finding the e-mail program that's right for you is really a matter of trial and error. Since most e-mail software is free (that's right—totally gratis), you can afford to try different programs until you find one you like. Here are some guidelines to get you started:

➤ If UNIX is your platform of choice (or necessity), try the Mail program that comes built-in with most UNIX systems (see Chapter 8). Most UNIX networks also feature the programs Pine (Chapter 9) and Elm (Chapter 10), so you can try these out as well.

➤ Windows users have a wide selection, but Eudora (Chapter 11) and Pegasus Mail (Chapter 12) are the two most popular.

➤ The DOS world doesn't have a wealth of choices but there are versions of Pegasus Mail (Chapter 12) and Pine (Chapter 9) you can check out.

➤ The Mac mavens in the crowd have choices similar to those enjoyed by Windows types. Again, though, choosy Mac users choose Eudora (Chapter 11) and Pegasus Mail (Chapter 12).

➤ Many people use one of the suites of Internet applications that are now available. In this case, you're probably better off sticking with the mail program that comes with the suite, since the various programs are designed to work with one another. The most popular suites right now are Internet Chameleon (Chapter 13) and Internet In A Box (Chapter 14).

➤ Finally, if you access the Net through one of the major commercial online services, you can just use the built-in e-mail system that the service provides. This book covers the e-mail systems of America Online (Chapter 15), CompuServe (Chapter 16), Prodigy (Chapter 17), and Delphi (Chapter 18).

What's This Netiquette Stuff I Keep Hearing About?

The Net is a huge, unwieldy mass with no central "powers-that-be" that can dictate content or standards. This is, for the most part, a good thing because it means there's no censorship and no one can wield authority arbitrarily. To prevent this organized chaos from degenerating into mere anarchy, however, a set of guidelines has been put together over the years. These guidelines are known, collectively, as *netiquette* (*network etiquette*), and they offer suggestions on the proper way to interact with the Internet's denizens. You can think of netiquette as a sort Emily Post/Miss Manners guide to proper Net behavior. To give you a taste of what I mean, here are some netiquette highlights to consider:

➤ Keep your messages brief and to the point, and make sure you clean up any spelling slips or grammatical gaffes before shipping it out.

➤ Make sure the Subject lines of your messages are detailed enough so they explain what your message is all about.

➤ Don't SHOUT by writing your missives entirely in uppercase letters.

➤ Don't bother other people by sending them test messages. If you must test a program, send a message to yourself.

➤ Don't quote another person's e-mail prose without their permission, except if you're responding to their message.

➤ When replying to a message, be sure to quote enough of the original message to put your reply into the proper context.

To sink your teeth into more netiquette niceties, head to Chapter 4, "You Send Me: Some Stuff About Sending E-Mail."

What's a Flame?

The vast majority of e-mail correspondence is civil and courteous, but with millions of participants all over the world, it's inevitable that some folks will rub each other the wrong way. When this happens, the combatants may exchange emotionally charged, caustic, often obscene messages called *flames*. When enough of these messages change hands, an out-and-out *flame war* develops. These usually burn themselves out after a while, and then the participants can get back to more interesting things.

There are many more flame facts in Chapter 5, "Learning the Lingo: E-Mail Jargon and Acronyms."

What Are These :-) Symbols I Keep Seeing?

One of the problems with written communication (especially for people who don't express themselves in writing very well, or for whom English is not their native tongue) is that it's easy to be misunderstood. In face-to-face conversation, a smile, wink, or change in voice inflection alerts the other person that you're being humorous, wry, sarcastic, or whatever. This is a lot harder to accomplish in an e-mail message, so several *smileys* (or *emoticons*) have been developed over the years. Smileys are symbol combinations designed to let everyone know your current feelings. For example, to let people know you're being humorous, you'd use the following smiley: :-). (To get the full effect, tilt your head to the left.) Other smileys can let people know you're sad :-(or winking ;-). You'll find lots more in Chapter 5, "Learning the Lingo: E-Mail Jargon and Acronyms."

My Friends Use a Different E-Mail System. Can I Still Send Them Mail?

Sure! As e-mail treads its inevitable course towards universality, most of the current crop of mail systems have built *gateways* so they can exchange dispatches with the Internet. So, in most cases, sending a message to a different system is a simple matter of adjusting the e-mail address accordingly. I provide the details for exchanging mail with several systems in Chapter 4, "You Send Me: Some Stuff About Sending E-Mail." If you need to bone up on Internet addressing, the place to be is Chapter 3, "A Basic E-Mail Primer."

Is E-Mail Secure?

In a word, no. The Net's open architecture allows programmers to write interesting and useful new Internet services, but it also allows unscrupulous snoops to lurk where they don't belong. In particular, the e-mail system has two problems: it's not that hard for someone else to read your e-mail, and it's fairly easy to forge an e-mail address. If security is a must for you, then you'll want to create an industrial-strength password for your home directory, use encryption for your most sensitive messages, and use an anonymous remailer when you need to send something incognito. This is all covered in detail in Chapter 6, "Stopping E-Snoops with E-Mail Security."

What's a Mailing List?

A mailing list is a system that sends out regular e-mail messages to its subscribers. Each list covers a specific topic, and there are dozens of lists to choose from. You may also hear them called LISTSERVs, since that's the most popular brand of list. To learn everything you need to know about mailing lists, check out Chapter 19, "Messing Around with Mailing Lists."

What Else Can I Do with E-Mail?

Most people only use the Internet e-mail system to fire dispatches back and forth with their buddies and coworkers, but these people are missing out on half the fun because you can use e-mail to access all kinds of other Internet services. You can order files from other computers (see Chapter 20), read Usenet (Chapter 21), access Gopher and the World Wide Web (Chapter 24), fax documents (Chapter 22), and even play games (Chapter 23).

Chapter 2

An Introduction to the Internet

In This Chapter

➤ A prosaic definition of the Internet

➤ A more useful definition of the Internet

➤ A look at some Net services

➤ Lots of useful background info that should make your e-mail travails a bit more comprehensible

Before we can appreciate how the Internet e-mail system works, we need to step back a bit and look at the big picture: the Internet itself. What is this thing we call the Net? What good is it, really? How does it affect you? What kind of stuff can you do with it? This chapter provides the answers to all of these queries and more. The tidbits you glean here should serve you in good stead when we get down to e-mail brass tacks in Chapter 3.

The Internet Nitty-Gritty

First off, let's get the boring definition of the Internet out of the way: The Internet is (yawn) an international collection of networks.

Okay, so what's a network?

Good question. A *network* is a collection of two or more computers (usually dozens or hundreds) connected via special cables so they can share stuff, such as files and printers. These networks are typically owned by large organizations, such as universities, research labs, and corporations. The Internet's job, in a nutshell, is to connect these networks using high-speed phone lines, fiber-optic cables, or, occasionally, satellite links.

Hmmm. So could you say that the Internet is a connected collection of collected connections?

Well, you could say that, but you'd just make everyone's head hurt. A network of networks is probably the simplest way to look at it. If an analogy would help, think of the Net as a giant city where the houses are computers. A neighborhood where the houses are connected with side streets is like an individual network connected via cables. In turn, each neighborhood is connected to other neighborhoods via larger roads and avenues or, for longer trips, by highways and expressways. The point is that in any city you can get from your house to any other house by traveling along a particular set of streets, roads, and highways.

The Internet works the same way: you can "travel" to other computers on the Net by "following" the various communications lines that make up the Net's infrastructure. (The real good news is that you can do this even if, like me, you have a lousy sense of direction. You just tell your software where you want to go and it will pick out the best route automatically, behind the scenes.)

Sounds good, but what if I don't belong to one of these big-time schools, labs, or corporations that have their networks jacked in to the Internet?

Ah, that's where the *access providers* come in. These are businesses that set up an Internet connection and then sell access to any Dick or Jane who needs it. You pay a fee (it's often an hourly rate, but you can get monthly or yearly fees that give you so many hours per month), dial in with your modem, and start surfing.

Redefining the Internet

This dull "network of networks" definition is okay for starters, but it really doesn't describe the Internet as it exists today, or capture the diversity and utility (or the frustration) of this most complex of human creations. It also tells us nothing about why the Net holds such fascination for computer pros and amateurs alike. Here, then, is a more realistic definition of the Internet:

The Internet is a means of communication. This is the big one for our purposes in this book. Many Internet types are only interested in sending mail back and forth between their friends and colleagues (and even complete strangers). I'll talk more about this later in this chapter (and, indeed, throughout the rest of this book).

The Internet is an information resource. To say the least. The Internet has literally thousands and thousands of computers that are jammed to the hilt with documents, books, pictures, and other information resources. Whether you're researching a thesis or just have an unquenchable thirst for knowledge, the Internet has something for everyone. (Be forewarned, however, that because these resources are so vast and so poorly organized, the patience of a saint is a real asset when looking for things on the Net.)

The Internet is a warehouse. If you scour your own computer, you'll probably find a few hundred or even a few thousand files scattered here and there. Imagine all those files multiplied by the millions of Net computers and you get some idea of the massive numbers of documents, graphics, sounds, and programs stored around the Internet. Happily, there are a number of tools (some of which I describe later in this chapter) that you can use to locate and grab these files.

The Internet is a community. Behind everything you see on the Internet—the messages, the documents, the software—there stands the person (or persons) who created it. Untold numbers of Net enthusiasts have spent countless hours assembling information, writing software, and answering questions. Amazingly, all this toiling in obscurity somehow managed to create a massive structure that works (most of the time) *without* the need for any semblance of central authority or governing body.

Having said that, however, I don't want to be accused of viewing the Net through rose-colored glasses. Any endeavor that boasts millions of participants is bound to attract its fair share of bozos, buttheads, and bellyachers. Hey, that's life; but overall, the Net denizens you'll encounter will be surprisingly helpful and generous, and are only too willing to engage in random acts of senseless kindness.

An Overview of the Internet Services

In Part 3 of this book, I'll be showing you how to use electronic mail as a substitute for various Internet services. In other parts of the book, I'll be showing you how to use these services to get more e-mail info, or to find e-mail software. Just to make sure we're always on the same page, let's review some of the available services you can use to interact with the various parts of the Internet:

FTP Short for File Transfer Protocol, FTP is the most common way to bring files from a particular Net locale onto your computer. You'll almost always use *anonymous* FTP, where you log in to the other computer under the name *anonymous* and you use your e-mail address as your password. Typical FTP instructions will include a *host name* (the Internet name of the computer storing the file; for example, **ftp.microsoft.com**), the *directory* (the file's storage location inside the computer; for example, **/pub/software**), and the name of the file itself.

Usenet Usenet is a collection of topics available for discussion. These discussion groups (or *newsgroups*, as they're normally called) are open to all and sundry, and they cover everything from Amazon women to Zima.

Gopher A Gopher is a system that displays Internet documents and services as menu options. You just select a menu choice and the Gopher will either display a document, another menu, or transfer you to a different gopher system. Gopher descriptions always include an *address* (the Internet location of the gopher system) and one or more menu options to select.

World Wide Web Throughout this book, you'll catch me saying things such as "To find out more about proper e-mail security, see Chapter 6, "Stopping E-Snoops with E-Mail Security." These instructions let you jump easily from the current page to another part of the book to get more info. This is, essentially, the way the World Wide Web works. Each Web document serves two purposes: it contains information that's useful in and of itself, and it contains specially marked words or phrases that serve as "links" to other Web documents. If you select the link, the Web loads the other document automatically. The descriptions of World Wide Web documents are called *uniform resource locators (URLs)*, and they look something like this:

http://www.mcp.com/general/mcpusa.html

Mailing Lists This is a system that sends out regular e-mail messages related to a specific topic. For example, if home beer making is your thing, then you'd definitely want to subscribe to the Homebrew mailing list to get recipes, how-to articles, beer festival announcements, and more. You usually subscribe by sending an e-mail message to the list's subscription address.

Telnet This is a program that lets you log in to another computer on the Internet and use its resources as though they existed on your machine. For example, you can often telnet to a computer to use its newsreader software. Of course, not every computer will let just anyone barge in unannounced. In many cases, you'll need to have an account on that machine, and you'll be required to enter your user id and password to log in. Still, there are plenty of computers that are happy to allow guests. For example, there are a number of online libraries you can telnet to and use their electronic card catalogs. Telnet descriptions require only the Internet address of the computer and, in some cases, a specific user id.

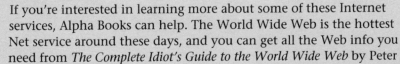

If you're interested in learning more about some of these Internet services, Alpha Books can help. The World Wide Web is the hottest Net service around these days, and you can get all the Web info you need from *The Complete Idiot's Guide to the World Wide Web* by Peter Kent or *The Complete Idiot's Guide to Mosaic* by Joe Kraynak. If you'd like to get in on the Usenet fun, may I not-so-humbly suggest *The Complete Idiot's Guide to Usenet* by Paul McFedries.

The Least You Need to Know

This chapter gave you a quick-and-dirty introduction to the Internet and its myriad services. Here's a summary of what you need to know as a budding e-mail maven:

➤ A network is a collection of two or more computers linked via cables that enable them to share data, programs, and printers.

➤ In its most drab guise, the Internet is an international network of networks.

➤ In reality, the Net is better described as a means of communication, an information resource, a warehouse, and a community.

➤ Common Internet services are FTP, Usenet, Gopher, the World Wide Web, mailing lists, and Telnet.

Chapter 3

A Brief E-Mail Primer

In This Chapter

> ➤ Understanding the e-mail thing

> ➤ The ins and outs of Internet addresses

> ➤ The parts of an e-mail message

> ➤ Reviews of e-mail software

> ➤ Lots of useful e-mail detail for newcomers

As you'll see throughout this book, one of the nicest things about Internet e-mail is that it's the most self-contained of all the Internet services. Features such as FTP, Gopher, and the World Wide Web require road trips on the Net's highways and byways to find what you need. With e-mail, though, you can stay "home" and send out missives to others, or have their messages delivered right to your "door." It's about as painless as the Net can get.

Still, this whole idea of sending messages back and forth in cyberspace is a mysterious business, to say the least. How are messages created and sent? How do they know where to go? How do we read the mail that comes our way? This chapter is designed to remove some of the mystery from the e-mail process by giving you some basic, and oh-so-nontechnical, background info.

How This E-Mail Malarkey Fits In

Chapter 2, "An Introduction to the Internet," gave you the big Net picture. Now let's narrow our focus a little and see if we can knock some sense into the real subject of this book: Internet e-mail. The next few sections give you some useful background info that'll prepare you for the ordeal to come.

How Does the E-Mail System Work?

You'll recall that earlier I used the analogy of a city connected by streets and highways to explain the Internet. This metaphor should serve quite nicely to explain how electronic mail works.

The first thing you need to know is that each computer on the Internet (or, in the case of commercial service providers, such as CompuServe, each user) has a unique *e-mail address*. Just like the full address of a house, your e-mail address tells everyone the exact location they can use to send stuff to you. These addresses can be confusing, so let's look closely at some examples. For starters, consider my Internet e-mail address:

paulmcf@hookup.net

This address has the following four parts:

paulmcf   This is my user name. Most user names are a single word representing either the person's first name, last name, or (like mine) a combination of the two names. Some companies insist that the user name be both the first name and last name separated by a period (for example, **paul.mcfedries**). Other e-mail systems will use different conventions. CompuServe, for example, uses two numbers separated by a period.

@   This symbol (it's pronounced "at") separates the "who" part of the address (the part to the left of the @ sign) and the "where" part (the part to the right of the @ sign).

hookup   This is the Internet name (in geekspeak, it's called the *domain name*) of my access provider (HookUp Communications). It tells you where my mailbox is located.

net   The last part tells you what type of organization you're dealing with. In this case, "net" means HookUp is a networking company. Table 3.1 lists the other organization types you'll run into in your e-mail travails. Notice, too, how **hookup**

and **net** are separated by a period. You pronounce this as "dot," so the entire address reads as "paulmcf at hookup dot net."

Table 3.1 Internet Organization Types

Type	What It Represents
com	Commercial business
edu	Educational institution
gov	Government
int	International organization
mil	Military
net	Networking organization
org	Nonprofit organization

My e-mail address is a relatively straightforward affair. Here's one that's a bit more complex:

biff@math.utoronto.ca

Again, the address begins with a user name (**biff**, in this case) and the @ sign. The **utoronto** part means this person is located at the University of Toronto. How come it doesn't have an "edu" at the end? Well, many newer e-mail addresses are foregoing the old "type" designations in favor of geographical designations (or *geographical domains* as the pocket protector crowd calls them). In this case, the **ca** tells you that the University of Toronto is located in Canada. Table 3.2 lists a few other common geographical domains. (Note that, in a bit of geographical chauvinism, most U.S. e-mail addresses don't bother with the country code.)

The **math** part of the address is called a *subdomain*, and it's used to narrow things down a bit. Universities and other large organizations usually have a number of different networks. At the University of Toronto, for example, there are probably separate networks for the mathematics department, the physics department, the chemistry department, and so on. The **math** subdomain tells you this person is part of the mathematics department's network.

15

Table 3.2 Some Internet Geographical Domains

Code	The Country It Represents
at	Austria
au	Australia
ca	Canada
ch	Switzerland
de	Germany
dk	Denmark
es	Spain
fi	Finland
fr	France
jp	Japan
nz	New Zealand
uk	United Kingdom
us	United States

Once you know a person's (or a company's) e-mail address, you're laughing. You just fire up your e-mail software, compose a message, tell the software the address of the recipient, and then send it off. In the same way that the post office can use the address on an envelope or package to track down the recipient, so, too, does the Internet e-mail system know how to locate the specified e-mail address. You just sit back and let the Net do all the dirty work.

A Quick Peek Under the Hood

One of the nice things about the Internet e-mail system is that, to use it, you don't have to know how its plumbing works. The missives you fire out, and the dispatches that come your way, are all routed automatically, without any help from the likes of you and me. However, one of the characteristics of the Internet is that its innards are never that far away. The programs we use to surf the Net are only a thin, shiny veneer covering the Net's guts.

So it pays, then, to know at least a little about the underlying mechanisms that make the Internet go. This will come in handy, for example, in some of the chapters in Part 2 where I tell you how to set up e-mail programs such as Eudora, Pegasus Mail, and Chameleon Mail. It'll also give you just enough background to let you pose intelligent questions to your system administrator, just in case some things go awry.

How Does My Mail Get There from Here?

When you dress up an e-mail message and send it out into the cold, cruel world of the Internet, it actually goes on quite a journey. The route it takes, the places it visits, and the sights it sees will vary from message to message, but the basic itinerary is easy to spell out:

1. A special e-mail computer on your network (or on your access provider's network) wraps up the message in an electronic "envelope" (that has, like a regular envelope, the recipient's address and your return address, among other things) and sends it out.

2. Since there will only rarely be a direct connection between your network and the recipient's network, the mail will make a number of stops at intermediate networks along the way. At each stop, another e-mail computer temporarily stores the message while it figures out the best way to relay the message toward its ultimate destination. When that's done, the message is sent on its merry way and the whole thing repeats at the next digital roadside rest stop.

3. Eventually, the message finds its way to the recipient's network where an e-mail computer routes it to the person's mailbox. (If the recipient uses a networked e-mail program that doesn't understand Netspeak—such as Microsoft Mail or cc:Mail—the message will have to go through another computer called a *gateway* that converts the message into something the program can make sense out of.)

This may sound like an awful lot of work just to send an e-mail note, but it's quite efficient for two reasons:

➤ The message is traveling at such phenomenal speeds that even the longest hop between networks happens in less than the blink of an eye.

➤ Almost all of the Net's e-mail computers use the same mechanism—it's called the Simple Mail Transport Protocol, or SMTP, for short—to transport the messages.

> The special e-mail computers that send out your e-mail message and pass it along to its destination are called **SMTP servers.** You'll also see these computers referred to as **SMTP relay hosts**, **mail gateways**, or **mail hosts.**

17

How Do I Get E-Mail If I'm Not on a Network?

If you use an access provider to do the Internet thing, there's no direct way to get an e-mail message onto your computer (since you're not jacked into a network full time). You could use the telnet service to log in to your access provider's network and read the mail directly from your mailbox, but most people prefer to store their private messages on their own hard disk.

To solve this problem, your access provider has probably set up a special account for you on one of its computers. This is called a *Post Office Protocol (POP) account*, and the computer it's set up on is called a *POP server*. POP essentially turns the server into the electronic equivalent of a post office. When people send messages to your e-mail address, the messages are stored in a special mailbox all your own. You can then use an e-mail program such as Eudora, Pegasus Mail, AIR Mail, or Chameleon Mail (all of which are covered in Part 2 of this book) to log in to this account, grab the messages, store them on your computer, and then clean out the mailbox.

The Pros and Cons of E-Mail

Okay, so the system seems to work pretty well, but is e-mail a good thing or a bad thing? Well, since e-mail represents (for most people) a completely new way to communicate with others, it should come as no surprise that it's certainly no panacea. Like anything new, it has its ups and more than its share of downs, as the following lists show.

The pros:

➤ *E-mail is easy.* The hardest part of Internet e-mail (or any Net service, for that matter) is getting connected to the Internet in the first place. Once you've made it through that trial by fire, however, the rest is no sweat. All you need is the appropriate software that runs on your computer. There are no yucky stamps to lick, no impossible-to-decipher waybills to fill out, and no trips in the freezing cold to mailboxes.

➤ *E-mail is fast.* No matter where you're sending your message, whether it's on the other side of town or on the other side of the planet, even the most rambling missive still takes only seconds or, at most, minutes to reach its destination. Nowadays, whenever I send regular mail (or *snail mail* as e-mail aficionados snidely refer to mail sent through the post office), I shudder to think it's actually going to take *days* to reach its destination. How primitive!

➤ *E-mail is cheap.* Outside of your normal online connection charges, Internet e-mail costs precisely nothing (although some commercial e-mail systems do charge a nominal fee after you've sent a certain number of messages or characters). Unlike with long distance telephone calls, you pay no more for messages sent to London, Ontario or London, England than to London, Ohio.

18

➤ *E-mail messages are easily stored.* Because they're electronic, saving an e-mail message you've received (and calling it back up again later on) is a breeze. And the electronic nature of e-mail helps to save natural resources such as trees and we don't have to bother with things such as slimy fax paper.

➤ *E-mail is practically universal.* Not only do millions of people on the Internet use e-mail, but every major e-mail system in the world has built-in electronic "bridges" (called *gateways*) that allow their users to send messages to and receive messages from the Internet. Yeah, sure, your aunt in Boise may not be wired, but just give the old gal some time.

The cons:

➤ *E-mail is impersonal.* Unlike in a mano-a-mano exchange, it's tough to get across facial expressions and other nuances in e-mail prose. Even a telephone conversation relies on oral cues such as inflection and volume to convey subtleties such as sarcasm and wry humor. There are ways around these e-mail constraints (I'll tell you about them in Chapter 5, "Learning the Lingo: E-Mail Jargon and Acronyms"), but your overall range of expression is limited.

The impersonality of e-mail also leads to another problem: forgetting that, most of the time, a live human being will be reading your message. E-mail is so easy that you can throw together a message in a few minutes and send it packing with a single keystroke or mouse click. Once it's sent, there's no way to retrieve a message that was written in a fit of pique or anger.

➤ *E-mail can take over your life.* As you get more involved in the world of e-mail, you'll naturally start getting more correspondence. You'll be exchanging pleasantries with friends and colleagues, subscribing to mailing lists and online journals, and trading info with complete strangers. Before you know it, you can spend most of your day just reading and responding to the deluge.

Today, it's estimated that between 30 and 60 million people use e-mail and, on the Internet alone, send well over a *billion* messages a month. These messages range in length from a few dozen words to a few thousand, but let's take 500 words as the average. That means Net e-mail types send more than 500 billion words a month scurrying around the world. Too big a number to comprehend? Okay, let's knock it down to size: 500 billion words a month is the equivalent of sending the manuscript of this book 10,000 times *every hour of every day*.

➤ *E-mail security is lax, at best.* As your e-mail messages wend their way to their destinations, they have to pass through other, public, systems. Anyone with the right amount of technical know-how can easily intercept your mail and snoop through it without you or the recipient knowing. E-mail security is such an important topic that I've devoted an entire chapter to it (see Chapter 6, "Stopping E-Snoops with E-Mail Security").

➤ *E-mail messages are easily stored.* Hey, wait a minute! I thought that was a pro. Well, it is, but there's a downside to this easy storage. If you say nasty things about your boss or a colleague in a message, a saved copy of your tirade could easily resurface and come back to haunt you sometime in the future. A good rule to follow is to assume your message will be read by the general public and to write accordingly.

➤ *E-mail can only handle text.* The biggest advantage to using snail mail and couriers over e-mail is that you can send such things as Christmas presents and food. E-mail is a text-only medium, which can be very limiting. Things are getting better, though. Many new e-mail programs let you "attach" graphics, sound files, and other types of documents (I'll talk more about this in Chapter 4, "You Send Me: Some Stuff About Sending E-Mail").

Overall, though, I'd have to say the pros of e-mail easily outweigh the cons, so that, yes, e-mail *is* a good thing after all (so it's safe to keep reading).

Message Anatomy

So you can make heads or tails of the messages you read, let's inspect a typical specimen to see what's what. As you can see in the following example, a message has three main parts: the *header*, the *body*, and the *signature*.

```
Date: Sat, 1 Apr 95 13:45 GMT
To: htarlek@tweedledumb.com
From: vbassoon@buyordye.com (Vital Bassoon)
Subject: An incorrect shipment. AGAIN!
Cc: acarlson@tweedledumb.com


Herb,
Those Neanderthals in your Shipping department have done it again!
This time they sent me 5 skids of "Wavy Locks" perm lotion instead
of 5 boxes of "Wavy Lay's" potato chips! Either you hire people with
at least a double-digit IQ, or I'll find a new distributor!!!

Vital Bassoon
Buy or Dye Convenience Store and Hair Salon
Toad Suck, Arkansas
"At Intel, quality is job 0.9999992362"
```

The Header

The first few lines constitute the header and represent the message's vital statistics. There are lots of obscure things that can appear in a header (especially the headers of messages you receive), but only a few truly useful items:

Date   This is the date and time the message was sent. The time given is usually Greenwich Mean Time (GMT) which is five hours earlier than Eastern Standard Time. (You'll also see GMT referred to as Universal Time, or UT.)

To   This is the e-mail address of the recipient.

From   This is the e-mail address and (usually) the real name of the person who sent the message.

Subject   This is a one-line description of what the message is all about. This line is crucial because most Netizens with busy e-mail in-boxes decide whether or not they'll read a message just by scanning the Subject line. To ensure your missives get read, make the Subject line detailed enough that it accurately reflects what your message talks about.

Cc   This line shows the e-mail addresses of people who received copies of the message.

The Body

The body is the content of the message, and it's always separated from the header by a blank line. When composing the body, be sure to use only the so-called *printable ASCII characters*, which is just a fancy designation for the letters, numbers, and symbols you can eyeball on your keyboard. For more tips about putting together a message body, see Chapter 4, "You Send Me: Some Stuff About Sending E-Mail."

The Signature

The message's signature is an addendum that appears as the last few lines of the message. Its purpose is to let the folks out there reading your e-mail know a little more about the Renaissance man or woman who sent it. Although signatures are optional, most people use them because they can add a friendly touch to your correspondence. You can put anything you like in your signature, but most people just put their name, their company name and address, their other e-mail addresses (if they have multiples), and maybe a quote or two that fits in with their character. (One of my favorite signature quotes—or *sig quotes*, as they're often called—came from Ken Rietz of the Ashbury College Department of Mathematics: "And just how did the fool and his money get together in the first place?")

Some signatures are absurdly elaborate, but most Internet types get upset at any signature that extends for more than four lines. (This is called "wasting bandwidth" and I'll talk more about it in Chapter 5, "Learning the Lingo: E-Mail Jargon and Acronyms.") Some e-mail software lets you create a separate signature file so you don't have to type it in yourself every time. In UNIX systems, you should use your favorite UNIX editor (such as **vi**) to enter your signature into a text file and then save the file as **.signature** in your home directory.

What E-Mail Software Should I Use?

Once you are connected to the Internet, all you need to start enjoying e-mail is the appropriate software. If you're not sure what to use, here's a quick review of the various packages that I cover in Part 2:

UNIX mail   This is the e-mail software that comes with every UNIX installation. It doesn't have all the features that the other programs do, but if you're running UNIX, it's an easy way to get started. See Chapter 8, "Yer Basic UNIX Mail Program."

Pine   This is an extremely easy-to-use UNIX e-mail program. It's perfect for new e-mail users or those who don't get a lot of mail. Chapter 9, "Riding Pine's Pony Express," tells all.

Elm   This is another simple UNIX mail program. Unlike Pine, though, Elm can grow with you (pardon the pun) as you get more experienced and start receiving a larger volume of mail. Check out Chapter 10, "Cruising Down Elm Street," to get started.

Eudora   This is a very popular program that runs under Windows and the Mac, so you know right off the bat that the interface is very simple. The program—especially the commercial version—is loaded with features that can make your e-mail life a lot easier. I cover all the versions of Eudora in Chapter 11, "Getting Graphical with Eudora."

Pegasus Mail   This is one of the most powerful and full-featured of the non-UNIX mail programs. Despite this power, it's very beginner-friendly so you'll have no trouble getting up and running. Chapter 12, "Taming Pegasus Mail," covers the Windows and Mac versions.

Chameleon Mail   This is the e-mail software that comes bundled with the *Internet Chameleon* suite of applications. It's kind of clunky to set up, but it gets the job done once it's ready. See Chapter 13, "The Karma of Chameleon Mail."

AIR Mail   This program comes as part of the *Internet In A Box* and *AIR Series* software suites. It lacks some of the features that make Eudora and Pegasus Mail so easy to use, but it's adequate for simple mail tasks. It's covered in Chapter 14, "Taking Flight with AIR Mail."

What Else Can You Do with E-Mail?

Although most e-mail consists of correspondence between two or more people, there's more to e-mail life than exchanging the latest gossip with your electronic pen pals. Here's a list of just a few of the e-mail jollies you can get:

➤ You can grab files from other Net computers just like you were using FTP. You can even use an e-mail version of Archie to find files. See Chapter 20, "Using E-Mail to Find and Retrieve Files," to see how it's done.

➤ You can read and post to Usenet newsgroups. Forget the newsreader; Chapter 21, "Postal Posting: Usenet Through E-Mail," shows you how to access Usenet from the friendly confines of your e-mail software.

➤ You can do some Gopher tunneling by following the instructions outlined in Chapter 24, "More Mail Chauvinism: Miscellaneous E-Mail Coolness."

➤ You can even access the World Wide Web (sans all the snazzy graphics, of course) through e-mail. Chapter 24, "More Mail Chauvinism: Miscellaneous E-Mail Coolness," gives you the lowdown.

➤ You can fax documents. E-mail faxing is explained in full in Chapter 22, "Stacks of Fax Hacks: Faxing Via E-Mail."

➤ You can play games. The Net has dozens of games that progress by exchanging e-mail messages. Turn to Chapter 23, "The Way-Out World of Play-By-E-Mail Games," to get the scoop on this popular Internet pastime.

The Least You Need to Know

This chapter led you through a few basics of e-mail. Here are some things to chew on before forging ahead:

➤ Internet e-mail addresses usually consist of a user name, followed by an @ sign, followed by the location of the user (which can include a domain name, one or more subdomains, and either an organization type or a country code).

➤ E-mail is easy, fast, cheap, archivable, and practically universal. On the other hand, it's also impersonal, voluminous, insecure, and restricted to text.

➤ Every e-mail message contains a header, the body text, and a signature.

➤ You can also use e-mail to get files, use Usenet and Gopher, access the World Wide Web, fax documents, and play cool games.

Chapter 4

You Send Me: Some Stuff About Sending E-Mail

In This Chapter

➤ The etiquette of sending e-mail

➤ How to send messages between different e-mail systems

➤ How to send nontext data through the e-mail system

➤ Some savory sending snacks that'll help you get this sending thing down pat

At its simplest, e-mail boils down to just two things: receiving messages and sending them. Receiving e-mail from others is no big deal: you get it, you read it, and then you either save it or toss it in whatever electronic version of a trash bin your mail software provides. Next!

Sending e-mail out into the ether, though, is another story altogether. When composing your missives, there are etiquette guidelines you should follow; when filling out the To: line in the header, you may have to jump through an extra hoop or two if the message is headed for a non-Internet address (such as CompuServe or MCI Mail); and if you need to send nontext data, such as a graphics file or a database, you have to set things up right or the recipient will receive a jumbled mess. This chapter tackles all of these sending subjects so your electronic postal duties will go as smoothly as possible.

Minding Your E-Mail Manners

One of the first things you notice when you drift around the Net is that it attracts more than its share of bohemians, nonconformists, and rugged individualists. Despite all these people surfing to the beat of a different drum, the Net resolutely refuses to degenerate into mere anarchy. Oh sure, you get the odd every-nerd-for-himself hurly-burly, but civility reigns the vast majority of the time.

Usually, most Netizens are just too busy with their researching and rubbernecking to cause trouble, but there's another mechanism that helps keep everyone in line: it's called *netiquette* (a portmanteau of *network etiquette*). Netiquette is a collection of suggested behavioral norms designed to grease the wheels of Net social discourse. Scofflaws who defy the netiquette rules can expect to see a few reprimands in their e-mail In box. To help you stay on the good side of the Internet community, the next few sections tell you everything you need to know about the netiquette involved in sending e-mail.

The Three B's of Composing E-Mail

Back in the long-gone days when I was a good corporate citizen, my boss used to call his secrets for successful presentations "the three B's": be good, be brief, begone. These simple prescriptions also form a small chunk of the basic netiquette landscape. Being good means writing in clear, understandable prose that isn't marred by sloppy spelling or flagrant grammar violations. Also, if you use some facts or statistics, cite the appropriate references to placate the doubting Thomases who'll want to check things for themselves.

Being brief means getting right to the point without indulging in a rambling preamble. Always assume your addressee is plowing through a stack of e-mail and has no time or patience for verbosity. State your business and then practice the third "B": begone!

DON'T SHOUT!

When writing with your high-end word processor, you probably use italics (or, more rarely, underlining) to emphasize important words or phrases. But because e-mail just uses plain vanilla text (that is, no fancy formatting options allowed), you may think that, in cyberspace, no one can hear you scream. That's not true, however. In fact, many e-mail scribes add emphasis to their epistles by using UPPERCASE LETTERS. This works, but please use uppercase sparingly. AN ENTIRE MESSAGE WRITTEN IN CAPITAL LETTERS FEELS LIKE YOU'RE SHOUTING, WHICH IS OKAY FOR USED-CAR SALESMEN ON LATE-NIGHT TV, BUT IS INAPPROPRIATE IN THE MORE SEDATE WORLD OF E-MAIL CORRESPONDENCE.

There are other ways to add emphasis to your e-mail prose. For example, you can *bracket* a word with asterisks. To find out more about these and other e-mail conventions, see Chapter 5, "Learning the Lingo: E-Mail Jargon and Acronyms."

on the other hand, you occasionally see e-mail messages written entirely in lower-case letters from lazy susans, toms, dicks, and harrys who can't muster the energy to reach out for the shift key. this, too, is taboo because it makes the text quite difficult to read. Just use the normal capitalization practices (uppercase for the beginning of sentences, proper names, and so on), and everyone'll be happy.

Avoid Tabs and Other Weirdo Characters

The Internet mail system works fine most of the time, but it's a temperamental, finicky beast. As long as things are just so, the mail should get through and your recipient will be able to read your well-crafted thoughts. But if you throw any kind of monkey wrench into the works, well, who knows what can happen. One of these monkey wrenches involves using characters that aren't part of the alphanumeric array on your keyboard. (By that, I mean the letters, numbers, and symbols such as $, ?, and %.) Tossing in Tabs or any of the so-called *control characters* (characters created by holding down the **Ctrl** key and pressing a letter or number), can throw your e-mail software for a loop.

Take Your Subject Lines Seriously

As I mentioned in Chapter 3, busy e-mail readers often use the contents of the Subject line to make a snap judgment about whether or not to bother reading a message. (This is especially true if the recipient doesn't know you from Adam.) The majority of mail mavens *hate* Subject lines that are either ridiculously vague (such as "Info required" or "Please help!") or absurdly general (such as "An e-mail message" or "Mail"), and they'll just press their mail software's "delete button" without giving the message a second thought. (In fact, there's a kind of illicit thrill involved in deleting an unread message, so don't give the person any excuse to exercise this indulgence.) Give your Subject line some thought and make it descriptive enough so the reader can tell at a glance what your dispatch is about.

Experiment with Yourself

When you're just starting out with e-mail, you'll likely want to try a test drive or two to work out the kinks. Unless you can enlist a friend or colleague as a willing guinea pig, don't send out messages to just anybody because, believe me, they have better things to do than read a bunch of "Testing 1..2..3.." messages. The best way to perform e-mail shakedowns is to send the tests to your own mail address. If things seem to be working fine, I hereby volunteer to be the recipient of your first "real" message. Send a note to **paulmcf@hookup.net** and let me know how the weather is in your neck of the woods.

More Snippets of Sending Sensitivity

The following, in no particular order, are a few more netiquette gems that'll help make sure you always put your best sending foot forward.

Don't Quote Me on That (Unless I Say So!)

If you receive private e-mail correspondence from someone, it's considered impolite to quote them in another message without their permission. You're probably also violating copyright law, because the author of an e-mail message has a copyright on any and all messages they send. There's even an acronym that covers this point with admirable succinctness: YOYOW—you own your own words. (See Chapter 5, "Learning the Lingo: E-Mail Jargon and Acronyms," for more acronym fun.)

Include Original Text When Replying

When replying to a message, include quotes from the original message for context. Few things are more frustrating in e-mail than to receive a reply that just says "Great idea, let's do it!" or "That's the dumbest thing I've ever heard." Which great idea or dumb thing are they talking about? To make sure the other person knows what you're responding to, include the appropriate lines from the original message in your reply. You'll need to use some judgment here, though. Quoting the entire message is wasteful (especially if the message was a long one), and should be avoided at all costs. Just include enough of the original to put your response into context.

When you want to respond to a message, make sure you use your e-mail software's Reply feature. This feature provides you with three advantages: 1) It automatically addresses the reply to the original sender; 2) It adds "Re:" to the Subject line so the original sender knows which message is being responded to; 3) It gives you the option of including some or all of the original message in the reply. I'll talk more about the Reply feature when we look at specific e-mail programs in Part 2.

Restrict Message Width to 65 Characters

Many people read their mail using terminals that display text across the screen in 80 columns. To keep your messages looking their best, limit your line lengths to no more than 80 characters. In fact, you should probably restrict your lines to 65 characters or so because many systems break up lines that are any longer. Another good reason to use shorter lines is that, when you include part of the original message in your reply, the quoted material from the original is indicated, usually, with a greater than sign (>) to the left of the line. If, as sometimes happens, people start quoting these quotes, the >s can start adding up. So restricting your lines to 65 columns will give everyone plenty of room.

Don't Get Carried Away with Your Signature

As I mentioned in Chapter 3, keep your signatures down to a dull roar. Believe me, *nobody* is interested in seeing your résumé or your *curriculum vitae* at the end of every message you send. The accepted maximum length for a signature is four lines.

Forgive Small Mistakes

If you see a message with spelling mistakes, incorrect grammar, or minor factual blunders, resist the urge to "flame" the perpetrator. (In e-mail lingo, a *flame* is a nasty, caustic message designed to put Internet scofflaws in their place. I'll talk more about them in Chapter 5.) For one thing, the international flavor of e-mail just about guarantees a large percentage of participants for whom English isn't their primary language. For another, I hope you have better things to do than to nitpick every little slip of the keyboard that comes your way.

Can I Get There from Here? Sending Mail Between Systems

Let's say you're schmoozing at some highfalutin cocktail party and you meet someone who could send a lot of business your way. Dreams of new powerboats dance in your head as they say, "Here's my card. E-mail me and we'll do lunch." You look at the card and—groan!—they have an MCI Mail address! Now what? Or suppose you're a CompuServe user and your best buddy has just gotten an Internet e-mail account. How on earth are the two of you supposed to shoot the digital breeze?

These kinds of scenarios are increasingly common because, while there are tens of millions of people exchanging electronic mail on the Net, there are tens of millions more who use other systems, such as MCI Mail, AT&T Mail, CompuServe, and America Online.

Are all these systems just countries unto themselves where fraternization is strictly taboo? Well, they used to be, but things have changed. Now, most e-mail systems have opened their borders (by installing things called, appropriately enough, *gateways*) to allow e-mail travelers safe passage. The next few sections show you how to exchange mail with the citizens of various other e-mail nations.

The following sections assume you're familiar with the Internet's arcane address formats. If you're not, you may want to head back to Chapter 3, "A Brief E-Mail Primer," to bone up on the essentials.

Exchanging Mail with America Online

America Online (AOL) is a commercial online service that boasts an increasing array of Internet services, including an e-mail gateway. I'll talk more about AOL's well-designed e-mail system in Chapter 15, "Mail Bonding with America Online," but let's see how internauts and America Onliners can exchange e-mail epistles.

Every AOL subscriber has a unique *screen name* that identifies him or her to the AOL system. The e-mail address takes the general form *screenname*@aol.com, where *screenname* is their screen name *in lowercase letters and without spaces*. For example, if you wanted to send e-mail from the Internet to an AOL user with a screen name of Will Tell, you'd use the following address:

willtell@aol.com

Sending mail from AOL to the Internet is the soul of simplicity. When composing a message, just enter the person's Internet e-mail address in the **To** box. For example, AOL types can send e-mail to me by entering the following address:

paulmcf@hookup.net

Exchanging Mail with AT&T Mail

AT&T Mail is a commercial e-mail service that assigns each of its subscribers a unique *user name*. The e-mail address of an AT&T Mail subscriber uses the general format *username*@attmail.com, where *username* is the person's user name (duh). For example, to send e-mail from the Internet to an AT&T Mail subscriber with the user name **jsprat**, you'd use this address:

jsprat@attmail.com

Sending messages from AT&T Mail to the Internet is a little more complicated. The general form is **internet!***domain***!***user*, where ***domain*** is the domain name from the Internet address (that is, the part to the right of the @ sign) and ***user*** is the user name from the Internet address (the part to the left of the @ sign). For example, to send mail to my Internet address (**paulmcf@hookup.net**), you'd use the following address:

internet!hookup.net!paulmcf

Exchanging Mail with CompuServe

CompuServe is one of the largest and oldest of the big-time online services. It's slowly adding more and more Internet services, but it has had a gateway for Internet e-mail since 1989. (See Chapter 16, "E-Mail Correspondence the CompuServe Way," to get the goods on the CompuServe e-mail system.) Each CompuServe subscriber is assigned a unique user id number that's actually two numbers separated by a comma (such as 12345,6789).

The e-mail address of a CompuServe user is simple. It takes the generic format ***idnumber*@compuserve.com**, where ***idnumber*** is the subscriber's user id number *with the comma replaced by a period.* For example, if the person's CompuServe user id is 12345,6789, then his e-mail address would look like this:

12345.6789@compuserve.com

Missives sent from CompuServe to the Internet use e-mail addresses that take the form **INTERNET:***user@domain*, where ***user@domain*** is the person's regular Internet e-mail address. So any CompuServe user who wants to drop me (**paulmcf@hookup.net**) a line would send his note to the following address:

INTERNET:paulmcf@hookup.net

Exchanging Mail with Delphi

Of all the major commercial online services, Delphi was the first to provide full Internet access, so it should come as no surprise that it also sports an e-mail gateway to the Net. (I talk about the Delphi mail system in Chapter 18, "Delphi's Mail Delivery.")

Each Delphi subscriber has a unique user name. To send mail to Delphi from the Internet, use the general format ***username*@delphi.com**, where ***username*** is the user name of the Delphi subscriber you're writing to. For example, to send a message to a Delphi subscriber with the user name **ucowboy**, you'd use the following address:

ucowboy@delphi.com

Sending mail from Delphi to the Net is only slightly more complicated. The format to use for the address is **internet"***user@domain***"**, where ***user@domain*** is the person's Internet e-mail address. Note that there are no spaces in this address and that you have to include both quotation marks. For example, here's the address a Delphi user would enter at the **To:** prompt to send me (**paulmcf@hookup.net**) a dispatch:

> internet"paulmcf@hookup.net"

Exchanging Mail with GEnie

General Electric's GEnie online service also has an Internet e-mail gateway. GEnie subscribers have a unique user name, so Internet types send mail to GEnie users with the following generic address: ***username*@genie.geis.com**. For example, to send e-mail to a GEnie subscriber with a user name of **m.hari3**, you'd use the following address:

> m.hari3@genie.geis.com

Sending mail from GEnie to the Internet is fairly straightforward. For the address, you just use the person's Internet e-mail address, and you attach **@INET#** at the end, like so: ***user@domain*@INET#**. For example, GEnie users who want to send messages to yours truly (**paulmcf@hookup.net**), would send their notes to the following locale:

> paulmcf@hookup.net@INET#

Exchanging Mail with MCI Mail

MCI Mail is another popular commercial e-mail service that has offered a gateway to the Internet for a number of years. When you sign up with MCI Mail, you get not one, but *three* separate means of identification: an MCI id number that looks like a seven-digit telephone number (such as 123-4567), an MCI id name (such as **mpeeved**), and a full user name (such as **Millicent Peeved**).

To send Internet mail to an MCI Mail user, you can address the message using any of these generic formats:

> *idnumber*@mcimail.com
>
> *idname*@mcimail.com
>
> *full_name*@mcimail.com

Notice that the space in the user's full name gets replaced by an underscore (_). Also, if you're using the MCI id number, you remove the dash. So, in the examples I used above, you could use any of the following addresses:

1234567@mcimail.com

mpeeved@mcimail.com

Millicent_Peeved@mcimail.com

To send correspondence to an Internet e-mail address, MCI Mail users need to follow a three-step procedure:

1. Start a new message as you normally would (by typing **create** at the **Command:** prompt and pressing **Enter**). When MCI Mail displays the **To:** prompt, type the name of the person or company you're sending the message to, followed by **(EMS)**, followed by **Enter**. For example, to send mail to me, enter **Paul McFedries (EMS)** and press **Enter**.

2. At the **EMS:** prompt, type **Internet** and press **Enter**.

3. At the **MBX:** prompt, type the Internet e-mail address and press **Enter**. To send mail to me, for example, type **paulmcf@hookup.net** and press **Enter**.

Exchanging Mail with Prodigy

Prodigy is another of the commercial online services that provides an Internet e-mail gateway. Note, however, that to exchange e-letters with the Net, you have to fork out an extra $14.95 for the E-Mail Connection program. (Check out Chapter 17, "Perusing the E-Mail Connection for Prodigy," to learn how to download this software from Prodigy, as well as how to work with Prodigy's e-mail system.)

When sending mail to a Prodigy user from the Net, you use an address of the form *userid*@**prodigy.com**, where *userid* is the unique identification Prodigy assigns to its users. For example, if the Prodigy person you want to contact has the user id **abcd01a**, then you'd mail your correspondence to the following address:

abcd01a@prodigy.com

Sending mail from Prodigy to the Internet is a breeze. When composing the message in E-Mail Connection, just use the person's Internet e-mail address. For example, Prodigy types can send e-mail to me by entering the following address:

paulmcf@hookup.net

The seven systems we looked at in this section represent only the most popular of the dozens of e-mail systems available worldwide. If you'd like instructions about exchanging mail with a system we didn't cover, head for Usenet and look in the **comp.mail.misc** newsgroup for the article "Updated Inter-Network Mail Guide," by Scott Yanoff. If you don't see the article, you can get it via anonymous FTP from **rtfm.mit.edu**. Change to the **/pub/usenet-by-group/comp.mail.misc** directory and get the file **Updated_Inter-Network_Mail_Guide**.

Sending Sounds, Graphics, and Other Nontext Files

Looked at in the simplest possible terms (my favorite way of dealing with anything that has to do with computers), the files you work with come in two flavors: text and nontext. Text files are those that contain only the letters, numbers, and symbols you can peck out on your keyboard (and a few other characters that we don't need to worry about). Nontext files include graphic images, sounds, and things you create with your applications, such as spreadsheets and databases. For reasons that are, thankfully, completely unimportant to us, you'll often hear nerdy types referring to nontext files as *binary* files.

As I've mentioned before, the Internet e-mail system only knows how to deal with text, so you'd think that sending nontext files would be strictly *verboten*. Well, you'd be partially right. It turns out that you *can* send nontext files if you convert them into text before you send them. Here's the general procedure:

1. Using one of the programs discussed below, convert the nontext file into a text file.

2. In your e-mail software, compose a new message and then "attach" the new text file to the message. (How you attach a file to a message depends on the mail program you're using. I'll tell you how it's done in the appropriate chapters in Part 2.)

3. Send the message.

4. When the recipient gets the message, they save it to a separate file.

5. The recipient converts this file back into its original nontext form.

There are actually a fistful of ways to perform steps 1 and 5, but the next few sections take you through the three most popular.

The UNIX Solution: Uuencode and Uudecode

The UNIX **uuencode** program will convert a nontext file into a jumble of text characters. (Uuencode stands for "UNIX-to-UNIX encode" and it's pronounced "you-you-encode.")

To put **uuencode** through its paces, you enter a command in the following general format and then press **Enter**:

uuencode *NonTextFileName EncodedFileName*.uue

Here, ***NonTextFileName*** is the name of the nontext file you want to convert and ***EncodedFileName*.uue** is the name you want to give to the encoded file. Notice the .uue extension at the end of the encoded file name; this reminds you (and the recipient) that the file has been uuencoded. For example, suppose you want to encode a graphics file named RAPTOR.GIF. Here's the command you enter:

uuencode raptor.gif raptor.uue

When you compose your mail message, you attach the file RAPTOR.UUE and fire it off. The recipient saves the message to a file (they can use any name for the file, but adding a .uue extension is probably a good idea) and then uses the **uudecode** program to convert the file back to its original, nontext glory:

uudecode *EncodedFileName*.uue

Uudecode examines ***EncodedFileName*.**uue and creates a new, nontext file that has the name of the original nontext file. For example, if the recipient saved the above message as RAPTOR.UUE, they'd decode it with the following command:

uudecode raptor.uue

Uudecode would automatically create a new file named RAPTOR.GIF.

If you use an MS-DOS-compatible PC or Macintosh, you can still get in on the uuencode/uudecode action:

➤ For DOS, you can use the *Uuencode for PC* and *Uudecode for PC* programs. To get them, anonymous FTP to **oak.oakland.edu** and look in the **/pub/msdos/decode** directory for a file named **uuexe*???*.zip**. (The ***???*** stands for the current version of the programs. As I write this, the current version is 5.32, so the file is called **uuexe532.zip**.) Also, the DOS version of Pegasus Mail has a uuencode feature.

➤ For Windows, if you use either the *Internet In A Box* or the *AIR NFS* Internet suites, you get a Windows program called UUCODE that will both encode and decode files. Also, the commercial version of Eudora (see Chapter 11, "Getting Graphical with Eudora") and the Windows version of Pegasus Mail (see Chapter 12) have built-in uuencoding.

➤ For the Mac, you can get the Uulite program by anonymous FTP at **plaza.aarnet.edu.au** in the directory **/micros/mac/info-mac/cmp**. The file to download is **uu-lite-??.hqx**, where the **??** is the current version (1.5 is the latest, so the file is **uu-lite-15.hqx**).

35

The Mac Solution: BinHex

The standard format for converting text to nontext in the Mac world is called *BinHex* (which, rather obtusely, stands for "binary-to-hexadecimal"). If you use the Eudora mail software, I'll show you how to use it to BinHex files in Chapter 11, "Getting Graphical with Eudora."

If you don't have Eudora, you can still do the BinHex thing. Anonymous FTP to **boombox.micro.umn.edu** and head for the directory **/pub/binhex/Mac**. The file you need is called **BinHex**. To convert a file with BinHex, double-click on the program icon to run the program. Then select the **File** menu's **Application -> Upload** command (or press **Command-U**). In the standard file dialog box that appears, select the file you want to convert and then click on the **Open** button. In the dialog box that appears, enter a name for the text file, select a folder, and then click on **Save**.

To convert a text file back into the original file, run BinHex and select the **File** menu's **Download -> Application** command (or press **Command-D**). Select the text format file and click the **Open** button.

The above site also has a DOS version of BinHex called *PC BinHex*. Look in the directory **/pub/binhex/MSDOS** and grab the file **binhex.exe**. To convert a file, start PC BinHex, press **F2**, select the file from the dialog box, and press **Enter**. PC BinHex creates a new, encoded file with the extension **hqx**. For example, if the original file is NONTEXT.DOC, the binhexed file will be named NONTEXT.HQX. To restore the file to its original nontext format, start PC BinHex, press **F3**, select the file in the dialog box, and press **Enter**.

You can do the BinHex thing in Windows if you use either Eudora (check out Chapter 11 for details) or Pegasus Mail (covered in Chapter 12).

The (Almost) Universal Solution: MIME

All this encoding and decoding of files is a royal pain-in-the-you-know-what, not only for you but also for your poor, beleaguered recipient. Wouldn't life be great if we could just attach the file we want to send to a message and then have the software worry about the conversion to text and back again?

Well, my friends, I'm here today to tell you that there's good news: the automatic conversion of nontext files to e-mail-friendly text *is* a reality. A few of the Net's big-time brainiacs got together and created a new standard for sending nontext stuff through the mail: MIME (which stands for Multimedia Internet Mail Extensions, which is, if nothing else, an impressive mouthful). If both you and your recipient have mail software that supports the MIME standard, then the whole process becomes a veritable walk in the park. You just attach the nontext file and send the message. When the recipient reads the message, MIME automatically extracts the file, converts it back to its former self, and stores it in a new file. Easy with a capital E.

The kicker, of course, is that you and your correspondent both need a mail program that can handle this MIME stuff. Fortunately, MIME is such a good idea that most popular mail software supports it. In particular, MIME is built into Pine, Elm, Eudora, Pegasus Mail, and the commercial version of Chameleon Mail (all of which are covered in Part 2).

The Least You Need to Know

This chapter gave you some pointers on sending e-mail messages. Here's a summary of the most important factoids:

➤ E-mail etiquette includes things like keeping your dispatches short and to the point, avoiding UPPERCASE SHOUTING, creating meaningful Subject lines, and quoting from the original message in your replies.

➤ Most of the world's e-mail systems have gateways that allow them to exchange e-mail with the Internet community.

➤ To send nontext files through the e-mail system, you need to convert them into text and then have the recipient convert them back.

➤ Common conversion solutions include uuencode and uudecode, BinHex, and MIME.

Chapter 5

Learning the Lingo: E-Mail Jargon and Acronyms

In This Chapter

➤ Understanding the inevitable Net jargon

➤ Unraveling the mysteries of Net acronyms

➤ Learning how to convey moods and emotions with smileys

➤ Filters, flaming, forwarding, and other e-mail f-words

➤ Your field guide to e-mail flora and fauna

As you'd expect with anything that boasts millions of participants, the Internet is home to a wide variety of characters. In particular, the Net seems to attract more than its fair share of three kinds of folks: neologists, jargonauts, and nymrods.

Neologists are people who coin new words and phrases either by making them up out of the blue, by enlisting existing words to perform new duties, or by combining two or more words into a new creation (the offspring of these lexical unions are called *portmanteaus*—a word coined by the inveterate neologist, Lewis Carroll).

Jargonauts are Net surfers who seek out new words and new phrases and who boldly try to get these coinages into general circulation by using them as often as possible.

Nymrods are Net types who, without even the slightest sting of conscience or pang of doubt, insist on turning every multiword computer term into an acronym.

As you interact with the Internet through your e-mail account, you're bound to run into many examples of each kind of Net word hound. This means you'll be exposed to all kinds of new jargon, acronyms, and symbols that could threaten to render your incoming missives unintelligible. To help you decipher these electronic Dead Sea Scrolls, this chapter presents translations of the most common Net neologisms and acronyms. (For a more extensive list of Internet argot, browse through the Speak Like a Geek glossary at the back of this book.)

Your Handy English-Internet Phrase Book

As I've said, learning the online vernacular is important if you hope to understand what the heck some Net denizens are talking about. At the same time, it'll also help if you can add to your e-mail messages a few choice morsels of Net patois (or *Netois*, as I guess you could call it; oops, there goes another neologism!). Experienced globetrotters maintain that you'll be greeted more warmly and treated more kindly by the locals if you learn a few key words and phrases in the language of the country you're visiting. This could easily be applied to the online world as well, so that jargon becomes a kind of *lingua franca* for the Net set. To get you on your way, here are some translations of a few common Internet idioms, with a special emphasis on e-mail-related terms:

attachment   A file that's linked to an e-mail message and hitches a ride to the recipient when the message is sent. See Chapter 4, "You Send Me: Some Stuff About Sending E-Mail," to learn how to send nontext files as attachments.

bandwidth   A measure of how much stuff can be stuffed through a transmission medium, such as a phone line or network cable. To put it another way, bandwidth measures how much information can be sent between any two Internet sites. Since bandwidth is a finite commodity, many Net veterans are constantly cautioning profligate users against wasting bandwidth. In e-mail circles, this means keeping messages short and to the point, attaching large nontext files (especially graphics) only if you have to, quoting a minimal amount of the original article in a reply, and avoiding useless *flame wars* (I describe what these are later in this chapter). Bandwidth is measured in *baud* or *bits per second* (defined below).

baud   This is a measure of how much bandwidth a transmission medium has. Its technical definition is "level transitions per second," but only the truly nerdy have any idea what that means. *Bits per second* (see next definition) is the more common measure because it's at least comprehensible to the likes of you and me.

bits per second (bps)   Another, more common, measure of bandwidth. Here, a *bit* is the fundamental unit of computer information where, for example, it takes eight bits to describe a single character. So a transmission medium with a bandwidth of, say, 8 bps

40

would send data at the pathetically slow rate of one character per second. Bandwidth is more normally measured in kilobits per second (Kbps—thousands of bits per second). So, for example, a 14.4 Kbps modem can handle 14,400 bits per second. In the high end, bandwidth is measured in megabits per second (Mbps—millions of bits per second).

You'll often see Net types talking about "T1" or "T3" lines. A T1 line is a telephone trunk line (usually consisting of fiber-optic cables) with a bandwidth of 1.544 Mbps. "T3" lines are ultra-high bandwidth trunk lines that can transfer data at a whopping 45.21 Mbps. These two types of lines provide the basic infrastructure of the Internet. Regionally (that is, within a state or within several adjoining states), networks usually are connected via T1 lines; this is called a *regional backbone*. Each of these regional backbones is then connected to the main Internet backbone—called NFSNet—which spans the country [...]. To [...]

— MYMAIL

— INBOX →

— CREATE MAIL

— TO: Levreault@ ALLTEL.NET

— Address book

— ITINERARY

— bitofblarney.com

[...] message that gets sent to a recipient [...] (the e-mail address in the To line) or [...] the Cc line).

[...] an e-mail system if a message can't be d[...]

fi[...] that scans incoming messages and a[...] contents of, say, the From or Subject li[...] automatically delete messages sent from a pa[...] *lter*). The UNIX programs Filter and Pr[...] Mail and Eudora (the commercial ve[...]

fla[...] message. See "The Incendiary Internet: Pla[...] er for a complete look at Net fla[...]

foo[...] eholders in descriptions and instructions[...] to the */foo* directory on a UNIX syst[...] s a generic placeholder for a directory nan[...] o" and "bar" are used, like so: "To FTP[...] and: *mget foo bar*." "Foobar" is often used[...] litary acronym FUBAR (bowdlerized vers[...] more rare, placeholder words are **baz** and[...]

forward To pass along a received message to another e-mail address. If you have a UNIX system and you have multiple e-mail addresses, there's a way to automatically forward mail from one address to another. In your home directory, create a new text file (using, say, the **vi** editor) and include in it a single line: the e-mail address where you want the mail forwarded. Save the file with the name **.forward** (yes, the dot at the beginning is part of the name).

luser A portmanteau of "loser" and "user." Someone who doesn't haven't the faintest idea what they're doing and, more importantly, refuses to do anything about it.

mail bomb To send numerous (and usually long) e-mail messages to a person's e-mail address (this is also called **e-mail terrorism**). Although I didn't mention it in Chapter 4 (it is, fortunately, still very rare), mail bombing is a definite netiquette no-no.

mailbox The file where your incoming messages are stored. Some e-mail software lets you divide your mailbox into different *folders* (such as one for business mail, one for personal mail, and so on).

net. A prefix used by Internet types who spend *way* too much time online. These people like to add "net." in front of just about anything even remotely connected to the Internet. For example, a newcomer to the Net becomes a *net.newcomer*; an online session becomes a *net.session*. That kind of thing. However, there are a few "net." constructions that have achieved mainstream status: *net.police* (self-appointed netiquette watchdogs who flame offenders), *net.gods* and *net.deities* (Internet old-timers who've achieved celebrity status), and *net.characters* (irritating internauts who post Usenet articles that are designed only to attract attention to themselves).

newbie A person who is (or acts like they are) new to the Internet. Since this term is almost always used insultingly, most Net neophytes try to behave as non-newbie-like as possible. The best way to avoid this label is to bone up on netiquette (see Chapter 4, "You Send Me: Some Stuff About Sending E-Mail").

postmaster The overworked, underpaid person in an e-mail system that has the responsibility of making sure the system runs smoothly, and troubleshooting problems when it doesn't.

sig quote A quotation added to a signature. Most people choose quotes that reflect their character or their politics.

spam Irrelevant prattle that has nothing whatsoever to do with the current topic under discussion. Aimless drivel noticeably lacking in any kind of point or cohesion.

surf To travel through cyberspace.

The Incendiary Internet: Playing the Flame Game

Everyone—even the calmest and most level-headed among us—has a particular bugaboo or bête noire that gets under his skin and makes his blood boil. In the real world, it could be people who drive too slow in the fast lane, discourteous types who butt ahead of you in line, or those annoying, late-night infomercials. In the online world, it could be a thoughtless remark, a misunderstood attempt at humor, or a vicious mail bomb.

Whatever the reason, the immediate reaction usually is to pull out the electronic version of your poison pen and compose an emotionally charged, scathing reply dripping with sarcasm and venomous abuse. Such messages are called *flames*, and they're an unfortunate fact of life on the Net. Firing off a particularly inventive flame may make *you* feel better, but it's likely effect will be to make the recipient madder than a hoot owl. They will, almost certainly, flame your flame, and before you know, a full-blown *flame war* will have broken out.

When the urge to flame hits, give yourself some time to cool off by going for a walk, taking a shower, or just yelling at the top of your lungs for a few minutes.

Flaming has become such an integral part of Internet culture that it has developed its own subgenre of colorful lingo and phrases. Here's a brief primer on flame jargon:

asbestos long johns   What e-mailers put on (metaphorically speaking, of course) before sending a message they expect will get flamed. Other popular flame-retardant garments are *asbestos overcoats* and *asbestos underwear*.

burble   Similar to a flame, except that the burbler is considered to be dumb, incompetent, or ignorant.

dictionary flame   A flame that criticizes someone for spelling or grammatical gaffes.

firefighters   People who attempt to put out flame wars before they get out of hand.

flamage   The content of a flame. This word seems to be a portmanteau of the words "flame" and "verbiage."

flame bait   Provocative material in a message that will likely elicit flames in response.

flame warrior   A person who surfs the Net looking for flame bait. Someone who tries to start flame wars intentionally.

flamer   A person who flames regularly.

rave   A particularly irritating type of flame in which the writer rambles on *ad nauseum*, even after a flame war has ended.

An Initial Look at Internet Acronyms

For most new users, acronyms are the bugbears and hobgoblins of computer life. They imply a hidden world of meaning that only the cognoscente (those "in the know") are privy to. The Internet, in particular, is a maddeningly rich source of TLAs (three-letter acronyms) and other ciphers. To help you survive the inevitable onslaught of Internet acronymy, here's a list of the most commonly used initials in Net discourse:

AAMOF	As a matter of fact.
AFAIK	As far as I know.
BTW	By the way.
CU	See you (as in "see you later").
DIIK	Damned if I know.
F2F	Face-to-face.
FAQ	Frequently Asked Questions. These are lists that appear in many Usenet newsgroups to provide answers to questions that new-comers ask over and over.
FAWOMPT	Frequently argued waste of my precious time.
FAWOMFT	Frequently argued waste of my foolish time (bowdlerized version; substitute your favorite f-word).
FOAF	Friend of a friend. Used to imply that information was obtained third-hand, or worse.
FOTCL	Falling off the chair laughing.
FTF	Face-to-face.
FYA	For your amusement.
FYI	For your information.
HHOK	Ha ha, only kidding.
HHOJ	Ha ha, only joking.
HHOS	Ha ha, only serious. (Used with ironic jokes and satire that contain some truth.)
IANAL	I am not a lawyer.
IMCO	In my considered opinion.

44

IMHO	In my humble opinion. (Although, in practice, opinions prefaced by IMHO are rarely humble. See IMNSHO, below.)
IMO	In my opinion.
IMNSHO	In my not so humble opinion. (This more accurately reflects most of the opinions one sees on the Internet!)
IOW	In other words.
IWBNI	It would be nice if.
IYFEG	Insert your favorite ethnic group. Used in off-color and offensive jokes and stories to avoid insulting any particular ethnic group, race, religion, or sex. You'll sometimes see *ethnic* instead.
KISS	Keep it simple, stupid.
LOL	Laughing out loud.
MEGO	My eyes glaze over.
MOTAS	Member of the appropriate sex.
MOTOS	Member of the opposite sex.
MOTSS	Member of the same sex.
MUD	Multiple User Dimension (or Multiple User Dungeon). A text-based, role-playing fantasy adventure game.
NRN	No response necessary.
OIC	Oh, I see.
OS	Operating system.
OTOH	On the other hand.
OTT	Over the top.
PD	Public domain.
PMJI	Pardon my jumping in.
PONA	Person of no account. Used disparagingly to describe someone who isn't part of the Internet set (that is, someone who doesn't have an Internet account).
ROTF	Rolling on the floor.
ROTFL	Rolling on the floor laughing.

ROTFLOL	Rolling on the floor laughing out loud.
RSN	Real soon now (read: never).
RTFF	Read the fine FAQ. (See RTFM.)
RTFM	Read the fabulous manual. (Another bowdlerized version; insert your own f-word.) This is an admonition to users (usually newbies) that they should try to answer a question themselves before asking for help. This may seem harsh, but self-reliance is a fundamental characteristic of Internet life. Most Net types have figured things out for themselves, and they expect everyone else to do the same. This means reading hardware and software manuals, and in Usenet, checking out the FAQ lists newsgroups.
SO	Significant other.
TFS	Thanks for sharing.
TIA	Thanks in advance.
TIC	Tongue in cheek.
TPTB	The powers that be.
TTFN	Ta-ta for now.
TTYL	Talk to you later.
WRT	With respect to.
YABA	Yet another bloody acronym.
YMMV	Your mileage may vary. This acronym means the advice/info/instructions just given may not work for you exactly as described.

If you come across an acronym that's not covered here, there are some Net resources you can turn to. The World Wide Web Acronym Server lets you look up acronyms or find acronyms whose expansion contains a particular word. Surf to the following page to check it out:

http://curia.ucc.ie/info/net/acronyms/acro.html

Gopher users can head to the Manchester Computing Centre at **info.mcc.ac.uk**. Select **Miscellaneous Items**, then **Acronym dictionary**, and then **Acronym dictionary (keyword search)**. If you'd like to access the acronym server via e-mail, you'll find the instructions in Chapter 24, "More Mail Chauvinism: Miscellaneous E-Mail Coolness."

Internet Hieroglyphics: Smileys

Flame wars ignite for a variety of reasons: derogatory material, the skewering of one sacred cow or another, or just for the heck of it (see *flame warrior* definition). One of the most common reasons is someone misinterpreting a wryly humorous, sarcastic, or ironic remark as insulting or offensive. The problem is that the nuances and subtleties of wry humor and sarcasm are difficult to convey in print. *You* know your intent, but someone else (especially someone for whom English isn't their first language) may see things completely differently.

To help prevent such misunderstandings, and to grease the wheels of Net social interaction, cute little symbols called *smileys* (or, more rarely, *emoticons*) have been developed. The name comes from the following combination of symbols: :-). If you rotate this page clockwise so the left edge is at the top, you'll see that this combination looks like a smiling face. You'd use it to indicate to your readers that the previous statement was intended to be humorous, or at least unserious.

Smileys are an easy way to convey meaning in your online writings, but don't lean on them too heavily. Overusing smileys not only means your writing isn't as clear as it could be, but it'll also automatically brand you as a dreaded newbie or as terminally cute.

The basic smiley is the one you'll encounter most often, but there are all kinds of others to tilt your head over (some of which are useful, most of which are downright silly). Here's a sampling:

Smiley	Meaning
:-)	Ha ha, just kidding (or, general friendly greeting).
:-D	That's hilarious (smiling broadly or laughing).
;-)	(Winking) Nudge, nudge, wink, wink; I'm flirting or being ironic.
:-(	I'm unhappy.
;-(	I'm crying.
:-|	I'm indifferent—well whatever, never mind.
:-#	My lips are sealed.
:-/	I'm skeptical.
:->	I'm being sarcastic.
:-V	I'm shouting.

continues

47

Smiley	Meaning
;^)	I'm smirking.
%-)	I've been staring at this screen for too long!
:-p	Nyah, nyah, I'm sticking out my tongue at you.
:-)~	I'm drooling.
%-S	Drunk me home, I'm drive.

You can also use smileys to paint a little picture of yourself or of someone/something else. Here are a few:

Smiley	Meaning
8-)	Wears glasses.
=l:-)x	Wearing a top hat and bow tie.
*<:-)	Wearing a stocking cap (or could be Santa Claus).
7:^)	Ronald Reagan.
):0_ |O|= |_o=	Cow.

E-Mail Miscellania

To round out our tour of the sights and sounds you'll come across in the e-mail world, let's look at a few miscellaneous conventions and symbols:

Adding emphasis to your messages. In Chapter 4, I told you that you can add emphasis to your messages by using UPPERCASE letters. However, many people interpret uppercase words as shouting, so other emphasis conventions are normally used. The most common is to bracket a word or phrase with asterisks, like *this*. You'll occasionally see other characters around a word, such as the _underscore_, the exclamation !mark!, and the greater than and less than >signs<. To get degrees of emphasis, some people use multiple characters, like ****this**** or like >>>>>this<<<<<. Rarely, you'll also see words "underlined" with carets (^), as shown here:

```
Why does everyone hate poor Barney the Dinosaur?
                                ^^^^^^^^
```

Conveying mood with nonsmileys. As you saw in the last section, smileys are a handy way to make sure your messages aren't misunderstood. However, many people find those little faces to be insufferably cute and so wouldn't be caught dead using them. Instead, they use the following "nonsmileys."

Symbol	What It Means
<g>	Grinning, smiling
<vbg>	Very big grin
<eg>	Evil grin
<veg>	Very evil grin
<l>	Laughing
<lol>	Laughing out loud
<i>	Irony
<s>	Sighing
<jk>	Just kidding
<>	No comment

Simulating a backspace. In oral conversation, you can achieve an ironic effect by saying one thing, and then saying "Oops, I mean," and then saying something else. To simulate this effect in writing, you can use the ^H symbol. Let's look at an example: "Would someone please tell this bozo^H^H^H^Hperson that ads aren't allowed in this newsgroup?" You'd read this as "Would someone please tell this bozo—oops, I mean person—that ads aren't allowed in this newsgroup?" The idea is that you add as many ^Hs as there are letters in the word you're trying to "backspace" out. Why ^H? Well, the caret (^) stands for the Ctrl key on a keyboard, so ^H actually represents the key combination Ctrl+H. And, in some UNIX systems, you press Ctrl+H to delete the character to the left of the cursor.

The Least You Need to Know

This chapter presented you with a field guide to the flora and fauna of Internet e-mail. Here's a review of some of the sites we saw along the way:

➤ The Internet is a jargon-lover's heaven, where new phrases and terms are minted with frightening regularity. Fortunately, if you want to talk the talk, there are really only a few "must know" words. These include *bandwidth*, *bounce message*, *foo*, *forward*, *spam*, and *surf*.

➤ A flame is an emotionally charged article that contains caustic, rabid rebuttals combined with vicious, personal ridicule. Exchanging multiple flames with multiple flamers constitutes a flame war.

➤ In general, you should try to avoid flaming because it just wastes bandwidth that could be used for more productive pursuits.

➤ One of the biggest causes of flame wars is the misinterpretation of an otherwise-harmless bit of humor or irony. To avoid these misunderstandings, use smileys to make your intentions clear. Just try not to overdo it. If smileys are just too darn cute, use nonsmileys such as <g> (grin) or <s> (sigh).

➤ The most common way to add emphasis to words or phrases is to surround them with *asterisks*.

Chapter 6

Stopping E-Snoops with E-Mail Security

> **In This Chapter**
>
> ➤ Why e-mail security is an issue
>
> ➤ Building a bullet-proof password
>
> ➤ Understanding Pretty Good Privacy encryption
>
> ➤ Using anonymous remailers
>
> ➤ Some precautionary tales about e-mail security

In any liberal democratic society, we expect our privacy to be respected at all times by our fellow citizens, by corporations, and by governments. Whether, in this age of Social Security numbers, photo radar, and credit bureaus, this right to privacy still has any meaning is a topic for another time and place. (If you have access to Usenet, the newsgroup **alt.privacy** is a good place to start.) Our concern in this chapter is to protect whatever privacy we do have in the more anarchic realm of the Internet in general, and the Internet e-mail system in particular.

Why All the Fuss About E-Mail Security?

If you made a list of the various tenets that constitute the Internet ethos, one of them would be that information should be free and easily accessible to all. This admirably egalitarian view is one of the reasons the Internet has been so successful. The composition of the Net's building blocks (the software that allows the various networks to communicate with each other and exchange data) is public knowledge, so it's relatively easy to write software that performs functions over the Net. In turn, the "information is free" ethic leads many of these software developers to make their creations free to all and sundry. So, once you're wired, you can easily put together a suite of Internet applications, and your total cost would be precisely nothing! (In fact, many of the e-mail programs we'll look at in Part 2 are freebies.)

The downside to all this openness (you knew there had to be a downside) is that it also makes it easy for the malicious and the malevolent to get into all kinds of mischief. By studying the published standards for how the Internet works, crackers (as hackers who've succumbed to the dark side of the Force are called) can apply their knowledge of programming and computer systems to compromise these systems and bypass the normal Internet operating procedures.

In the e-mail world, this leads to two major security issues: privacy and authenticity.

The Privacy Problem

Remember all the fuss a while back when some cellular snoop managed to listen in on a phone conversation between Princess Diana and "Squidgy," her alleged (and bizarrely nicknamed) lover? The problem with cellular phones, of course, is that their transmissions are just microwave radio signals that travel willy-nilly through the air just like any other radio signal. With a simple receiver, anyone can tour through the appropriate frequencies, intercept these transmissions, and listen in on what were supposed to be private conversations.

All Internet communication—files, World Wide Web pages, e-mail, etc.—is divided into small chunks called **packets** that are sent individually and reassembled when they reach their destination. For this reason, the Net's electronic eavesdroppers are called **packet sniffers**.

Internet e-mail suffers from a similar problem. When you send a message, it doesn't travel directly to the recipient but, instead, it must first pass through a number of other systems. Remember the analogy back in Chapter 3 where I likened a message traveling through the Net to driving from one city neighborhood to another along a system of roads and highways? Well, on the Net, these roads and highways often have "checkpoints" that messages must pass through on their journey.

These checkpoints are just computers on some other network, and at each stop there's always the possibility that someone with enough know-how will intercept your message, read it, and then send it on its way. Neither you nor your recipient would ever be the wiser. In this sense, using Internet e-mail is no different from sending snail mail messages on the back of a postcard.

The Authenticity Problem

You may recall a famous story from the seventies in which the sportscaster Howard Cosell was doing a Monday Night Football broadcast and received what he thought was a call from the boxer Muhammad Ali. At the time, Ali was in Zaire preparing to fight George Foreman, so this was a real coup for Cosell. In fact, he even did a brief interview with Ali right on the air to a nationwide TV audience. Much to Mr. Cosell's chagrin (not to mention his embarrassment), the call turned out to be a hoax (the caller was actually somewhere in the Midwest, I think).

This brings us to the second e-mail security problem: authentication. When you receive a message, the header's From line tells you the e-mail address of the person who sent the missive. Or does it? The Internet e-mail system is such an open book that it turns out to be fairly easy to forge another person's e-mail address! Now, obviously, if you get a message from **president@whitehouse.gov** or **billg@microsoft.com**, you can pretty well guess you're dealing with a forgery (depending on the social circles you run in). However, if you get flamed by a total stranger, or if someone you know inexplicably asks for your credit card number, there's no way to tell whether the message is on the up-and-up.

Is This All a Bunch of Paranoid Fearmongering?

Well, perhaps we *should* keep some perspective here. Tens of millions of e-mail messages are sent every day, so what, really, are the chances of someone picking out *your* message to spy on? Besides, only criminals and other undesirables really need to keep their communications private, right?

Wrong! I mean, you "hide" most of your paper mail inside an envelope don't you? Does that make you a criminal? Of course not, and what if your e-mail dispatches include sensitive material, such as payroll data, credit card or Social Security numbers, financial info, research results, or trade secrets? You'll probably want to protect these decidedly noncriminal messages, so you have every right to be at least a little paranoid. And you can forget that "safety in numbers" argument. Someone looking for your e-mail messages wouldn't have to sift through the millions of dispatches that are posted daily. It's possible to scan mail messages passing through a site and do "keyword searches" to intercept those that contain particular words, phrases, names, or even e-mail addresses.

As for e-forgeries, it's true that they're still quite rare, if only because the necessary know-how is well beyond the skills of the vast majority of Netizens. But, still, they *do* happen. Why just a few months ago (in late 1994), some prankster forged a Microsoft press release that stated the company had bought the Vatican! The very idea sounds preposterous, but Microsoft actually had to put out their own press release to confirm the other was a fake!

In the end, it comes down to a matter of principle. With more and more people jumping on the Net bandwagon every day, with the possibility that all correspondence will be done via e-mail getting closer and closer to reality, and with the prospect of Net financial transactions looming large, e-mail security will have to become as much of a "right" as the privacy we enjoy in our own homes.

Your First Line of Defense: Your Password

The system administrator of your UNIX network or access provider will have provided you with a password to use when you log in. This password means that only you and the system administrator can access your home directory and, more importantly, read your incoming e-mail. The first rule of good password protection is to change this password as soon as you can. (For UNIX systems, you use the **passwd** command to do this. If you're not sure, contact your system administrator to get the appropriate instructions.)

The big question is, "Which password do I use to provide the maximum protection without sacrificing convenience?" Keeping in mind that the whole point of a password is to select one that nobody can guess, here are some guidelines to follow when choosing a password:

Don't be too obvious. Since forgetting a password is inconvenient, many people use meaningful words or numbers so their password will be easier to remember. This means they often use extremely obvious things like their name, the name of a family member or colleague, their birth date or social security number, or even their system user name! Being this obvious is just asking for trouble.

Don't use single words. Many crackers break into accounts by using "dictionary programs" that try every word in the dictionary. So, yes, "xiphoid" is an obscure word that no person would ever guess, but a good dictionary program will figure it out in seconds flat. Using two or more words in your password (or *pass phrase*, as multiword passwords are called) is still easy to remember and would take much longer to crack by a brute force program.

Put lousy spelling to good use. If, like me, your spelling leaves little to be desired, your password may the one place where it comes in handy. Misspelling a word or words in your password will really throw those crackers a curve.

Use passwords that are at least eight characters long. Shorter passwords are susceptible to programs that just try every letter combination. You can combine the 26 letters of the alphabet into about 12 million different five-letter word combinations, which is no big deal for a fast program. If you bump things up to 8-letter passwords, however, the total number of combos rises to 200 *billion*, which would take even the fastest computer quite a while. If you use 12-letter passwords, as many experts recommend, the number of combinations go beyond mind-boggling: 90 *quadrillion* or 90,000 trillion!

If you do forget your password, it's no big deal. Just tell your system administrator and he will be able to assign you a new one.

Mix upper- and lowercase letters. Almost all password systems are case-sensitive, which means that if your password is, say, *YUMMY ZIMA*, trying *yummy zima* won't work. So you can really throw snoops for a loop by mixing the case. Something such as *yuMmY zIMa* would be almost impossible to figure out.

Add numbers to your password. You can throw a few more permutations and combinations into the mix by adding a few numbers to your password. In fact, some systems insist on passwords that include at least a couple of numbers.

Throw in a few punctuation marks and symbols. For extra variety, toss in one or more punctuation marks or special symbols such as % or #.

Try using acronyms. One of the best ways to get a password that appears random, but is easy to remember, is to create an acronym out of a favorite quotation, saying, or book title. For example, if you've just read *The Seven Habits of Highly Effective People*, then you could use the password *T7HoHEP*.

Don't write down your password. After going to all this trouble to create an indestructible password, don't blow it by writing it down on a sticky note and then attaching it to your keyboard or monitor! Even writing it down on a piece of paper and then throwing out the paper is dangerous. Determined crackers have been known to go through a company's trash looking for passwords (this is known as *dumpster diving*).

Don't tell your password to anyone. If you've thought of a particularly clever password, don't suddenly become unclever and tell someone. Your password should be stored in your head alongside all those "wasted youth" things you don't want anyone to know about.

Change your password regularly. If you change you password often (say, once a month or so), then even if some skulker does get access to your account, at least they'll only have it for a relatively short period of time.

PGP: A Pretty Good Precaution

Back in Chapter 4, "You Send Me: Some Stuff About Sending E-Mail," we looked at a few programs that can *encode* nontext files into text so they can be sent as part of an e-mail message. If you examine these encoded files, they look like just a random jumble of characters, so you may think that you can use this encoding stuff to protect the privacy of *all* your e-mail. Unfortunately, it's trivial to *decode* these files, so anyone with enough savvy to intercept your e-mail would certainly have no trouble translating your messages back to their original form.

No, the real secret to truly private e-mail is *encryption*. Like simple encoding, encryption transforms text into an unreadable dog's breakfast of letters and numbers. Unlike encoding, however, it's extremely difficult to translate an encrypted file back to its original state. In fact, it's possible to set things up so that the *only* person capable of decrypting an encrypted message is the recipient!

Basic encryption uses mind-numbingly complex mathematics to scramble the contents of a file. In simple terms, encryption is effective because *how* a file gets encrypted depends on a certain *key* value that gets fed into the encryption formulas. Here's how the key makes encryption so powerful:

➤ You have to use the same key value to *de*crypt the file. Without the key, it's impossible to restore the file to its original state. So the idea, then, is to supply your recipient with the key (either in person or over some secure means of communication) so they can decrypt the file when they get it. In this sense, encryption is analogous to a lock and the key value is analogous to a physical key. You can't open the lock unless you have the right key.

➤ If you change the key, the file gets encrypted in a completely different way. This means that even if one key somehow falls into the wrong hands, security won't be compromised as long as you change the key value regularly.

However, the greatest strength of this kind of system—the key value—is also its greatest weakness. In particular, making sure that both parties have the same key is the weak link in the chain. The idea of meeting face-to-face to exchange keys seems to defeat the whole purpose of e-mail. And if you have a "secure means of communication" for transmitting the key, then why not use it to transmit your message!

To get around the inconvenience of this so-called "single-key" encryption system, a new "double-key" method was invented. Amazingly, with double-key encryption, you can send encrypted files to total strangers *and they're the only ones who'll be able to decrypt them*. In the next few sections, we'll look at the software that performs this small miracle: *Pretty Good Privacy* (or *PGP* as it's normally called).

What Is PGP?

As I've said, PGP is a double-key system. This means that each person uses two keys: a "public" key and a "private" (or "secret") key. The public key is made available to all and sundry, either by sending it out or by placing it in special "key databases." The private key stays on your computer and can only be used by someone who knows its password. (This is, or should be, a different password than the one you use to log in to your Internet provider.)

The main idea here is that each person's public key and private key are related to each other. This means that whenever you use a particular public key to encrypt a message, *only* the person who has the corresponding private key can decrypt it. You can't even decrypt it yourself! Here's how PGP works:

If you're sending a file to someone:

> **To ensure privacy,** you grab his public key and you use it to encrypt the message with PGP. You then send him the message, and he uses his private key to decrypt it (again, using his version of the PGP software).

> **To ensure authenticity,** (that is, to prove the message came from you), you'd encrypt the message using your private key. This doesn't change the actual text of the message, but it does create a digital "signature" that identifies the file as your own. The recipient would then use your public key to verify that this signature is valid. Note that you can combine both of these procedures if you want to send a message that is both private and verifiably authentic.

If someone is sending a file to you, the procedure is just the opposite:

> **To ensure privacy,** the sender would get hold of your public key and use it to encrypt the message. When you receive the message, you'd use your private key to decrypt it.

> **To ensure authenticity,** the sender encrypts the message using his private key to create his own signature. You'd then use the sender's public key to verify that the signature is valid.

If it sounds complicated, well yes, I guess it is. The good news, though, is that PGP handles all the complexities behind the scenes. It's actually a lot easier to use PGP than it is to understand how the program works (thank goodness!). However, I've saved the best news for last: PGP is free! That's right: you get this incredibly sophisticated and useful program for the same price as the air you breathe. Sound too good to be true? Not really. You see, the program's developer, Phil Zimmerman, is one of the Net's staunchest privacy advocates, so PGP is his way of furthering the cause. (He calls PGP "public-key encryption for the masses.")

If you're worried about things such as technical support and upgrades, there is a commercial version of PGP that costs around $100. It's put out by a company called ViaCrypt at the following address:

9033 N. 24th Avenue
Phoenix, AZ 85021-2847
Phone: (602) 944-0773
Fax: (602) 943-2601
E-mail: vbiacrypt@acm.com or 70304.41@compuserve.com

Where Can I Get My Hands on PGP?

The main site for PGP is at MIT. Unfortunately, the U.S. State Department has all kinds of weird rules regarding the export of cryptography products, so getting PGP requires jumping through a few hoops. Here's the basic procedure (for U.S. citizens only; all others see the instructions that follow these instructions):

When you look inside the PGP directory, you'll see many other files, which you can safely ignore.

1. Anonymous FTP to **net-dist.mit.edu** and head for the directory **/pub/PGP**.

2. Read the files **mitlicen.txt** and **rsalicen.txt** and agree to their terms.

3. Telnet to **net-dist.mit.edu** and, at the **login** prompt, type **getpgp** and press **Enter**.

4. You'll see a series of questions on the screen. For each one, type **yes** (if applicable) and press **Enter**. You'll then see a message similar to the following:

```
To get PGP 2.6.2 use anonymous FTP to net-dist.mit.edu and look in the
directory:
                /pub/PGP/dist/U.S.-only-5f19
```

5. Make a note of the directory and press **Ctrl+C** to end the telnet session.

6. Anonymous FTP to **net-dist.mit.edu** and grab the PGP files from the indicated directory. For DOS, get **pgp262.zip**; for the Mac, get **macpgp26.hqx**; for UNIX, get **pgp262.tar.gz** (source code only). Note that the numbers in the file names may change as new versions of PGP are released.

If you need to use e-mail to get PGP, see Chapter 20, "Using E-Mail to Find and Retrieve Files." Here's a list of some other anonymous FTP sites that carry PGP (again, each of these sites are for U.S. citizens only):

Site	Directory	Instructions File
ftp.csn.net	/mpj	README.MPJ
ftp.netcom.com	/pub/mp/mpj	README.MPJ
ftp.eff.org	/pub/Net_info/Tools/Crypto	README.Dist
ftp.gibbon.com	/pub/pgp	README

Canadian users can get their privacy-starved mitts on PGP by anonymous FTPing to **ftp.wimsey.bc.ca**, looking in the directory **/pub/crypto/software**, and following the instructions in the **README** file. For all other nationalities, you can get sites and instructions in the article "Where to get the latest PGP (Pretty Good Privacy) FAQ," which is posted regularly to the **alt.security.pgp** newsgroup in Usenet. If you don't see it there, anonymous FTP to **rtfm.mit.edu**, jump to the directory **/pub/usenet-by-group/ alt.security.pgp** and grab the file **Where_to_get_the_latest_PGP_(Pretty Good Privacy)_FAQ**.

Once you have the PGP file, decompress it (see Chapter 20 for more info on decompressing files), and then read the file SETUP.DOC to get specific instructions on how to install PGP.

Where Can I Get More Info?

The best place to go for more info on PGP is the Usenet newsgroup **alt.security.pgp**. This is the place to be to get technical help with PGP, learn about new releases, and talk about the politics and legal ramifications of encryption in general and PGP in particular. Before diving in, though, be sure to read the Frequently Asked Questions (FAQ) lists for **alt.security.pgp**. There are five, in all:

```
alt.security.pgp FAQ (Part 1/5)
alt.security.pgp FAQ (Part 2/5)
alt.security.pgp FAQ (Part 3/5)
alt.security.pgp FAQ (Part 4/5)
alt.security.pgp FAQ (Part 5/5)
```

You can also get these files via anonymous FTP from **rtfm.mit.edu**. You'll find them in the directory **/pub/usenet-by-group/news.answers/pgp-faq** under the file names **part1**, **part2**, **part3**, **part4**, and **part5**.

Another great resource for PGP info is the book *The Complete Idiot's Guide to Protecting Yourself on the Internet*.

E-Mail Incognito: Anonymous Remailing Services

What do you do if you want to send a message to, say, a mailing list, but you don't want anyone to know who sent it? For example, someone still "in the closet" may want to post to one of the gay and lesbian lists, or someone who actually *likes* Shannon Doherty may want to defend her in the *90210* list. For these situations, the Net has a number of anonymous remailing services that will forward your mail and strip out any references to your home site or your e-mail address.

The anon.penet.fi Anonymous E-Mail Service

The most commonly used service for mailing clandestine messages is **anon.penet.fi** (yes, it *is* in Finland). Here's how it works:

1. Start a new mail message and address it to **anon@anon.penet.fi**.

2. Enter the subject of your message.

3. In the first line of the message, enter **X-Anon-To:** *address*, where *address* is the e-mail address of the recipient. For example, if you wanted to post to a mailing list with the address **in-the-closet@motss.mil**, you'd enter the following:

   X-Anon-To: in-the-closet@motss.mil

4. Enter a blank line and then type in the rest of the message. (Make sure, of course, that you don't add a real signature to the end of the message.)

5. Send the message.

The first time you send a message to the service, you'll receive a response telling you your anonymous "code name" (it will be something like *an123456*). This is the only ID that readers of your article will see. If anyone sends an e-mail response to that ID (that is, to **an123456@anon.penet.fi**), the service will automatically forward it to your mailbox.

The next thing you need to do is set up a password for your anonymous postings. (This is an extra security measure designed to make sure nobody finds out who's behind your code name.) Send an e-mail message to **password@anon.penet.fi** and include the password you want to use in the message body. When the password has been accepted, you're ready to start mailing anonymously to **anon@anon.penet.fi**. The top of each message should look something like this:

```
X-Anon-To: put the recipient's e-mail address here
X-Anon-Password: put your password here
The next line must be blank
```

Instead of those impersonal letters and numbers in your code name, you can assign yourself a jaunty nickname. To do this, send an e-mail message to **nick@anon.penet.fi**, and enter the nickname you want to use in the Subject line.

Instead of always adding the **X-Anon-To:** line at the top of the message body, you can simply specify the recipient's e-mail address as part of the To: line in the header. In general, if you're sending a message to *user@domain*, then your To: line becomes *user%domain***@anon.penet.fi**. (Notice how the @ sign in the recipient's address gets changed to a percent sign: %.) For example, if you're sending a message to **in-the-closet@motss.mil**, your To: line would look like this:

```
in-the-closet%motss.mil@anon.penet.fi
```

A Note About the Cypherpunk Remailers

One of the problems with the **anon.penet.fi** service is that anyone intercepting the message before it gets to Finland will know your secret. Even if you encrypt the message, you'll still have to leave the recipient's address (the **X-Anon-To:** part) unencrypted so **anon.penet.fi** knows where to send the mail. If you're looking for the maximum security possible, you can try the cypherpunk remailing services.

A *cypherpunk* is anyone who believes encryption software should be freely available and that users should always have the right to encrypt their e-mail messages. (Note that there's nothing in this description that requires cypherpunks to be punks. In fact, many of the staunchest cypherpunks are actually old geezers like me in their thirties and forties!) In their eternally vigilant quest for maintaining their privacy rights, the cypherpunk movement has set up a number of different anonymous remailers. Some of these services actually let you encrypt the portion of the message that specifies its ultimate destination (the remailing header). For more info on the cypherpunk remailers, see Part 3 of the **alt.security.pgp** FAQ (as mentioned earlier in this chapter.)

Another security issue you need to be aware of is viruses. When you're transferring files to your computer, you'll want to make sure you don't accidentally pick up one of these nasty little programs along the way. Chapter 20, "Using E-Mail to Find and Retrieve Files," gives you some tips for avoiding viruses and tells you where to pick up some good antivirus software.

The Least You Need to Know

There you have our quick look at e-mail security. It really is an important topic, so just to make sure things sink in properly, here's a curtain call for some of the main points:

➤ The openness of the Internet is what makes it both reliable (most of the time, anyway) and cheap, but it also makes it easier for the ethically challenged to stick their noses where they don't belong.

➤ In e-mail circles, there are two main types of security breaches: privacy and authenticity. Privacy is a problem because any technically savvy spook can read your mail without your knowing; authenticity is a problem because it's relatively easy to forge an e-mail address.

➤ All your security precautions should begin with setting up a snoop-proof password. To that end, don't make your password obvious; use multiple words; make passwords at least eight characters long; and throw in some mixed case, numbers, and symbols.

➤ Encryption protects the privacy of your e-mail by making it nearly impossible to decipher without the key value. Pretty Good Privacy makes encryption easy by using both a public key and private key and by allowing you to add both privacy and authenticity to your messages.

➤ To hide your name and e-mail address from a message, use the **anon.penet.fi** anonymous remailing service. You can also use the cypherpunk remailers for maximum anonymity.

Chapter 7

Where's Waldo (and Wanda, Too)? Finding an Address

In This Chapter

➤ Finding addresses from USENET posts

➤ Interrogating Whois databases

➤ Cranking up the Knowbot Information Service

➤ Thumbing through Gopher phone books

➤ Umpteen almost-useful techniques for locating long-lost e-mail addresses

These days, a business card or letterhead just doesn't have the right cachet if it lacks some kind of e-mail address. In fact, I've exchanged cards with people who've *apologized* to me because the old card they were giving me didn't have their e-mail address and their new, e-mail-enhanced cards hadn't arrived yet. (I'll tell you one thing about the Internet: I'll bet it's been a boon to business card manufacturers!)

Anyway, the point is that e-mail addresses are becoming commonplace, and will someday be as ubiquitous as telephone numbers. What happens, though, if you want to contact someone by electronic mail but you don't have a business card or letter that gives you his e-mail address? The phone companies have directory assistance numbers you can call; does the Net have an analogous service? Sadly, no, there's no central repository for

Internet e-mail addresses. All is not lost, however. There are a number of tools you can wield in an attempt to track down your would-be recipient. They don't always work, but they're the best we have at the moment, and they're the subject of this chapter.

Getting Addresses from USENET

Lots of people on the Internet like to drop in on USENET newsgroups at least occasionally. Many of these folks also enjoy putting their two-cent's worth in by posting their own articles in USENET. If you think the person you're trying to track down may have sent in a USENET article, then you may be in luck. Jonathan Kamens at the Massachusetts Institute of Technology (MIT) maintains a list of the names and e-mail addresses of all the people who've posted an article to USENET in the past year. (Technically, Jonathan's list keeps track of all the From lines in USENET posts. These From lines always include an e-mail address, and most also include a name.) You can send in a request to MIT to search for a particular name, and you'll get a message back telling you if there were any matches.

Here's how it works:

1. Start a new e-mail message and address it to **mail-server@rtfm.mit.edu**.

2. Leave the Subject line blank and enter the following in the message body: **send usenet-addresses/*name***, where ***name*** is the name of the person you're looking for. (You can enter the last name, the first name, or both.) If you want to run multiple searches (say, because you're not sure of the exact spelling of the name), you can enter separate **send** commands on different lines, like so:

```
send usenet-addresses/limbaugh
send usenet-addresses/limbaw
send usenet-addresses/limmbah
```

3. Send the message.

When you receive your reply, if any matches were found, they'll be listed something like the following (this was the result of a search for the name "McFedries"):

```
paulmcf@hookup.net (Paul McFedries)  (Dec 2 94)
Paul McFedries <pmcfedries@delphi.com>  (Nov 23 94)
paulmcf@noc.tor.hookup.net  (Nov 17 94)
```

As you can see, it's possible to get multiple matches for the same person if he has used different systems to post to USENET. If you're not sure which one to use, I'd suggest starting with the one that has the most recent date.

Whois You Gonna Call?

The Internet may not have an official phone book, but there are a number of services called *white pages directories* that try to fill in the gaps. These services typically enable you to search a database of names to get the info you need, but the databases are usually restricted to individual organizations or universities.

One such service is called *Whois*. Whois is a program that lets you search a *Whois database* that contains a list of names. If the program finds a match, it displays the person's full name, his e-mail address, and his company's address and phone number. Most Whois databases are set up for specific companies, though, so the vast majority of internauts won't be listed.

How you use Whois depends on the system you're running. The next section looks at the UNIX **whois** command, and then we'll examine telnetting to a Whois database, using DOS, Windows, or Mac programs, and using e-mail.

The UNIX whois Command

Many UNIX systems have a **whois** command you can try. In the simplest case, you use this command by typing **whois**, a space, and the last name of the person you want to find. When you press **Enter**, Whois searches its database and then displays the matches it found. For example, to look for a person with the last name *Kirk*, you'd enter the following command:

whois kirk

Of course, you may get a few Kirks, so you can narrow things down a tad by entering both the first name and last name. For example, to find James Kirk, you'd enter the following command:

whois kirk,james

Notice that you need to separate the last name and the first name with a comma. You may still end up with multiple matches, though. For example, **whois** may display the following:

```
Kirk, James T. (JTK7)    jtkirk@ncc1701.org   (123) 555-1212
Kirk, James X. (JXK4)    kirk@spock.com       (456) 555-9876
```

If James T. Kirk is the one you want, you can specify his record by running another **whois** command on the letters and numbers in brackets beside his name (JTK7, in the above example; this is called an *alias*):

whois !jtk7

The exclamation mark tells **whois** that you just want to search for an alias.

You may be wondering which Whois database you've been searching all this time. Well, your system administrator will have set up a default database that will likely be one of the following:

➤ Your organization's Whois database, if it has one.

➤ The Department of Defense Whois database. This database used to contain names from all over the Internet, so many systems set it up as the default. Nowadays, though, it just contains info on people in the U.S. Department of Defense.

➤ The InterNIC Registration Services Whois database. This is a general listing of some Internet e-mail addresses. It's more global than the company-specific databases, but it's still mostly just contact names for organizations.

If you want to use a different database, you need to specify the name of the appropriate Whois *host* (or Whois *server* as the geeks would say). For example, suppose you want to search the Whois database at North Carolina State. Its Whois host is **whois.ncsu.edu**, so your **whois** command to search for "Kirk" would look something like this:

whois -h whois.ncsu.edu kirk

Notice how you type **-h** (the "h" is for "host"), followed by a space, followed by the host address.

To get to the InterNIC Registration Services host, use the address **whois.internic.net**; for the Department of Defense host, use **nic.ddn.mil**. To get a list of hosts, anonymous FTP to **sibd.mit.edu**, step into the directory **/pub/whois**, and get the file **whois-servers.list**.

Other Ways to Access Whois

The UNIX **whois** command isn't the only way to do the Whois thing. Here's a summary of a few other methods you can add to your arsenal:

➤ Some Whois hosts are open to the public, so you can telnet to them. If you're asked for a user name, type **whois** and press **Enter**. You should see a **Whois:** prompt. (If not, type **whois** and press **Enter** to get it.) Now you just enter the name you want to search for and press **Enter**.

➤ If you want to use the InterNIC Registrations Services host, you can search it with e-mail. Send a message to **whois@whois.internic.net** and use the Subject line **whois** *name*, where *name* is the name of the person you want to find. (Don't put anything in the message body.) To get more info, you'd send a message with the Subject line **whois help**.

➤ If you use a system other than UNIX, you may be able to find Whois software you can use right on your computer. For example, the next figure shows the Whois program that comes with the Internet Chameleon suite of applications. I've also heard of a another Windows program (anonymous FTP to **bitsy.mit.edu** and look in the **/pub/dos/potluck** directory for the file **winwhois.exe**), but I haven't tried it out.

The Whois program from the Internet Chameleon collection.

Reach Out and KIS Someone: The Knowbot Information Service

A *knowbot* is an independent, automated program that seeks out information on other computer systems and sends back reports on its progress. (The name is a portmanteau of the phrase *knowledge robot*.) Although the technology isn't quite up to snuff as yet, you'll someday be able to send knowbots out into the Net looking for, say, haggis recipes or any documents that contain the words "Travolta," "come-back," and "miraculous."

While we're waiting breathlessly for this technology to arrive, there is a knowbot (albeit a primitive one) up and running that can help you search for an e-mail address. It's part of the *Knowbot Information Service* (KIS) and it searches Whois databases, a list of MCI Mail customers, and some other sites, for a name you enter.

67

To use the service, follow these steps:

1. Crank up a new e-mail message and address it to **kis@cnri.reston.va.us**.

2. Don't bother with the Subject line, and enter the following in the message body: **query** *name*, where *name* is the name of the person you want to find. (You can enter the last name, the first name, or both.)

3. Fire off the message.

Before long, you'll get a return message showing the results. The figure below shows part of reply generated by a search for the name "Cringely." As you can see, a match was found in the MCI Mail system. (The person's e-mail address isn't shown in the figure but, trust me, it's there.)

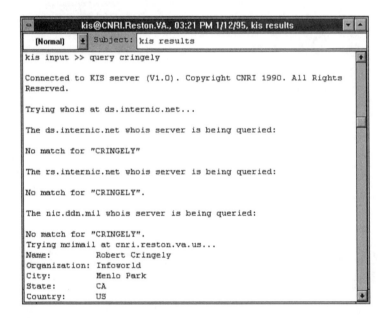

Part of the output from a KIS query.

Gopher Phone Books

If you have access to the Internet Gopher service, you can take advantage of the "phone books" that many Gopher sites offer. To see what I mean, let's work through an example Gopher session: finding a person who either attends or works at the Albert Einstein College of Medicine. Here's the procedure:

1. Start by using your Gopher software to burrow to the University of Minnesota's Gopher at **gopher.micro.umn.edu.**

2. When you get the main menu, select the **Phone Books** item. The Gopher displays the Phone Books menu.

3. Select **Phone books at other institutions**.

4. When the next menu appears, select the geographical area you want to work with. For our example, select **North America**. Now you'll see a menu that displays the names of a bunch of organizations in the selected area.

5. Select the organization you want to search. For the example, you'd select **Albert Einstein College of Medicine**. Now the Gopher displays a form for the search. The layout of this depends on the institution, but the form shown in the figure below is typical.

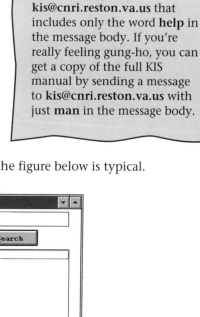

KIS actually has a number of commands you can use besides **query**. To get a list of the commands, send an e-mail message to **kis@cnri.reston.va.us** that includes only the word **help** in the message body. If you're really feeling gung-ho, you can get a copy of the full KIS manual by sending a message to **kis@cnri.reston.va.us** with just **man** in the message body.

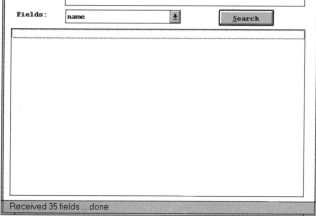

You'll use a form such as this one to search for the person you want.

6. Type the name of the person and then select **Search**. The Gopher displays the results of the search.

Checking Out Mailing List Subscribers

If you know the person you want to track down subscribes to a particular mailing list (because, say, you saw a contribution from that person sometime in the past), you can try to get your hands on a list of the list's subscribers. There are three ways to go about this:

➤ If the list's subscription address is **listserv@*somewhere***, send a message to this address with just the following command in the message body (where **listname** is the name of the mailing list):

review *listname*

➤ If the list's subscription address is **majordomo@*somewhere***, use this address to e-mail a message that has just the following in the message body (again, **listname** is the name of the mailing list):

who *listname*

➤ For all other mailing lists, send a message to the **listname-request@*somewhere*** address and ask, politely, if you can have a list of the subscribers.

If you're on shaky ground with all this talk about listservs and majordomos, have no fear. You'll be getting the full mailing list treatment in Chapter 19, "Messing Around with Mailing Lists."

Things to Try When You Get Desperate

If the techniques we've looked at so far don't work, there are still a few other last ditch things you can try. Here's a summary:

Post a Message to USENET

USENET has a newsgroup that caters specifically to people looking for e-mail addresses. In the group **soc.net-people**, you'll see all kinds of posts with Subject lines like "Looking for Muffy VanSlyke." I have no idea if these people ever get any results, but I figure it can't hurt to try. You'll probably improve your chances of getting a positive reply if you include details, such as what city you think the person lives in, how old they are, and so on.

Read the FAQ

The newsgroup **soc.net-people** is also home to an article called "FAQ: How to find people's E-mail addresses." This article appears regularly and it contains not only the things we've talked about in this chapter, but all kinds of more obscure techniques that the stout-hearted may want to try. If you don't see the article, anonymous FTP to **rtfm.mit.edu**, change to the directory **/pub/usenet-by-group/news.answers**, and grab the file named **finding-addresses**.

Read Another FAQ

Speaking of FAQs, if you're hunting for someone in a college or university, you may find the three-part article "FAQ: College E-mail Addresses," helpful. It's posted regularly to **soc.college** and **soc.net-people** and it gives advice about finding professors, students, and other academicians. You'll also find lots of info on tracking down people at specific institutions. If you can't get the article in one of the newsgroups, you can get it from **rtfm.mit.edu** in the **/pub/usenet-by-group/news.answers/mail/college-email** directory. Download the files **part1**, **part2**, and **part3**.

Try the Netfind Service

If you have some idea about where the person is located (say, their city, state, province, or organization), the *Netfind* program may be of help. Netfind scours the Net's various white pages directories looking for a specified name and location. It's a bit more complex than the other services, so I won't cover it in detail. If you have the Netfind program on your computer (it's a UNIX program), type **man netfind** to get some instructions. If you don't have access to the Netfind program, there are public "Netfind servers" you can telnet to and use the program on their nickel. The article "FAQ: How to find people's E-mail Addresses," that I previously mentioned has a list of these sites.

Try the Postmaster

All Internet sites have a *postmaster* who looks after the various electronic mail chores for that site. If you know the domain name of the site where the person you're trying to find has his e-mail address, you may be able to enlist the postmaster's help. Just send an e-mail message to **postmaster@*domain***, where ***domain*** is the domain name of the site. Most postmasters won't just fork over an e-mail address, but you can ask them to forward your message to the person. Here's an example message you could send to find, say, Bill A. Bong at **atlantis.com**:

Why can't you just get the postmaster to send the person's e-mail address to you? Well, for one thing, most postmasters are *way* too busy to send out responses to every bozo looking for an e-mail address. For another, in Internet circles, it's considered rude to give out or publicly advertise a person's e-mail address without his permission.

```
To: postmaster@atlantis.com
Subject: Is there a Bill A. Bong in the house?

Dear Postmaster,
I understand that Bill A. Bong has an e-mail address at your site.
Would you be so kind as to forward this message to him for me.

Thank you for your time.

Dear Bill,
Hey, how are ya! If this message gets to you, send me some e-mail
so I can get your address.
```

Pick Up the Phone!

You'd be amazed how many people would rather brave the muddy waters of Whois databases and Gopher phone books than simply pick up the phone and ask the person or the person's secretary for his e-mail address! Admittedly, one of the side effects of heavy e-mail use is an almost comical aversion to telephone conversions (no, really; just wait and see), but there are times when you should just bite the bullet and pick up the phone.

The Least You Need to Know

This chapter gave you a sampling of just a few of the many Internet services that are available to help you find someone's e-mail moniker. Not all of the tools are particularly useful, but, hey, whaddya want for nothing!? Anyway, for what it's worth, here's a rehash of the techniques we looked at:

➤ MIT hoards the e-mail addresses of all the people who posted to a USENET newsgroup in the past year. To search this list for a name, send an e-mail message to **mail-server@rtfm.mit.edu** and include **send usenet-addresses/*name*** in the message body.

➤ Use the UNIX **whois** command to search for a name in a Whois database.

➤ The Knowbot Information Service uses a knowbot to check various sites for a name. Send an e-mail message to **kis@cnri.reston.va.us** with **query *name*** in the message body.

➤ If you tunnel through Gopherspace regularly, look for menu items that access "phone books" from various institutions around the world.

➤ If the person has posted an article to a mailing list, get a copy of the list's subscribers. For a LISTSERV list, send the message **review** *listname*; for a Majordomo list, send the message **who** *listname*.

➤ If all else fails, try posting a request to the USENET newsgroup **soc.net-people** or reading the FAQs that appear in the group. You can also try the Netfind program, the postmaster at the person's site, or a simple telephone call.

Part 2
A Guide to Popular E-Mail Software

My parents are Scottish, so they have many good "old country" expressions for various situations. One of my favorites is "fine words butter no parsnips," which means, basically, that all the theory in the world won't accomplish anything practical. So, after many a fine word in Part 1, our job now is to start buttering a parsnip or two. Specifically, it's time to start learning how to get things done in the e-mail world. To that end, the eleven chapters in Part 2 show you the ins and outs of the most popular e-mail programs available today. We'll cover software for UNIX, Windows, and the Mac, as well as the Big Four online services: America Online, CompuServe, Prodigy, and Delphi.

MODEM PROBLEMS

Chapter 8

Yer Basic UNIX Mail Program

In This Chapter

➤ Displaying your mail

➤ Replying to an e-mail message

➤ Saving and deleting messages

➤ Composing and sending e-mail messages

➤ A no-muss, no-fuss primer for a no-muss, no-fuss program

When it comes to the Internet, UNIX is Numero Uno, the Big Cheese, the Top Dog, the Head Honcho, the Big Kahuna. Yeah, sure, there are plenty of DOS, Windows, and Macintosh machines dialing in to the Net these days, but they're really just paying obeisance to the great UNIX lords and their all-knowing, all-seeing, all-powerful deities-cum-servers. If you're one of the blessed UNIX flock, you almost certainly have an e-mail program built right into your system. Actually, you probably have several e-mail packages to choose from, but there's one that's standard on almost every UNIX installation. It's called **mail** and it's the subject of this chapter.

Cranking Up the mail Program

Well, since brass tacks wait for no one (or something like that), let's get right to the business at hand. To start the **mail** program, just type **mail** at the UNIX prompt and press **Enter**. That's it. No keyboard contortions or convoluted UNIX syntax to master. If you have mail waiting to be read, your screen will show a printout similar to the following:

```
SCO System V Mail (version 3.2) Type ? for help.
"/usr/spool/mail/paulmcf": 3 messages 3 new
 N  3 orex@thebes.gov    Tue Apr 4 21:58  31/1381 Need help with riddle!
 N  2 athena@olympia.com Tue Apr 4 15:42  18/940  Father needs headache remedy
>N  1 apollo@delphi.com  Tue Apr 4 13:01  53/2743 Re: Request for stock trends
```

The first line tells you which version of **mail** you're using and tells you that you can enter **?** to get help (I'll talk about this a little later). The second line shows the name of your system mailbox, how many messages are waiting, and how many of them are new or unread. From there, the rest of the text gives you short, one-line descriptions of each message. These so-called *header summaries* are usually divided into six columns. Using the first header summary as an example, let's see what each column means:

N	The first column tells you the status of the message. This will usually be N (new), U (unread), or blank (read).
3	This is the message number (in the order in which it was received).
orex@thebes.gov	This is the e-mail address of the person who sent the message.
Tue Apr 4 21:58	This is the date and time the message was sent.
31/1381	These numbers tell you the number of lines and the number of characters in the message (including the header).
Need help with riddle!	This is the Subject line of the message.

After the last header summary, you'll see the **mail** program's ampersand (&) prompt with a blinking cursor beside it. This is where you'll be entering the commands that make **mail** do your bidding.

Running mail Commands

Before we pull out our digital machetes and start cutting our way through the jungle of **mail**'s commands, here are some tidbits that will help you work with these commands:

➤ To run any command, type the command name and press **Enter**.

➤ Most of the commands have two forms: a full name and an abbreviation. For example, the command that displays a message is called **print**, and its abbreviation is **p**.

➤ Many of **mail**'s commands can operate on either the *current message* or on a group of messages. What's the current message? Well, if you look at the preceding header summaries, you'll notice that message 1 has a greater-than sign (>) on the far left. This symbol tells you that message 1 is the current message.

If all you want to do is a quick check of your mail without doing any reading or sending, you have a couple of choices. To see the header summaries, type **mail -H** at the UNIX prompt and press **Enter**. **mail** will display the summaries and drop you back at the UNIX prompt. To see just the sender's e-mail address and the message dates and times, type **from** and press **Enter**.

➤ If you want a command to operate on a message other than the current one, you specify the message number as part of the command. For example, to display message number 5, you'd type **print 5** (or just **p 5**) and press **Enter**. Notice the space between the command and the message number. Similarly, you can specify multiple messages for a command. For example, the **delete** (or **d**) command deletes messages. To delete messages 5, 6, and 7, you'd type **delete 5–7** (or **d 5–7**) and press **Enter**. (Here, the designation 5–7 is called a *message list*.) To make our lives a bit easier, **mail** also has a few other ways to specify messages, and I've listed them all in Table 8.1 on the following page.

Working with mail's Header Summaries

What do you do if you're not sure which message is the current one? The easiest course is to type an equal sign (=) and press **Enter**. **mail** will display the message number and return you to the & prompt. If you need the big picture, though, you'll want to redisplay the header summaries. You can do that by typing **headers** (or just **h**) and pressing **Enter**.

If you're really popular on a particular day, you may have more than a screenful's worth of messages in the header summary. In this case, type **z** and press **Enter** to see the next page of summaries. To return to the previous page, type **z-** and press **Enter**.

Table 8.1 Specifying Messages in mail

Use This	To Specify
n	Message number *n*. For example, **d 1** deletes message number 1.
n-m	Message number *n* through *m*. For example, **d 2–3** deletes messages 2 and 3.
^	The first message. Note that this applies to the first *undeleted* message. For example, if you delete message 1, then any command that uses the caret (^) will apply to message number 2.
$	The last message.
*	All the messages.
address	All messages with *address* in the From line.
/*string*	All messages that contain *string* in the Subject line.
:d	All deleted messages.
:n	All new messages.
:o	All old messages.
:r	All read messages.
:u	All unread messages.

Reading Your Mail

Okay, that's enough of that. Now that **mail** is waiting patiently for you to do something, let's start with reading your mail (if you have any, that is). To read a message, use the **print** command (or its abbreviation, **p**). Alternatively, you can just press **Enter** and **mail** will do two things:

➤ It will display the current message.

➤ It will move the current message marker to the *next* message.

This means you can read all your messages in order just by continuously pressing **Enter**. If you need to go back to the previous message, you can press the minus (-) key.

If you receive a lengthy message, the whole thing may not fit in a single screen. In this case, **mail** courteously pauses after one screenful. In most cases, you'll see a prompt at the bottom of the screen that looks like this:

— —More— — (25%)

This tells you that you've seen only 25% of the message so far. To see more, press the **spacebar**; if you need to go back one screen, press **b** instead. When **mail** has displayed the entire message, it returns you to the & prompt or displays the next mail message.

Replying to a Message

Lots of messages that come your way will be FYI only, and you won't have to deal with them any further (unless you want to save them or delete them; see the instructions later in this chapter). There will be plenty of messages, however, where you'll want to reply to the sender in some fashion. **mail** gives you two options for replying:

➤ If you want to reply only to the author of the message, use the **reply** (or **r**) command.

➤ If you want to reply to the author of the message *and* any other recipients that are listed in the Cc (courtesy copy) line, use the **Reply** (or **R**) command.

Just to keep us all on our toes (and thoroughly confused, to boot), some versions of **mail** reverse the meanings of the **reply** and **Reply** commands. Before trying out a reply, type a question mark (**?**) and press **Enter** to see a list of commands for your version of **mail**.

In either case, you can enter the command by itself to reply to the current message, or you can use some of the symbols from Table 8.1, shown earlier, to reply to a different message. **mail** then displays the To, Subject, and (if you chose the **Reply** command) Cc lines for your reply and displays a blinking cursor where you can enter your text (this is called *input mode*). At this point, there are three main things you can do: adjust one or more of the header fields, insert the text from the original article into your reply, and/or type in your own contribution to the reply. You can read about each of these procedures in the next few sections.

Adjusting Header Lines While Composing a Message

Normally, you won't need to make any changes to the header of a reply because **mail** takes care of most of the dirty work for you. In particular, it addresses the To line to the original author of the message, it adds **Re:** to the Subject line of the original message, and (if you chose the **Reply** command) inserts the other recipients into the Cc line.

However, if you *do* need to change any of these fields (say, to add or remove recipients in the Cc line), **mail** is only too happy to oblige. You do this by entering various commands. The problem is, though, that **mail** is currently in input mode waiting for you to enter the text of your reply. So how is the program supposed to differentiate between the text of your message and the text of a command? The answer lies in a seldom-used character called *tilde*: ~. By typing this character and *then* typing your command, **mail** knows that you're not just adding text to the reply. In honor of the tilde, these commands are called *tilde escapes* and Table 8.2 lists some examples of the species that let you modify the header of the message you're composing (note that you press **Enter** after entering each command):

Table 8.2   Tilde Escape Commands for Modifying Headers

Tilde Escape	What It Does
~t *addr*	Adds the e-mail address given by *addr* to the To line. For example, ~**t paulmcf@hookup.net** adds "paulmcf@hookup.net" to the To line.
~s *subject*	Changes the Subject line to *subject*. For example, entering ~**s Re: What!!!** changes the Subject line to Re: What!!!.
~c *addr*	Adds the e-mail address given by *addr* to the Cc line.
~b *addr*	Adds the e-mail address given by *addr* to the Bcc (blind carbon copy) line.
~h	Displays all the header lines one at a time so you can edit each line. You can add text to a line or use Backspace to delete unwanted characters. When you finish with each line, press **Enter** to move on to the next one.

Inserting Text into a Message

As I mentioned back in Chapter 4, in the "Minding Your E-Mail Manners" section, it's polite to include some text from the original message in your reply, but only enough to put your response into context. In **mail**, you do this by using another tilde escape command: **~f**. Typing this command and pressing **Enter** causes **mail** to insert into the reply the

mail will only recognize the tilde escape commands when you're at the beginning of a new line.

original message in its entirety, header and all. I'll show you in the next section how to load the reply into a text editor so you can delete the lines you don't need.

A slightly different tilde escape command is **~m**. This command also inserts the original message into the reply, but it shifts the text a few spaces to the right. (Indenting text to the right is one way of differentiating between original text and new text. A much more common method is to preface each line in the original text with a greater-than sign (>). I'll show you how to do this in the next section.)

Finally, if you want to include the contents of another file in the reply (such as your **.signature** file), use the **~r** command. Note that for this command you also have to specify the name of the file. So, for example, to include your **.signature** file in the reply, you'd enter the following command:

```
~r .signature
```

What's a **.signature** file? It's nothing more than a simple text file that contains the signature you want to use with your messages. Use your favorite text editor to create the **.signature** file in your UNIX home directory.

Typing Text into a Message

If you type anything other than a tilde escape when you're in input mode, **mail** just adds the text to the message body of the reply. This means you can just start typing to compose your message. When you reach the end of a line, press **Enter** to start a new line. When you finish your message, press **Ctrl+D** to tell **mail** you're done. **mail** then sends the message on its cyberspatial journey.

Input mode, though, suffers from two glaring problems:

➤ Once you've entered a line, you can't go back and make changes. This will really make you pull out your hair if you notice a spelling mistake or some other boner in a previous line.

➤ If you've added text from the original message, there's no way to delete some of the chaff (especially the header from the original message) or add the greater-than signs (>) that are the normal indicators of original material.

The solution to both problems is to load your message into a good text editor and then go crazy. To do this, type **~e** and press **Enter**. **mail** will start the default text editor (which is usually **vi** or **Emacs**) and load your message. If you'd prefer to specify your favorite text editor (or, since this is UNIX we're talking about, the text editor you hate the least), enter the following tilde escape command:

```
~e editor
```

Here, *editor* is the name of the editor you want to use. For example, to specify the **vi** editor, type **~e vi** and press **Enter**.

Saving Messages for Posterity

As I've said, you should add greater-than signs (>) to the beginning of each line you're quoting from the original message (you should also add a space to make the quoted lines easier to read). If you have a boatload of quoted material (shame on you!) and you're using **vi**, entering the following command will automatically place the string ">" (that's greater-than followed by a space) at the beginning of every line:

```
:%s/^/> /
```

If someone sends you a particularly memorable message, you'll probably want to preserve it for the ages. The best way to do this is to save the message to its own file. **mail** gives you two options:

➤ If you want to preserve just the message body (i.e., no header), use the **write** (or **w**) command, like so:

```
write [message_list] filename
```

Here, [*message_list*] is the optional list of message numbers to write (if you leave this out, **mail**, as usual, works with the current message), and *filename* is the name of the file. For example, to save messages 3 and 4 in the file **Homebrew_Mailing_List**, you'd use the following command:

```
write 3-4 Homebrew_Mailing_List
```

➤ If you want to save both the message body *and* the header, use the **save** (or **s**) command, instead:

```
save [message_list] filename
```

Again, [*message_list*] is an optional list of message numbers and *filename* is the name you want to give to the file.

You should know that whichever command you use, if the filename you specify already exists, **mail** will simply append the message to the end of the file. This is a handy way to keep similar messages together. For example, you could set up a file for a particular mailing list you subscribe to and save the list's mailings to the same file each time. You could set up similar files for regular correspondents, messages from your system administrator, or even for current projects.

Deleting Expendable Messages

If you've read a message and you don't need to save it or even look at it again, you should delete it to keep your mailbox relatively tidy. To delete a message, you can either use the **delete** (or **d**) command to blow away any message(s), or the **dp** command, which deletes the current message and then displays (prints) the next message.

If you delete a message accidentally, you can recover it by using the **undelete** (or **u**) command.

Composing a New Message

When it's time to dazzle the world with your brilliant prose, **mail** gives you a couple of ways to start composing a new message. Here are the steps you need to follow:

1. Use either of the following methods to get things off to a rousing start:

   ➤ If you've already started **mail**, type **mail** (or **m**), a space, the e-mail address of the recipient, and then press **Enter**.

   ➤ If **mail** isn't up and running, type **mail** at the UNIX prompt, a space, the recipient's e-mail address, and then press **Enter**.

2. In either case, **mail** displays a **Subject** prompt. Type the subject of the message and press **Enter. mail** switches to input mode and displays the blinking cursor.

3. Type your message, pressing **Enter** when you come to the end of each line. Keep in mind that the tilde escape characters we looked at earlier will be in effect. In particular,

you can use these commands to change the header, add a file to the message, or load a text editor for fine-tuned work.

4. When your message is done, press **Ctrl+D** to send the message.

Quitting mail

When you've had just about all you can stand of this **mail** malarkey, you can quit the program by entering the **quit** (or **q**) command. This command preserves any changes you made to your mailbox, including deleting any messages that you saved to a file. If you don't want to preserve the mailbox changes, bail out using the **exit** (or **ex** or **x**) command.

A Summary of mail's Commands

Just so you have a handy reference for the **mail** procedures we looked at in this chapter, Table 8.3 lists the various commands and their options. Note that the table uses *[msgs]* to represent a message list (that is, a number, series of numbers, or a symbol that specifies which messages you want a command to work with). The square brackets tell you that the message list is optional in each case.

Table 8.3 A Summary of the mail Commands

Command	Abbreviation	What It Does
Working with Header Summaries		
headers *[msgs]*	h	Displays the list of header summaries.
z	-	Displays the next page of header summaries.
z-	-	Displays the last page of header summaries.
Displaying Messages		
Enter	-	Displays the next message.
- (minus)	-	Displays the previous message.
num	-	Displays message number *num*.
print *[msgs]*	p	Displays messages.

Command	Abbreviation	What It Does
Working with Messages		
=		Displays the current message number.
edit [*msgs*]	e	Loads messages into the editor.
reply [*msgs*]	r	Replies to the author of the specified message.
Reply [*msgs*]	R	Replies to the author and all recipients of the specified message.
write [*msgs*] *file*	w	Writes messages to *file* without the headers.
save [*msgs*] *file*	s	Saves messages to *file*, including the headers.
delete [*msgs*]	d	Deletes messages.
dp	-	Deletes the current message and displays the next message.
undelete [*msgs*]	u	Undeletes messages.
Miscellaneous Commands		
mail *addr*	m	Composes and sends a message to the e-mail address *addr*.
quit	q	Quits **mail** and saves the mailbox changes.
exit	ex or x	Quits **mail** and doesn't save changes.
?	-	Displays a summary if **mail**'s commands.

The Least You Need to Know

This chapter introduced you to the basic **mail** program that comes with most UNIX installations. Here's what we covered:

> ➤ To start **mail**, just type **mail** and press **Enter**. If you want to send a message, type **mail *addr***, where ***addr*** is the e-mail address of the recipient.

87

➤ To redisplay the list of header summaries, type **headers** (or **h**) and press **Enter**.

➤ If you want to read all your mail consecutively, press **Enter** at the start as well as after you've read each message.

➤ To reply to a message, use the **reply** (or **r**) command to reply only to the author. If you want to send the response to the author and to each recipient, use the **Reply** (or **R**) command instead.

➤ When composing a message (that is, in input mode), you can use the tilde escapes to enter commands. For example, ~**h** lets you change the header lines individually, ~**f** inserts the text from the original message in a reply, and ~**e** starts the text editor and loads the current message.

➤ To save a message, use the **write** (or **w**) command to include the headers or the **save** (or **s**) command to go headerless.

➤ You can handle your message-deleting chores with either the **delete** (or **d**) command, which can delete any specified message, or the **dp** command, which deletes the current message and displays the next one.

➤ To compose a new message while **mail** is running, use the **mail** (or **m**) command.

Riding Pine's Pony Express

The standard, garden-variety **mail** program that's built into most UNIX systems (and that we discussed in Chapter 8) is okay for light-duty e-mail chores. However, you only need to use it for a little while before its shortcomings become glaring: there's no way to send or receive nontext files; it can't store e-mail addresses you use regularly; and there's no convenient way to save and retrieve related messages you've received.

Happily, most UNIX installations also come equipped with another mail program called *Pine*. Pine (which stands for "Program for Internet News and E-mail") overcomes each of these faults and adds a few more handy features, besides. Does this mean Pine is obtuse and hard to learn? Thankfully, no. If anything, Pine's layout is even simpler and more sensible than **mail**'s. This chapter introduces you to the program and takes you through all the pertinent Pine particulars.

Pushing Off with Pine

There's no time like the present, as they say, so let's get right down to business. To start Pine, type **pine** at the UNIX prompt, and press **Enter**. Pine ponders life for a few seconds and then displays its MAIN MENU screen, as shown in this figure.

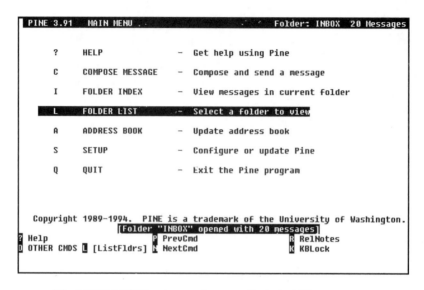

```
PINE 3.91    MAIN MENU                          Folder: INBOX   20 Messages


       ?    HELP              -  Get help using Pine

       C    COMPOSE MESSAGE   -  Compose and send a message

       I    FOLDER INDEX      -  View messages in current folder

       L    FOLDER LIST       -  Select a folder to view

       A    ADDRESS BOOK      -  Update address book

       S    SETUP             -  Configure or update Pine

       Q    QUIT              -  Exit the Pine program



     Copyright 1989-1994.  PINE is a trademark of the University of Washington.
                    [Folder "INBOX" opened with 20 messages]
? Help                       P PrevCmd                    R RelNotes
O OTHER CMDS L [ListFldrs] N NextCmd                      K KBLock
```

The MAIN MENU you see when you first start Pine.

The MAIN MENU, like all of Pine's screens, is divided into three sections:

➤ The top line of the screen is called the *status line*, and it tells you the version of Pine you're using, the screen name, the folder you're using (I'll explain what a folder is in the next section), and how many messages are in the folder.

➤ The area below the top line is a work area where you'll select items from menus and lists, read messages, compose new messages, and more.

➤ The bottom three lines display reports on recent Pine actions (such as **Folder "INBOX" opened with 20 messages** shown in the preceding figure) and show you some of the Pine commands that are currently at your disposal.

Making Pine Do Something

Before we examine the various trees in Pine's forest, we should first figure out how to make Pine do our bidding. Here's a rundown of the basics:

➤ All Pine commands and menu items have a *selection letter* that sets the command in motion. There are two ways to determine the appropriate letter for the command you want to run: 1) Menu items show the selection letter to the left of the item. In the MAIN MENU, for example, the selection letter for the **COMPOSE MESSAGE** item is **C**; 2) The bottom two lines of the Pine screen list the available commands and display their selection letters to the left of the command name. For example, the selection letter for the PrevCmd command is **P**.

➤ When entering your selection letters, it doesn't matter if you enter the letter as uppercase or lowercase.

➤ There's always a default menu item or command that you can run just by pressing **Enter**. There are two ways to figure out which item/command is currently the default: 1) If you're viewing a menu or list, the default item will be highlighted (in the MAIN MENU shown in the preceding picture, the **FOLDER LIST** item is highlighted, so it's the default; 2) The bottom line of the screen shows the default command in square brackets. For example, when you first display the MAIN MENU, the default command is shown as **[ListFldrs]** (see the preceding picture).

➤ As I've said, the default item in a menu or list is highlighted, but you can change the default menu item by moving the highlight up or down. To move up, press **P** (for "Previous"); to move down, press **N** (for "Next") or use the arrow keys. This is especially handy in lists of messages, because many Pine commands (such as **Reply** and **Delete**) operate on the currently highlighted message.

➤ There are three important commands that will be available in most of Pine's screens:

    ?   The **Help** command brings up a *context-sensitive* HELP screen. (Context-sensitive means the HELP screen that appears is related to whatever Pine screen you're currently slaving away in.)

    O   The **OTHER CMDS** command displays more commands at the bottom of the screen.

    M   The **Main Menu** command takes you back to the MAIN MENU.

➤ Some Pine commands will display a selection letter that looks like this: ^C. The caret (^) indicates that you have to hold down the **Ctrl** key when pressing the letter. So ^C means you hold down **Ctrl**, press C, and then release **Ctrl**. To be consistent with other parts of this book, I'll use the more standard notation **Ctrl+C** for these shortcuts.

A Note About Pine's Folders

One of the few things I miss about corporate life is having an efficient assistant to handle all those details I can never seem to get the hang of. In particular, I miss having my daily mail separated into nice, neat little stacks. There'd be a pile for memos, another one for correspondence from customers, another for magazines, and so on.

So one of the nice things about Pine is that I can at least separate my e-mail into electronic "piles" called *folders*. A folder is just a file that can hold e-mail messages. When you first start Pine, it sets up a basic folder called INBOX to hold all your incoming mail, but you're free to create however many folders you need. For example, you could set up a folder to hold notes from regular e-mail correspondents, from your system administrator, your best friend, or whomever. I'll give you the details about creating and selecting folders later on in this chapter.

Catching Up with Your E-Mail Messages

Okay, let's start putting Pine through its paces. In particular, this section will show you how to use Pine to read your e-mail messages.

Since we're just starting out with Pine, any messages you have to read will be stored in your INBOX folder. Conveniently, Pine opens the INBOX folder for you automatically when you load the program, so we can get right to it. (I'll show you how to open other folders later on.) The first thing you need to do is display the list of messages that are stored in the INBOX folder. You do this by pressing **I** to select the **FOLDER INDEX** item in the MAIN MENU. When you do, you'll see the FOLDER INDEX screen, as shown in the following figure.

```
  PINE 3.91    FOLDER INDEX            Folder: INBOX   Message 1 of 20

     1   Jan 13 Robert E. King      (3,728) NEW: VIRTED - Uses of VIRTUAL REAL
     2   Jan 13 RASCHKE             (3,511) NEW: CORELINK - Educational Goals a
   D 3   Jan 13 Lynn Craig          (3,232) NEW: rip-pol-econ - Review Internat
     4   Jan 13 Me, Myself and I    (3,048) NEW: TOP5 - Letterman-Style comedy
   D 5   Jan 13 Franklin Weston     (3,530) SEARCH: Literacy Training
     6   Jan 13 Gregory L. Jacknow  (3,504) NEW: MULT-ED - Multicultural Educat
     7   Jan 13 Jim Delaney         (3,576) NEW: WalkNet-L - Campus Safety Esco
 + A 8   Jan 14 Ian Worling         (1,272) Financial statements
 +   9   Jan 14 HookUp Support      (1,213) Re: Can't get mailx to pause when c
    10   Jan 14 bs293017@v9001.ntu  (3,431) integral solns.
    11   Jan 14 Mark R Panitz       (1,876) SEARCH: I love Lucy
    12   Jan 14 Christina G. Atchl  (2,967) NEW: MULTIAGE - Multiage Learning a
    13   Jan 14 DICK BANKS ADAPTIV  (3,012) NEW: ADVOCACY - Rights of people wi
    14   Jan 15 Benjie KE6BCU       (3,014) BBS service for IAMS now available
    15   Jan 15 CFS-L Moderator     (2,490) SEARCH: Women's Health list?
    16   Jan 15 Lori A. Martin      (2,996) CHANGE: STHL-L - Star Trek Humour L
    17   Jan 15 Harlan M.Woodring   (3,169) Do you know these books?
   N 18  Jan 16 Leigh Blue Caldwel  (4,188) Re: Do you know these books?
   N 19  Jan 16 Michael Ulm         (3,238) a few problems

 ? Help        M Main Menu  P PrevMsg    - PrevPage    D Delete     R Reply
 O OTHER CMDS  V [ViewMsg]  N NextMsg  Spc NextPage    U Undelete   F Forward
```

The FOLDER INDEX screen shows a list of messages waiting to be read.

The first two columns show the current status of each message. Table 9.1 lists the most common codes you'll see in your Pine travels.

Table 9.1 Status Codes for E-Mail Messages in Pine

Code	What It Means
A	You've replied to (answered) the message.
D	You've marked the message for deletion.
N	The message is new.
+	The message came directly to you (that is, it wasn't passed on to you by a mailing list, or you weren't listed in the Cc line of the message).

The rest of the columns show the message number, the date the message was sent, the author, the number of characters in the message, and the Subject line.

Sorting the Messages

By default, Pine sorts your messages in the order they arrived, with the earliest messages at the top. To change this sort order, press **$** to fire up the **SortIndex** command. Pine then displays the following prompt:

```
Choose type of sort, or Reverse of current sort :
```

The most common sort options are by Subject line (press **S**), by From line (press **F**), by size (press **Z**), by date sent (press **D**), and by arrival time (press **A**). You can also press **R** to reverse the current sort order. For example, if you reverse the order of the arrival sort, the latest messages will appear at the top. If you decide not to sort the messages after all, press **Ctrl+C** to cancel.

Selecting a Message to Read

To select a message, Pine gives you a cool half-dozen methods to get the job done. Here's the rundown:

➤ To move down one message, press **N** to select the **NextMsg** command.

➤ To move up one message, press **P** to select the **PrevMsg** command.

➤ If you have more messages than can fit on a single screen, press either the **Spacebar** or **+** (plus sign) to display the next page. To move back a page, press **-** (minus sign).

➤ To highlight the next new message, press **Tab** to run the **NextNew** command.

➤ To move to a specific message number, press **J** to select the **Jump** command. When you see the **Message number to jump to :** prompt, type the message number and press **Enter**.

➤ To find a message that contains a particular word or phrase in the author name or the Subject line, press **W** to run the **WhereIs** command. When Pine displays the **Word to search for :** prompt, type in your search text and press **Enter**. If Pine finds a match, it highlights the message. If that isn't the message you want, you can continue the search by pressing **W** and then pressing **Enter**.

Reading a Message

Now that you have your message highlighted, you can read what it has to say by pressing **V** to select the **ViewMsg** command. (This command is the default, so you can also just press **Enter**.) Pine loads up the message and displays it in the MESSAGE TEXT screen. If the entire message doesn't fit on the screen, you can move to the next page by pressing **Spacebar** or + (plus). To move back a page, press - (minus).

When you're done with the current message, press **N** (**NextMsg**) to move on to the next message, or press **P** (**PrevMsg**) to head back to the previous message. If all you want to do is read the next new message, press **Tab** (**NextNew**), instead.

When you've finished reading, you can either process the message (by replying to it, saving it, or deleting it; see the next few sections), or you can press **I** (**Index**) to get back to the FOLDER INDEX screen.

If the author of the message included an attachment, you'll see something like the following at the bottom of the header:

```
Parts/attachments:
  1 Shown    15 lines  Text
  2          64 KB     Image
```

The first "part" is the message text, and the second describes the attachment (a graphics file or "Image," in this case). Press **V** to select the **ViewAttch** command, highlight the attachment, and then press **S** to run the **Save** command. Pine should suggest a name for the file. If the name is okay, just press **Enter**. Otherwise, type your own name and press **Enter**. Press **E** to return to the message. Later, when you quit Pine, you can use the appropriate program (such as a graphics viewer) to check out the file in its native format.

Replying to a Message

If the author of a message is expecting some kind of response from you, or if you've thought of a witty rejoinder to a message, you need to use Pine's **Reply** command to compose and send a reply. To try this out, follow these steps:

1. Either highlight the message you'll be replying to in the FOLDER INDEX list, or display the message in the MESSAGE TEXT screen.

2. Press **R** to select the **Reply** command. Pine displays the following prompt:

   `Include original text in reply?`

3. If you want to include the original text (it's usually a good idea), press **Y** or **Enter** to select **Yes**. Otherwise, press **N** for **No**. Pine displays the COMPOSE MESSAGE REPLY screen. If you elected to include the original message text, it appears with greater-than signs (>) on the left (see figure below).

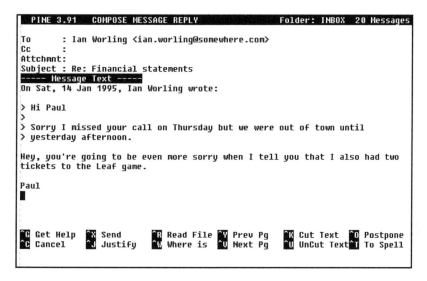

Pine's COMPOSE MESSAGE REPLY screen.

4. Use the keys listed in Table 9.2 to move around the screen, edit text, and remove unnecessary lines from the original message text.

95

Table 9.2 Some Keys to Use with Pine's Text Editor

Press	To
Arrow keys	Move one character in the arrow direction.
Ctrl+F	Move forward one character.
Ctrl+B	Move back one character.
Ctrl+E	Move to the end of the line.
Ctrl+A	Move to the beginning of the line.
Ctrl+N	Move to the next line.
Ctrl+P	Move to the previous line.
Ctrl+V	Move to the next page.
Ctrl+Y	Move to the previous page.
Ctrl+D	Delete the current character.
Ctrl+H	Delete the character to the left.
Ctrl+^	Set the beginning of marked text.
Ctrl+K	Cut marked text or delete the current line.
Ctrl+U	Paste cut text or undelete a line cut with Ctrl+K.

This notion of "marked text" may require a bit more explanation. Marked text is just highlighted text that you can cut out of the reply and, optionally, paste somewhere else. (Cutting large chunks of text is handy when, say, you want to get rid of a few lines from the original text of a message.) To try it out, first position the cursor at the beginning of the text. Now press **Ctrl+^**. Pine will display **Mark Set**. Now move the cursor to the end of the text and notice how Pine highlights the text as you move. Press **Ctrl+K** to cut the text out of the reply. If you want to paste the text in a different location, move the cursor to the spot you want, and then press **Ctrl+U**.

5. Enter your own text. Note, as well, that you're also free to edit the header lines as needed.

6. Press **Ctrl+X** to send the reply. Pine displays the following prompt to ask you to confirm you want the message sent:

   ```
   Send message ?
   ```

7. Press **Y** or **Enter** to select **Yes** and send the message on its merry way. If you change your mind, press **N** to select **No**, instead.

If you're wondering about other message options, such as attaching a nontext file, inserting a text file, and spell-checking the message, I'll postpone those until we talk about composing a new message (see the "Composing an Original Message" section later in this chapter).

Forwarding a Message to Another Address

You may occasionally receive a message that you think should be seen by someone else, or you may get a message delivered to your address that should have been sent to a different locale. In either case, Pine makes it easy to forward the message to another e-mail address. Here are the steps to follow to get this done:

1. Highlight or read the message you want to forward.

2. Press **F** to select the Forward command. Pine loads the message into the FORWARD MESSAGE screen.

3. In the **To** line, enter the e-mail address where you want the message sent.

4. Use the **Message Text** section to enter your own comments, if any.

5. Press **Ctrl+X** to send the reply and, when Pine displays the **Send message ?** prompt, select **Yes**.

Fiddling with Pine's Folders

As I mentioned earlier, Pine uses folders to store your messages. The basic INBOX folder is fine for reading your incoming mail, but if you want to save messages (as explained in the next section), you'll want to have different folders for different types of messages. To create a new folder, follow these instructions:

1. From Pine's MAIN MENU or FOLDER INDEX screen, press **L** to select the **ListFldrs** command. Pine displays the FOLDER LIST screen, as shown here.

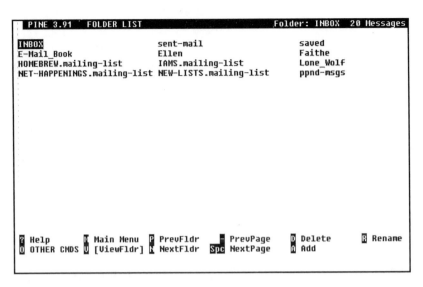

You use the FOLDER LIST screen to add new folders.

2. Press **A** to select the **Add** command. Pine displays the following prompt:

   ```
   Name of folder to add :
   ```

3. Type a name for the new folder; use only letters, numbers, periods (.), and under-scores (_) and then press **Enter**. Pine adds the folder to the list.

If you make a mistake while entering the folder name, press **Delete** to erase the offending characters. This works in any Pine prompt where you have to enter multiple characters.

To see the messages in a particular folder, highlight the folder name by pressing **N** (for **NextFldr**) or **P** (for **PrevFldr**), and then press **V** (for **ViewFldr**) or **Enter**. (If you have a lot of folders, an easier way to move around is to press **G** for the **GotoFldr** command. At the **GOTO folder** prompt, type the name of the folder and press **Enter**.)

If you want to change the name of a folder, highlight it in the FOLDER LIST, and then press **R** to select the **Rename** command. Use the **Rename folder to :** prompt to edit the name.

To get rid of a folder you don't use, press **D** to select the **Delete** command. When Pine asks if you really want to delete the folder, press **Y** or **Enter**.

Saving Messages in Folders

Okay, now that you're an expert with folders, let's see how you go about saving a message to a folder. Actually, it's pretty simple. With the message either displayed or highlighted in the FOLDER INDEX, press **S** to fire up the **Save** command. You'll then see the following prompt:

```
SAVE to folder [saved] :
```

The first time you run the **Save** command, it will default to the **saved** folder. At this point, you have three ways to proceed:

➤ If you want to use the **saved** folder, just press **Enter**.

➤ To use a different folder, type in its name and then press **Enter**.

➤ If you're not sure about the name of the folder, or if it's a long one and you're too lazy to type the whole thing, you can press **Ctrl+T** to display a list of all your folders. Highlight the one you want, and press **S** or **Enter** to choose the **Select** command. Pine automatically inserts the folder name in the above prompt. Now just press **Enter** to save the message.

In each case, Pine marks the original message for deletion. (I'll explain what this means in the next section.)

Expunging Expendable Messages

For our final message maintenance chore, I'll show you how to get rid of messages that you no longer want to bother with. Message deletion in Pine is actually a two-step process. First, you highlight the message and press **D** to run the **Delete** command. If you try this, you may be disappointed to see that nothing much seems to happen. What gives? How come the message wasn't blown away? Well Pine, being the cautious program that it is, actually only marks the message for deletion by changing its status to D. This way, if you accidentally run the **Delete** command on the wrong message, you can save your bacon by pressing **U** (for **Undelete**).

When you have all your expendable messages marked for deletion, you can perform the second step in Pine's deletion process and really get rid of them by pressing **X** to run the **eXpunge** command. When Pine asks you to confirm, press **Y** or **Enter**.

Adding Names to Pine's Address Book

One of Pine's nicest features is its address book. The address book is just a list of commonly used e-mail addresses that you can call up at any time. As you'll see in the next section, this is particularly handy when filling out the To line in a new message: no more memorizing e-mail addresses or writing them on sticky notes that always seem to get lost.

To display the address book, head back to the MAIN MENU, and then press A to run the **AddrBook** command. Here's how you add a new address:

1. Press **A** to select the **Add** command. Pine displays the following prompt:

   `New full name (Last, First):`

2. Type the person's name and press **Enter**. Another prompt appears:

   `Enter new nickname (one word and easy to remember):`

3. Type a nickname and press **Enter**. (You'll be using these nicknames when you compose your own e-mail missives, so make the nickname short and easy to remember.) Once again, Pine presents you with a prompt:

   `Enter new e-mail address:`

4. Type the person's e-mail address and then press **Enter**. Pine adds the new address to the book.

To make changes to an address, highlight it and press E or **Enter** to choose the **Edit** command. When Pine prompts you to choose a field, press either **N** (for **Nickname**), **F** (for **Fullname**), or **A** (for **Address**). If you've set up a folder for this person, you can have copies of the messages you send to them stored in the folder. Just press **G** to select **Fcc** (folder courtesy copy) and enter the name of the folder.

To delete an address, highlight it and press **D** for the **Delete** command. When Pine asks you to confirm the deletion, press **Y**.

Composing an Original Message

When you have something to get off your chest, then it's time to compose an original e-mail message and send it off. Here's how it's done in Pine:

1. From Pine's MAIN MENU, press **C** to select the **Compose** command. The COMPOSE MESSAGE screen appears, as shown in the next figure. This is essentially the same screen as the COMPOSE MESSAGE REPLY screen you saw earlier. In particular, you can use the same navigation and editing keys that I listed in Table 8.2.

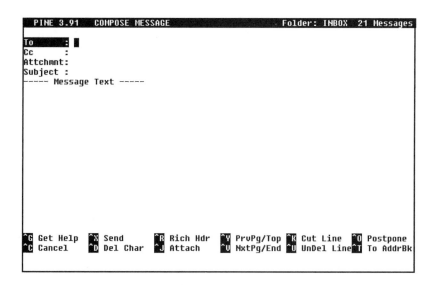

```
   PINE 3.91    COMPOSE MESSAGE                  Folder: INBOX   21 Messages
  To     :
  Cc     :
  Attchmnt:
  Subject :
  ----- Message Text -----




  ^G Get Help  ^X Send      ^R Rich Hdr  ^Y PrvPg/Top  ^K Cut Line    ^O Postpone
  ^C Cancel    ^D Del Char  ^J Attach    ^V NxtPg/End  ^U UnDel Line  ^T To AddrBk
```

Use the COMPOSE MESSAGE screen to create and send a new message.

2. In the **To** field, enter the e-mail address of the recipient. If the addressee is in your address book, just type in their nickname. (If you can't remember the nickname—I told you to make it short!—then press **Ctrl+T** to display the address book, highlight the address you want to use, and then press **S** or **Enter**.)

3. If necessary, fill in the **Cc** field. (Again, you can use nicknames from your address book.) If you're entering multiple addresses, separate each one with a comma.

4. Move to the **Subject** line and type in the subject of your message.

5. Place the cursor below the **Message Text** line and enter the message body.

6. When you're ready to roll, press **Ctrl+X** to send the message and, when Pine displays the **Send message ?** prompt, select **Yes**.

Attaching a File to Your Message

Pine, bless its electronic heart, supports the MIME thingy I told you about back in Chapter 4, in the "Sending Sounds, Graphics, and Other Nontext Files" section. This, you'll recall, means you can attach nontext files, such as graphics and databases to your dispatches.

If you want to attach a file to a message, first place the cursor in the **Attchmnt** field of the COMPOSE MESSAGE screen (or the COMPOSE MESSAGE REPLY screen). Now press **Ctrl+J** to select the **Attach** command, and Pine will display the following prompt:

101

```
File to attach:
```

Type in the name of the file you want to send and press **Enter**. Pine, ever persistent, prompts you again:

```
Attachment comment:
```

Type a comment, such as a description of the file and press **Enter**. Pine adds the filename to the **Attchmnt** field.

Spell-Checking the Message

People on the Net are remarkably tolerant of misspellings and such, but that's no excuse for sloppy spelling on your part. If spelling was never your strong suit (hey, I can relate), you'll be happy to know that Pine has its own spell-checker. You can try it out from either the COMPOSE MESSAGE or COMPOSE MESSAGE REPLY screens by pressing **Ctrl+T** to select the **To Spell** command. If Pine finds a word it doesn't recognize, you'll see a prompt similar to this:

```
Edit a replacement: tikcets
```

Either edit the word or, if the spelling is okay, press **Enter** to move on.

Quitting Pine

Shutting down Pine is no big whoop. You can just press **Q** (for **Quit**) at any screen (except COMPOSE MESSAGE and COMPOSE MESSAGE REPLY). Pine presents one last prompt, for old times sake:

```
Really quit pine?
```

Select **Y** or press **Enter** to get the heck out of there.

If you're looking to learn more about Pine, or to keep abreast of the latest releases, check out the Usenet newsgroup **comp.mail.pine**. You can use this group to ask questions and get technical help from fellow Pine aficionados.

The Least You Need to Know

This chapter showed you Pine's version of the better e-mail mousetrap. Now we'll indulge in a bit of Auld Lang Pine (sorry!) and take a nostalgic look back at some of this chapter's more memorable moments:

➤ To start Pine, type **pine** and press **Enter**.

➤ To read a message, press **I** to select **FOLDER INDEX** from the MAIN MENU, highlight the message, and then press **V**.

➤ To reply to a message, press **R**, enter your reply, and then press **Ctrl+X**.

➤ To forward a message, press **F**, type the forwarding address, and then press **Ctrl+X**.

➤ To save a message to a folder, press **S** and then enter the name of the folder.

➤ To mark a message for deletion, press **D**. To send the marked messages to oblivion, press **X**.

➤ To compose a new message, press **C** to select the **Compose** command. Enter the header data and message body, and then press **Ctrl+X**.

Chapter 10

Cruising Down Elm Street

In This Chapter

➤ Displaying and reading your e-mail

➤ Responding to an e-mail message

➤ Filing your correspondence in folders

➤ Composing new mail and sending it

➤ An embarrassment of Elm riches

This chapter presents the third and final installment of our series on UNIX e-mail software. In the previous episodes, we looked at the standard **mail** program (Chapter 8) and Pine (Chapter 9), and now we turn our attention to *Elm*. As you'll see, Elm and Pine are actually close cousins to each other. Not only are they both named after trees, but they both have similar, full-screen interfaces where you run commands with the touch of a key. Pine has a few more features (such as the handy address book), but Elm is simple, easy to learn, and is ideally suited for e-mail newcomers.

Embarking On Your First Elm Expedition

Outside of logging in to your system, there's no other preparation needed to use Elm. So, without further ado, start Elm by typing **elm** at the UNIX prompt and pressing **Enter**. If you're starting the program for the first time, you'll see the following note appear on your screen:

```
Notice:
This version of ELM requires the use of a .elm directory in your home
directory to store your elmrc and alias files. Shall I create the
directory .elm for you and set it up (y/n/q)? n
```

This somewhat mysterious message is just telling you that Elm needs to set up a few things in your home directory so the program can function properly. Happily, Elm will handle everything automatically, so just press **y** to set things in motion. When that chore is complete, Elm checks your mailbox and, if it finds any messages inside, it loads them up and displays some info about each one in its *Index* screen. This figure shows an example.

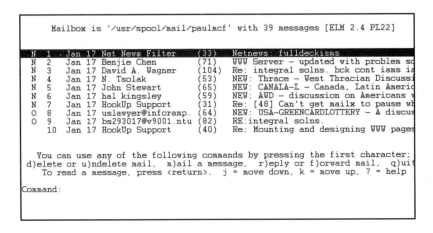

Elm's Index screen displays info about your messages.

The top line of the Index screen shows the name of your mailbox, the total number of messages therein, and the version of Elm you're using. The next 10 lines or so display your mailbox messages in the order you received them (with the most recent ones at the top). Each line represents a single message and is divided into six columns. Using the first message in the preceding picture as an example, here's what you'll find in each column:

N	The first column gives you the status of the message. This will usually be N (new), O (old; unread), D (deleted), or blank (read).
1	This is the message number.
Jan 17	The date the message was sent.
Net News Filter	The name or e-mail address of the person or service that sent the message.
(33)	The number of lines in the message (including the header).
Netnews: fulldeckisms	The Subject line of the message.

Below the messages, you'll see a menu of the most commonly used Elm commands. Since you'll be confronted with a similar menu in all the Elm screens, let's take a moment to try and knock some sense into it.

Don't see the command menu on your screen? You can display it by first pressing **o** to display the Elm Options Editor screen. Now press **M** to select the **M)enu display** option, press **Spacebar** until you see the value **ON**, and then press **Enter**. Now press **i** to return to the Index screen.

In most cases, you run an Elm command just by pressing a letter on your keyboard. The menu uses two methods to show you which keys to press. In the first method, the letter is part of the command name and Elm marks the letter with a right parenthesis, like so:

```
d)elete
```

In this case, you'd simply press **d** to delete the currently highlighted message. (I'll discuss deleting in more detail later on.) In the second method, if the character you press isn't part of the command name, the summary uses an equals sign (=), as shown here:

```
? = help
```

This means you'd press **?** to invoke Elm's online help system (see the next section, "Feeling Overwh-Elm-ed? Try the Help System,"). You should also keep in mind that Elm differentiates between uppercase and lowercase letters. So, for example, pressing **q** runs one command (quit), while pressing **Q** (**Shift+Q**), runs a different command (quick quit). (Both quit commands are explained in the "Quitting Elm" section later in this chapter.)

Feeling Overwh-Elm-ed? Try the Help System

The Elm menu only displays a few of the commands you have at your disposal. If you'd like to see a list of all the Elm commands, or if you'd like a reminder about which command a particular key will invoke, the online help system can ride to your rescue.

To try it out, press **?**. Elm displays the following prompt:

```
    Press the key you want help for. '?' for a key list, or "." to exit help
Help for key:
```

To display a help message that tells you what a specific key does, just press the key. For example, if you press **d**, you'll see the following message:

```
d = Mark the current message for future deletion
```

Go ahead and press any other keys you like. If you want to leave the help system, press period (.). If, instead, you'd prefer to see a list of all the commands and their corresponding keys, press **?**. You'll see a list like the one shown in the following figure. Press **Spacebar** to see more commands, or press **q** to get back to the Index screen.

```
   Command                          Elm 2.4 Action

    <RETURN>,<SPACE>        Display current message
     |                      Pipe current message or tagged messages to
                                a system command
    !                       Shell escape
    $                       Resynchronize folder
    ?                       This screen of information
    +, <RIGHT>              Display next index page
    -, <LEFT>               Display previous index page
    =                       Set current message to first message
    *                       Set current message to last message
    <NUMBER><RETURN>        Set current message to <NUMBER>
    /                       Search from/subjects for pattern
    //                      Search entire message texts for pattern
    >                       Save current message or tagged messages
                                to a folder
    <                       Scan current message for calendar entries
    a                       Alias, change to 'alias' mode
    b                       Bounce (remail) current message

Press <space> to continue, 'q' to return.
```

Press ? twice to see this list of Elm commands.

Reading Your Mail

Our first order of business will be to read whatever mail is waiting for you in your mailbox. The next couple of sections show you how to select a message and how to read the thing.

Picking Out a Message to Read

You'll have noticed by now that when you first see the Index screen, the message at the top is highlighted. (Actually, Elm highlights the first *unread* message at startup.) This bar is called the *current message pointer*, and it tells you which message your next command will operate on. To move the pointer and make a different message the current one, Elm gives you no less than seven—count 'em—seven methods:

➤ To move down one message, press **j**.

➤ To move up one message, press **k**.

➤ If you have more than 10 messages, they won't all fit on a single screen. To move to the next page of messages, press the plus sign (+). To move back a page, press the minus sign (-).

➤ To move to the first message, press the equals sign (=). To move to the last message, press the asterisk (*).

➤ To jump to a specific message number, press the number and then press **Enter**.

➤ To find a message that contains a particular word or phrase in the author name or the Subject line, press the slash (/). Elm displays the following prompt:

```
Match pattern:
```

Type in your search text and press **Enter**. If Pine finds a match, it highlights the message. If that isn't the message you want, you can continue the search by pressing the slash (/) and then pressing **Enter**.

➤ If you want to search for a message that contains a word or phrase in the message body, press the slash (/), and then press the backslash (/) again. Elm will display a slightly different prompt:

```
Match pattern (in entire message):
```

Again, type in your search text and press **Enter**.

Displaying the Selected Message

Once you have the message you want highlighted, you can read what it has to say by pressing **Enter** or **Spacebar**. Elm loads up the message and displays it on-screen. If the entire message doesn't fit, you'll see a status line at the bottom of the screen telling you how many lines are left and what percentage of the article you've read (see the next figure).

```
Message 2/39  From Benjie Chen                    Jan 17, 95 03:39:00 pm P

Return-Path: benjie@hh.sbay.org
Date: Tue, 17 Jan 95 15:39 PST
Sender: benjie@hh.sbay.org (Benjie KE6BCU)
Subject: WWW Server - updated with problem solving center and stuff
Designated-To: Internet Amateur Mathematics Society
Replied-From: Internet Amateur Mathematics Society
Precedence: bulk
Sender: iams@hh.sbay.org (Internet Amateur Mathematics Society)
X-Info: email to listserv@hh.sbay.org with "FAQ iams" in the message
X-Ignore: iams  Ignore this line. It's a mailing-list-loop detector.


I have updated/upgraded the www server.  The address is now
http://www.relay.net/~benjie/iams.html

New graphics and links.

I added a on-line problem solving page which has links to other
online solving groups and pages!!  Also check out the MathPro
link!  They have some very interesting stuff about math problem
There are 17 lines left (76%). Press <space> for more, or 'i' to return.
```

When you read a message, the status line at the bottom tells you how much more you have to slog through.

You can press the **Spacebar** to see the rest of the article, **j** to move to the next article, **k** to head back to the previous article, or **i** to return to the Index screen.

Saving an Attachment to a File

Elm is one of those e-mail programs that support the MIME attachments I told you about back in Chapter 4, in the "Sending Sounds, Graphics, and Other Nontext Files" section. So if someone sends you a dispatch with an attachment, Elm will display a note similar to the following at the bottom of the message:

```
Content-Description: some kind of description will appear here


This message contains data in an unrecognized format, image/gif,
which can either be viewed as text or written to a file.
```

```
What to you want to do with the image/gif
data?
1 — See it as text
2 — Write it to a file
3 — Just skip it
```

In this example, a graphics file (`image/gif`) has been received. To save the image to its own file, type **2** and then press **Enter**. Elm gives you a choice of accepting a suggested filename or entering your own. To accept the default name, just press **Enter**. Otherwise, type in the name of the file; use only letters, numbers, periods (.), and underscores (_) and press **Enter**.

> If you're in the middle of a long article and you'd like to return to the beginning, press **h**. This command actually displays the full header for the article, but at least it takes you back to the beginning.

Later, when you leave Elm, you can view the file using the appropriate software (such as a graphics program or viewer).

Talking Back: Sending a Reply

Did you think of a snappy comeback while reading a message? Or perhaps the message is part of a thread that's indulging in some witty repartee and you'd like to join in the fun. Whatever the reason, if you have a riposte, rejoinder, or retort you'd like to get on record, the reply message is the way to go. Here's how it's done in Elm:

1. Either use the Index screen to highlight the message you want to reply to, or read the message.

2. Press **r**. Elm displays the following prompt:

   ```
   Copy message? (y/n) n
   ```

3. If you want to insert a copy of the original message in your reply, press **y**. Otherwise, just press **Enter** to accept the default value **n**. Elm displays another prompt:

   ```
   Subject of message: Re: <original subject appears here>
   ```

4. Elm has conveniently added **Re:** to the beginning of the Subject line from the original message. If this is acceptable, press **Enter**. Otherwise, you can type your own subject and press **Enter**. The prompts just keep on comin'. Here's the next one:

   ```
   Copies to: <address>
   ```

5. If the original message had addresses in the Cc line, they'll appear in this prompt. You're free, though, to add or remove addresses. When you're done, press **Enter**. Elm now starts up the default text editor (this is usually **vi**) and, if applicable, loads

the original message. Elm also appends a greater-than sign (>) and a space to the beginning of each line of original text.

6. Use the editor to remove any unwanted lines from the original message.

7. Add your own text.

8. Exit the editor. (In **vi**, you exit by pressing **ZZ**. For more information on **vi**, check out *The Complete Idiot's Guide to UNIX*, by John McMullen.) Yet another prompt appears:

```
Please choose one of the following options by parenthesized letter: s
        e)dit message, edit h)eaders, s)end it, or f)orget it.
```

9. Press **e** to make changes to the message body; press **h** to adjust the header lines; press **s** to send the reply; or press **f** to forget the whole thing ever happened. If you select **h**, Elm displays the Message Header Edit Screen. Press the letter of the header line you want to change (for example, press C to adjust the Cc line), enter the new value, and then press **Enter**. When you're done, press **Enter** at the **Choice:** prompt.

Getting Elm to Add Your Signature Automatically

You may be wondering if there's any way to have Elm automatically add a signature to the end of your messages. Well, there is, but you have to jump through a hoop or two to get it done. Here are the required steps (these steps assume you've exited Elm and are at the UNIX prompt; see the "Quitting Elm" section to learn how to shut down Elm):

1. First of all, use your favorite text editor to create a **.signature** file in your home directory.

2. Now use your editor to load the file **elmrc** from the **.elm** directory that Elm created when you first started the program. (For example, if you're using **vi**, use the following command to load the **elmrc** file: **vi $HOME/.elm/elmrc**.)

3. Insert the following two lines anywhere in the file:

```
remotesignature = ~/.signature
localsignature = ~/.signature
```

Actually, you should first check to see if the lines are already in the file. If they are, they'll be disabled with number signs (#), like so:

```
### remotesignature = ~/.signature
### localsignature = ~/.signature
```

All you have to do is remove the number signs and you're in business.

4. Exit the editor.

Forwarding a Message to Another E-Mail Address

What happens if someone sends an e-mail message to your mailbox by mistake or if you want a colleague or friend to take a look at a message you received? The easiest thing to do is just forward the message to the appropriate e-mail address. Here's how it's done in Elm:

1. Use the Index screen to highlight the message you want to forward, or else display the message.

2. Press **f**. You'll see the following prompt:

   ```
   Edit outgoing message? (y/n) y
   ```

3. If you want to send the message as is, press **n**. Otherwise, if you want to add a note or two (such as, "Jones: Wait'll you get a load of this!"), just press **Enter** to accept the default value **y**. Elm displays another prompt:

   ```
   Send the message to:
   ```

4. Enter the e-mail address of the new recipient and press **Enter**. Now Elm, persistent as usual, prompts you with the Subject line.

5. Make your changes, if necessary, and then press **Enter**. The **Copies to:** prompt appears.

6. Enter anyone else's e-mail address you can think of and press **Enter**. If you elected to edit the message, Elm will load the text editor so you can go crazy.

7. When you're done, exit the text editor. Yet another prompt appears:

   ```
   Please choose one of the following options by parenthesized letter: s
             e)dit message, edit h)eaders, s)end it, or f)orget it.
   ```

8. Press **s** to forward the message, or select one of the other options.

Getting Rid of Messages You're Done With

If you've read a message and you don't need to save it (as described in the next section), you should delete it to keep your mailbox trim and tidy and to give yourself more room to maneuver around the Index screen.

To delete an unneeded missive, first highlight it in the Index screen and press **d**. Notice that Elm doesn't delete the message right off the bat. Instead, it just changes the message's status to **D**. This is called *marking the message for deletion*.

Why doesn't Elm just nuke the message without a second thought? Well, because *you* may have a second thought. You may decide you want to keep the message after all,

113

or you may realize you've deleted the wrong message. Since the message is only marked for deletion, you can "unmark" it by highlighting it and pressing **u**. (Note, however, that you won't be able to highlight the message using Elm's **j** (move down) and **k** (move up) keys. These commands only take you to you to *nondeleted* messages. Instead, you'll need to type in the number of the message and press **Enter**.)

Okay, so when do these marked messages get sent to kingdom come? There are two times:

➤ When you switch to a different folder (see the next section).

➤ When you exit the program.

In either case, you'll see the following prompt:

```
Delete messages? (y/n) n
```

To eradicate those pesky messages once and for all, press **y**.

Working with Folders

The mail that comes to your home first lands in your mailbox. Then, when you pick it up, you probably sort it accordingly: magazines go on the coffee table for later reading, bills go on the desk for later payment, flyers go to the bottom of the bird cage, and so on. You can also do the same kind of sorting with Elm. Your e-mail first arrives in your UNIX mailbox where you can read it, reply to it, or whatever. It doesn't take long, however, for the mailbox to get pretty crowded, and since Elm's Index screen can only show ten lines at a time, navigating all those messages can quickly become unwieldy.

The solution is to take advantage of Elm's *folders*. A folder is just a separate storage location for your e-mail. You can set up different folders for different kinds of mail and then move your messages into the appropriate folders. For example, you can have folders for mail from regular correspondents, notes from your system administrator, or for each mailing list you subscribe to. The next few sections show you how to work with folders in Elm.

Saving a Message to a Folder

Saving messages to a folder is easy as pie. First, use the Index screen to highlight the message you want to save. Now press **s** to display the following prompt:

```
Save message to: <suggestion>
```

Here, *suggestion* will be Elm's suggested folder name, which is usually the user name of the person who sent the message, *preceded by an equals sign* (=). For example, suppose you received a message from **scylla@charybdis.com**. The prompt may look like this:

```
Save message to: =scylla
```

If the suggestion is okay with you, just press **Enter**. Otherwise, press the equals sign (=), type the name you want to use for the folder, and then press **Enter**. (If the folder doesn't exist, Elm will be only too happy to create it for you.) The name can be up to 255 characters long, and it should consist only of letters, numbers, periods (.), and underscores (_). Note, too, that Elm marks the message for deletion (by changing the message's status to **D**) even though it is moving it to another folder.

Another thing to bear in mind is that Elm comes equipped with a three folders of its own:

➤ A **received** folder that you can use as a sort of general storage area for the mail you've read (and want to keep). As you'll see later, when you quit Elm, the program will ask if you want to move the messages you've read into the **received** folder.

➤ A **sent** folder that's useful for storing messages you send out so you always have a record of your compositions. How do you put sent messages into your mailbox? Well, there are two ways. The first method is to add your own e-mail address to the Cc line. Then, when you receive the copy, you can save it to the **sent** folder. The second method involves editing your **elmrc** file, as described earlier in this chapter (see the "Getting Elm to Add Your Signature Automatically" section). In this case, you need to add the following line to **elmrc**:

```
copy = ON
```

In this case, each time you ship out a message, Elm will automatically place a copy of it in the **sent** folder.

➤ In Elm's eyes, your incoming mailbox is also a folder. The name of this "folder" is the same as your user name.

Switching Folders

Now that you've saved a dispatch or two inside another folder, how do you get at them? Easy: you can switch folders by first pressing **c** to display the following prompt:

```
Change to which folder:
```

Type an equals sign (=) followed by the name of the folder, and then press **Enter**. For example, to switch to the "received" folder, type **=received** and press **Enter**. Actually, Elm's three built-in folders have short forms you can use, as shown in Table 10.1.

115

Table 10.1   Elm's Short Forms for Folder Names

Short Form	The Folder It Represents
>	=received
<	=sent
!	The incoming mailbox (e.g., **=paulmcf**)

So at the **Change to which folder:** prompt, you could change to, say, the **received** folder by typing greater-than (>) and pressing **Enter**.

When you switch folders, Elm checks to see if you have any deleted or read messages in the current folder. If you have deleted messages, you'll see the following prompt:

```
Delete messages (y/n) n
```

Press **y** to delete the messages or **Enter** (or **n**) to preserve them. If you've read some messages, you'll see this prompt:

```
Move read messages to "received" folder (y/n) n
```

Again, press **y** to move the messages to **received**, or **Enter** (or **n**) to leave them be. If you're switching from the mailbox folder, you may also see this prompt:

```
Keep unread messages in incoming mailbox (y/n) y
```

Press **Enter** (or **y**) to keep the unread messages in the mailbox.

Composing a New Message

Of course, you won't be spending all your time in Elm reading and replying to incoming correspondence. You'll also be doing your share of composing and sending out original messages to the four corners of the world. Here are the steps to plow through in Elm:

1. From the Index screen (it doesn't matter which folder is active), press **m**. Elm displays the following prompt:

   ```
   Send the message to:
   ```

2. Type in the e-mail address of the beneficiary of your brilliant prose and then press **Enter**. Elm displays another prompt:

   ```
   Subject of message:
   ```

3. Type the subject of your message (assume a maximum of 40 characters, to be safe) and press **Enter**. Hey, guess what? Elm displays another prompt:

```
Copies to:
```

4. If you're sending out multiple copies, enter the other e-mail address here (separated with commas) and then press **Enter**. Elm starts up the default text editor (probably **vi**).

5. Enter your message body.

6. Exit the editor (in **vi**, you exit by pressing **ZZ**). One last prompt appears:

```
Please choose one of the following options by parenthesized letter: s
        e)dit message, edit h)eaders, s)end it, or f)orget it.
```

7. Press **e** to edit the message body; press **h** to edit the header lines; press **s** to send the message; or press **f** to nix the operation altogether.

> If you're starting from the UNIX prompt, you can bypass steps 1–3 by starting Elm like this:
>
> ```
> elm -s 'subject' address
> ```
>
> Here, *subject* is the Subject line for the message and *address* is the e-mail address of the recipient. For example, to send a message to **orex@thebes.gov** with the Subject line `Riddle Answer?`, you'd start Elm like so:
>
> ```
> elm -s 'Riddle Answer?' orex@thebes.gov
> ```
>
> When Elm loads, it displays the **Subject of message:** prompt and your subject. Press **Enter** to get to the **Copies to:** prompt.

Quitting Elm

To bail out of Elm, press **q**. If you made changes to the current folder (such as deleting and reading some messages), Elm will prompt you as described in the "Switching Folders" section, earlier in this chapter. If you'd prefer to bypass the prompts and leave the folder unchanged, press **Q**, instead.

If you plan to use Elm as your regular e-mail program, you'll probably want to pay regular visits to the Usenet newsgroup **comp.mail.elm**. This group is the place to go to ask questions, get technical help, and learn about the latest releases. You'll also find a very useful article that's posted monthly (on the 15th) called "Elm Mail User Agent FAQ—Frequently Asked Questions."

The Least You Need to Know

This chapter rounded out our discussion of UNIX e-mail programs with a tour of the Elm e-mail package. Here's a rundown of some of the sights we saw along the route:

➤ To start Elm, type **elm** and press **Enter**. If you want to send a message, type **elm -s** *'subject' address*, where *subject* is the Subject line and *address* is the e-mail address of the recipient.

➤ To read a message, highlight it in the Index screen and then press **Enter**.

➤ To reply to the current message, press **r** and respond to Elm's incessant prompting.

➤ To forward a message, press **f** and follow the prompts.

➤ You can delete a garbage message by first highlighting the message and pressing **d**. When you switch folders or quit, Elm will ask if you want to delete the message.

➤ To save a message to a folder, press **s**, type an equals sign (=) followed by the name of the folder, and then press **Enter**.

➤ To compose a new message, press **m** and then do the prompt thing.

Getting Graphical with Eudora

Until a few years ago, the vast majority of Net citizens performed their electronic postal chores using either the standard UNIX **mail** software or one of its more full-featured descendants (such as the Pine and Elm programs we checked out in the last couple of chapters). These programs are admirably competent, but their interfaces lack, shall we say, a certain *panache*. Oh sure, the basics are easy enough to pick up, but some operations that should be routine (such as getting a signature at the bottom of your messages) throw up obstacles that are just too high for beginning and casual users to hurdle.

That's all changed in recent years as more and more e-mail packages come online that are designed for those of us who prefer the relative comforts of graphical environments, such as Windows and the Macintosh. Suddenly, tasks that used to take dozens of keystrokes while responding to umpteen command-line prompts can now be done with a simple click or two of a mouse. Suddenly, in other words, e-mail became easy.

This chapter looks at one of the first and still one of the most popular of the graphical e-mail programs: Eudora. I'll take you through all the basics of both the Windows and Mac versions, including configuring the program, reading and replying to messages, composing your own missives, and lots more.

Getting Your Hands on a Copy of Eudora

Eudora comes in two flavors: a commercial version that costs about $65, and a "freeware" version that costs exactly nothing. The freebie, of course, lacks some of the nice features of the retail package, but it's more than adequate for basic e-mail duties. Personally, I use the commercial version for all my mail maintenance, because it has a few doodads that are, to me, worth the price of admission (such as the ability to filter your incoming mail).

However, I do recommend starting off with the free Eudora so you can check it out and see if the two of you get along well together. To get a copy, anonymous FTP to **ftp.qualcomm.com** and then grab one of the following files:

➤ For the Windows version, head for the directory **/quest/windows/eudora/1.4** and download the file **eudor???.exe**. (The **???** stands for the version number of Eudora. The current version, for example, is 1.44, so the file name is **eudor144.zip**.) Once you have the file, use File Manager to create a separate directory for Eudora, copy EUDOR144.EXE (or whatever) into the directory, and then double-click on it. This will extract the program files you need to run Eudora. Now create a program item for Eudora in any Program Manager group (the name of the file that starts Eudora is WEUDORA.EXE).

➤ For the Mac version, jump to the directory **/quest/windows/mac/eudora/1.5** and get the file **eudora???.hqx**. (Again, the **???** will be whatever is the latest version. Right now, it's 1.51, so the file name is **eudora151.hqx**.) You'll need to use BinHex, StuffIt, or some other program to decode the file.

If you're interested in the commercial version of Eudora, you can either send an e-mail message to **eudora-sales@qualcomm.com** (don't bother with a Subject line or message body) to get more info, or you can call QUALCOMM Inc. at 1-800-238-3672.

Eudora works, in most cases, by using your modem to exchange pleasantries with your access provider's POP (Post Office Protocol) computer (as explained in Chapter 3). These exchanges use either SLIP (Serial Line Interface Protocol) or PPP (Point-to-Point Protocol) so the two machines can understand one another's lingo. So before you can use Eudora for sending or receiving e-mail, you need to dial up your access provider and establish either a SLIP or PPP connection. How you do this depends on how your Internet connection is set up:

➤ Many access providers supply their customers with a "dialer" program that will connect you automatically.

➤ If you have no dialer software, you need to use some kind of TCP/IP program to establish the connection. For Windows, you need *Trumpet WinSock* (available via anonymous FTP from **wuarchive.wustl.edu**; the file is **/pub/MSDOS_UPLOADS/ winsock/twsck???.zip**; the ??? stands for the current version of Trumpet WinSock— as I write this, the current version is 2.0b, so the filename is **twsck20b.zip**.). Use the program TCPMAN.EXE to connect. For the Mac, you can use MacTCP (available from Apple with system 7.x). In either case, setting up the programs is not for the faint of heart, so you should commandeer the nearest Internet guru and get her to set things up for you. If there's no nerd in sight (they're never around when you need them), try contacting the technical support folks at your access provider.

If you pay by the hour for your connection, or if you pay a monthly fee that limits the number of hours you can spend online, you may consider working "offline" until you're ready to send or receive mail. Working offline means you load Eudora *before* establishing a connection to your service provider. This way, you can configure the program, perform mail maintenance chores, and compose messages without running up your connection costs. Then, when you're ready for action, you can connect and send your messages or get your new mail.

Wondering where the name "Eudora" comes from? Well, according to Steve Dorner, the original program designer, he kept thinking of a short story called "Why I Live at the P.O." while he was writing the program. The author of that story was the great American writer Eudora Welty, so he named the program after her. (Which just goes to show that a hacker isn't necessarily a geek.)

Getting Eudora Off on the Right Foot

Okay, I'll assume since you've reached this part that Eudora is installed on your machine and you've established a connection to your Internet access provider (unless, of course, you've decided to work offline for a while). So far so good. You'll be happy to know that the hard part's over because from here on, everything will be a relative breeze. To get you on your way, the next couple of sections give you the lowdown on configuring Eudora. To follow along, you'll need to start the program by double-clicking on the Eudora icon.

First Things First: Configuring Eudora

Before we get to the nitty-gritty of reading and writing e-mail, you'll need to tell Eudora a little about yourself. To do that, pull down the Special menu and select the Configuration command. You'll see a Configuration dialog box similar to the one shown below. (Note that all of the figures in this chapter were taken from the commercial version of Eudora. If you are using the freeware version, your screens may appear slightly different.)

Use the Configuration dialog box to give Eudora your vital statistics.

This dialog box is jammed to the gills with options, but only a few are important. Here's a rundown:

POP Account   The e-mail sent to you is actually stored on a computer at your access provider that runs the Post Office Protocol (POP).

Real Name   This is the name that appears alongside your e-mail address in the From line of messages you send. For example, my e-mail address is **paulmcf@hookup.net**, so my From lines look like this:

```
paulmcf@hookup.net (Paul McFedries)
```

Connection Method (commercial version only)   Windows users should activate the **WinSock** option; Mac mavens should activate **MacTCP**.

SMTP Server   Eudora uses the Simple Mail Transport Protocol (SMTP) to send your messages (this, too, was explained back in Chapter 3). Use this field to enter the name of the computer at your access provider that runs their SMTP server. (If it's the same computer as your POP account, you can leave this field blank.)

Return Address   Eudora will normally use your POP account as the return address for your messages. If you want to use a different address for some reason, enter it in this field. (Double, no, *triple*-check the Return Address field if you use it. Entering the wrong address could send the replies to your messages off into la-la land, and you'd never be the wiser.)

Check For Mail Every   You can use this field to have Eudora automatically check your incoming mail at regular intervals. Unless you get a lot of mail, I'd just leave this field at 0 (no checking) and check for new mail by hand (as explained later on). If you want to try this feature, use a value of 15 or higher to reduce the workload on the beleaguered mail computer.

A Note About Eudora's Switches

One of Eudora's nicest touches is that the program is endlessly customizable. It may work just the way you like right out of the box, but you'll probably find that after a while, you'll wish the program did a thing or two differently. The good news is, it probably can! Most of these customization chores are handled through the Switches dialog box shown below. I'll discuss some of these options as we work through this chapter, but for now, I'll just tell you that you can display the dialog box by selecting the **S**pecial menu's **S**witches command.

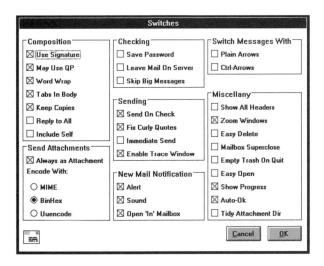

Use the options in the Switches dialog box to remake Eudora in your own image.

Getting and Reading Your Mail

All right, enough preparation. Let's get down to brass tacks and make Eudora do something useful. For starters, the next couple of sections show you how to check for incoming mail and, if you have any, to read whatever the Net hordes have sent your way.

Checking for New Mail

Unless you have Eudora checking your POP account at regular intervals (as described previously), you need to tell the program to access your account and see if there are any missives waiting there for you. You do this by pulling down the File menu and selecting the Check Mail command (you can also just press **Ctrl+M** in Windows or **Command-M** on the Mac). If this is the first time you're checking mail in this session, Eudora displays the Enter Password dialog box. Type in the password for your POP account and then click on **OK**. Eudora then logs in to the POP server and sniffs around for messages. If it doesn't find any, the commercial version displays a dialog box to tell you the bad news (click on **Sorry** to remove the dialog box). If there was a message or two, Eudora transfers them to your computer and displays a dialog box to let you know. In this case, click on **OK** to continue.

Handling Incoming Attachments

If one of the messages Eudora is retrieving has a file attached to it, you'll see the Save Attachment dialog box appear. Use this dialog box to select the directory (in Windows) or folder (on the Mac) where you want the attachment stored. You can also change Eudora's suggested name for the file. When you're ready, click on **OK**.

You can avoid this dialog box in the future by changing one of Eudora's configuration options. Select the Special menu's Configuration command to display the Configuration dialog box, and then do one of the following:

➤ In Windows, activate the **Auto Receive Attachment Directory** check box, click on the button beside it, select a directory in the Select Auto Receive Directory dialog box, and then select **Use Directory**. Select OK to return to Eudora.

➤ On the Mac, activate the **Automatically save attachments to** check box, and use the button below it to select a folder for your attachments. Click on **OK** to get back to Eudora.

In either case, Eudora will save the attached file to the specified directory or folder automatically and will display a note to that effect at the bottom of the message body.

Reading Messages from the In Mailbox

If you've received some fan mail or other Net notes, you'll need to display the In mailbox to read them. Eudora normally opens this mailbox for you automatically, but you can display it at any time by pulling down the Mailbox menu and selecting **In** (or by simply pressing **Ctrl+I** in Windows or **Command-I** on the Mac). The In mailbox is a window similar to the one shown here.

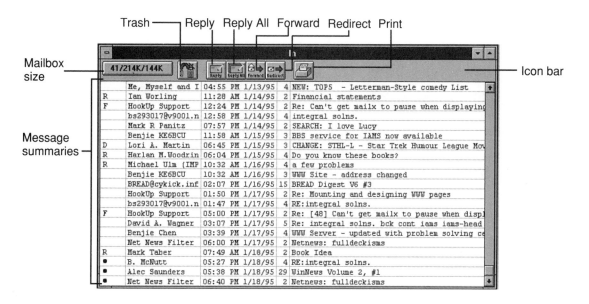

Eudora's In mailbox displays the messages you've received.

The In mailbox (like all of Eudora's mailboxes), has an icon bar below the title bar. I'll be talking about these buttons as we go along, but for now, let's see if we can make heads or tails of the numbers in the *Mailbox size* button. Basically, these values tell you how large the mailbox is. The first value is the number of messages in the mailbox; the second number is the total amount of space (in kilobytes) the messages take up on your hard disk; the third number is the amount of that space that is wasted. This wasted space is created when you delete messages or move them to other mailboxes. To reclaim the space for this mailbox only, click on the Mailbox size button. To reclaim the space for all your mailboxes, select the **Special** menu's Compact Mailboxes command.

Below the icon bar, you'll see the *message summaries*. Each line represents an individual message and gives you a bird's-eye view of the message's basic info. The first column tells you the message status:

- ●   You haven't read the message yet.

<blank> You've read the message.

R   You've replied to the message.

F   You've forwarded the message

D   You've redirected the message.

S   You've sent the message (Out mailbox only).

Q   You've queued the message to send it later (Out mailbox only).

The second column tells you the name of the message's author, then comes the date and time the message was sent, the number of kilobytes used by the message, and the last column shows the Subject line of the message.

To read a message, just double-click on it. Eudora opens a new window and loads the message for you.

Retorts and Rejoinders: Sending a Reply

If the sender asks you a question or is looking for some info, or if you just want to rebut an argument they've put forth, sending a reply message is the way to go. To try it out, first either highlight the message in your In mailbox (by clicking on it) or read the message. Now pull down the **Message** menu and select **Reply** (or you can press **Ctrl+R** in Windows or **Command-R** on the Mac). Alternatively, if you're reading the message, you can click on the **Reply** button in the icon bar. Eudora opens a new window (which I'll call the *message composition window*) similar to the one shown in the next figure and adds the following info to the message:

- ➤ The original author's e-mail address is stuffed into the To line.
- ➤ Your return address goes into the From line.
- ➤ "Re:" is tacked on to the original Subject line.
- ➤ The text of the original article is added with greater-than signs (>) as quote markers.

Signature   Encoding

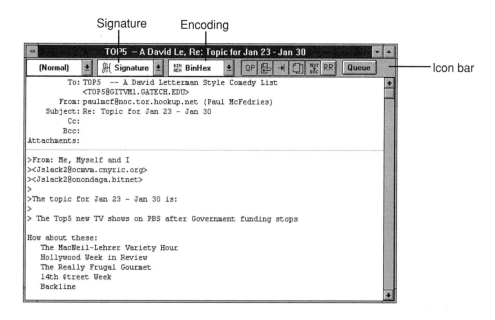

—— Icon bar

When you reply to a message, Eudora sets everything up all nice and pretty.

Now add in your two cent's worth, remove any unneeded lines from the original text, and make adjustments to the header, if necessary. When you're done, you can send the message by using one of the following methods:

➤ If you see a **Queue** button in the icon bar, click on it. (You can also either select the Message menu's Queue for Delivery command, or press **Ctrl+E** in Windows, **Command-E** on the Mac.) Eudora places the message in a holding area (the Out mailbox) so you can send it later. When you're ready to do your sending, select the File menu's Send Queued Messaged command (or press **Ctrl+T** in Windows or **Command-T** on the Mac). If you'd like to take a peek at the queued messages before shipping them out, select the Mailbox menu's Out command to display the Out mailbox.

➤ If you see a **Send** button in the icon bar, click on it to send the message right away. (If you prefer, you can also select Send Immediately from the Message Menu, or you can press **Ctrl+E** in Windows or **Command-E** on the Mac.)

Whether Eudora queues messages or sends them right away is controlled by the **Immediate Send** option in the Switches dialog box. When this check box is deactivated, you see the **Queue** button in the icon bar of the message composition window, and the Queue for Delivery command appears in the Message Menu. If this check box is activated, you get the **Send** button and the Send Immediately command, instead. Which method should you use? Well, if you're working offline, then you have no choice but to queue the messages until you connect. Otherwise, if you'll be sending lots of messages, it's best to queue them up and then send them all at once when you're going to be away from the computer for a while (at lunch, say, or at a meeting). If you're just firing off a quick message or two, sending immediately is the way to go. Note, as well, that you can change this on the fly for the current message. Just select the Message menu's Change Queueing command, and choose the method you want from the Change Queueing dialog box that appears.

Sending an Incoming Message to a Different Address

If you think a message you've received may be of interest to a colleague or friend, you can forward the message to their e-mail address. You can click on the Forward button at any time, so long as the message is highlighted. To forward the current message, pull down the Message menu and select Forward (or, if you're reading the message, you can also click on the **Forward** button). This works just like replying, except there are three differences to bear in mind:

➤ The To line is left blank for you to fill in with the address of the forwardee.

➤ The Subject line remains the same.

➤ The *entire* text of the original message (including the header) is added (with quote markers) to the message body.

After you've added any extra text or adjusted the header, you can send the message as usual.

A slightly different concept is that of *redirecting* a message to a different e-mail address. You'd do this, for example if someone sent a message to your mailbox by mistake. To do this, either select Redirect from the **Message** menu, or (if you're reading the message) click on the **Redirect** button. Again, Eudora leaves the To line blank so you can enter the redirected address, but the message text is left untouched.

Taking Out the Trash: Deleting Unneeded Messages

If you find your In mailbox getting crowded, you have two choices to ease the crunch: you can transfer some messages to a different mailbox (as explained in the next section), or you can delete messages you no longer need.

To delete the current message, pull down the Message menu, and select the **Delete** command (or you can save a bit of time by just clicking on the **Trash** button, pressing either **Delete** or **Ctrl+D** in Windows, or pressing **Command-D** on the Mac). If you have a bunch of messages you want to blow away, you can select multiple messages in any mailbox by using either of the following techniques:

➤ If the messages are consecutive, click on the first message you want to delete, hold down the **Shift** key, and then click on the last message you want to delete.

➤ If the messages are scattered willy-nilly, click on the first message you want to expunge, hold down the **Ctrl** key in Windows, or the Mac's **Command** key, and then click on the other messages that are trashable.

When you delete a message, Eudora simply transfers it to a mailbox called, appropriately enough, Trash. This way, if you accidentally delete a message, you can recover it by displaying the Trash mailbox (select Trash from the Mailbox menu), highlighting the message, and then selecting the Transfer menu's ->In command. If you're sure you want to get rid of the messages accumulating in the Trash mailbox, select the Empty Trash command from the Special menu.

Monkeying Around with Mailboxes

So far in our Eudora tour, we've seen three different mailboxes: In, Out, and Trash. These are built right in to Eudora, but the fact is that you're free to create any number of mailboxes yourself. Why on earth would you want to do this? Well, if you and your boss exchange a lot of e-mail, you can create a separate mailbox just for her messages. This makes her messages easier to find and it reduces the clutter in the In mailbox. You could also create mailboxes for each of the mailing lists you subscribe to, for announcements from your system administrator, for current projects on the go, or for each of your regular e-mail correspondents. There are, in short, a thousand-and-one uses for mailboxes, and this section tells you everything you need to know.

Setting up a new mailbox is no sweat. Just pull down the Mailbox menu and select the New command. In the New Mailbox dialog box that appears, type in the name of the mailbox, and then click on OK. That's it!

With your new mailbox ready for action, you can switch to it by pulling down the Mailbox menu and selecting the name of the mailbox from the list. Similarly, if you want to move the current message to your new mailbox, pull down the Transfer menu, and select your mailbox (its name will be prefaced with an arrow: ->).

Mailboxes are so handy that you'll probably find yourself creating all kinds to store various types of messages. To keep your Mailbox menu from overloading, however, you should consider creating *folders* to hold related mailboxes. For example, if you subscribe to several mailing lists, you could create a "Mailing Lists" folder and then create a mailbox for each list inside the folder.

To set up a folder, select the Mailbox menu's New command. In the New Mailbox dialog box, type in the name of the folder, activate the **Make it a Folder** check box, and then click on OK. Eudora creates the folder and then redisplays the New Mailbox dialog box so you can create a mailbox inside the folder. Type in the mailbox name and click on OK. As you can see in the figure below, the folders appear on the Mailbox menu, and their mailboxes appear in a cascade menu. When you want to add more mailboxes to the folder, select it from the Mailbox menu, and then select New in the cascade menu.

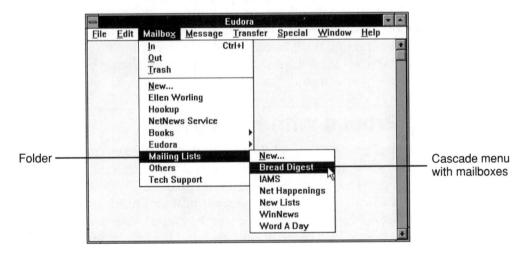

Eudora lets you set up folders to hold multiple mailboxes.

Composing an Original Message

If you have some information to exchange, a question to ask, or some wisdom to impart, you'll need to compose a new message and send it off to whomever will listen. Here's how it's done in Eudora:

1. Pull down the Message menu and select New Message (or press **Ctrl+N** in Windows or **Command-N** on the Mac). Eudora displays a new message composition window.

2. Fill in the header lines for the message. Note that if you'll be entering multiple addresses on the Cc line, you need to separate them with commas.

3. Type your message in the message body.

4. Set up your signature and attachments, as needed. (If you need details, check out the "Working with Signatures" and "Attaching Files to Outgoing Messages" sections earlier in this chapter.

5. Send or queue the message, as described in the "Retorts and Rejoinders: Sending a Reply" section.

Working with Signatures

A signature, as I explained back in the "Message Anatomy" section of Chapter 3, is a few lines of text that appears at the bottom of your messages to tell your addressees a bit more about yourself. Eudora makes it spectacularly easy to create and add signatures to your messages (compared to, say, most UNIX mail programs).

To create a signature, pull down the **Window** menu and select **Signature**. In the Signature window that appears, type in your signature (keeping in mind that anything more than four lines is overkill and could get you flamed). When you're done, pull down the File menu and select Close. When Eudora asks if you want to save your changes, click on the **Save** button. (Note: the commercial version of Eudora lets you create a second signature for special occasions. In this case, you'd select Alternate Signature from the Window menu.)

When you're creating a message, you can get Eudora to add your signature text to the end of a message by selecting **Signature** from the Signature drop-down list in the message composition window (if you're using the commercial version, you can also choose **Alternate Signature**).

Attaching Files to Outgoing Messages

Eudora has full support for reading and sending file attachments encoded with MIME, BinHex, and (in the commercial version) Uuencode. (If you're not sure about this encoding business, hike back to Chapter 4 and read the "Sending Sounds, Graphics, and Other Nontext Files" section to get the full scoop.)

If you're in the message composition window and want to attach a file to the message, first pull down the **Message** menu and select Attach Document (or press **Ctrl+H** in Windows or **Command-H** on the Mac). When the Attach Document dialog box appears, select the file you want to send, and then click on **OK**. Eudora adds the file name to the Attachments line in the header. Now use the Encoding drop-down list to select the type of encoding you want: **BinHex**, **MIME**, or **Uuencode** (again, you'll only see the **Uuencode** option in the commercial version).

Shutting Down Eudora

When you've completed your e-mail chores for the day, you can quit Eudora by pulling down the File menu and selecting the Exit command (or by pressing **Ctrl+Q** in Windows or **Command-Q** on the Mac).

If you become a dedicated Eudora fan, the Net has some resources you won't want to miss. For starters, there's a mailing list for aficionados of the freeware version that answers users questions and offers tips about Eudora. To subscribe, send an e-mail message to **majordomo@qualcomm.com**, leave the Subject line blank, and include only the following in the message body: **subscribe eudora_forum**. If you have access to the World Wide Web, be sure to check out the QUEST (QUALCOMM Enterprise Software Technologies) home page at the following locale:

http:/www.qualcomm.com/quest/QuestMain.html

This page has lots of hooray-for-QUALCOMM stuff, but there's a semi-annual newsletter called "Enterprise Times" that has some excellent articles.

The Least You Need to Know

This chapter took you on a tour of Eudora's handsome graphical approach to the Internet e-mail world. I'll tell you one thing: it sure beats the heck out of all those cryptic UNIX mail programs. In fact, that was so enjoyable (and, dare I say it, Eudorable) I think I'll go back for seconds:

➤ Once Eudora is installed, you crank it up by double-clicking on its icon. If you're just starting out, you'll need to configure Eudora for your Internet connection by pulling down the **S**pecial menu and selecting the Configuration command.

➤ To see if you have any mail waiting, select the File menu's Check **M**ail command (or press **Ctrl+M** in Windows or **Command-M** on the Mac). If this is the first time you're checking mail in this session, you'll also have to enter your POP account password. Once you get your messages, you can read them by double-clicking on them in the In mailbox window.

➤ To reply to the current message, select the Message menu's Reply command (or press **Ctrl+R** in Windows or **Command-R** on the Mac).

➤ If you need to forward the current message, pull down the Message menu and select Forward. If you'd prefer to redirect the message, choose the **Message** menu's Redirect command, instead.

➤ Message deleting is easy: just highlight the message and select Delete from the **Message** menu (or you can press either **Delete** or **Ctrl+D** in Windows, or **Command-D** on the Mac).

➤ If you'd like to use different mailboxes to store your messages, you can create them by selecting the Mailbox menu's New command.

➤ To compose a new message, pull down the Message menu, select New, and then fill in the message composition window.

Chapter 12

Taming Pegasus Mail

In This Chapter

➤ Giving your incoming mail the once-over

➤ Forwarding and replying to an e-mail message

➤ Using folders to organize your mail

➤ Working with address books

➤ Creating and sending new messages

➤ All you need to know about Pegasus Mail—an e-mail horse of a different color

Greek legend has it that when the great hero Perseus killed Medusa (a woman of such frightening countenance that, you'll recall, one glimpse of her would turn man and beast to stone), a fantastic, winged horse named Pegasus sprung from her body. Another hero, Bellerophon, tried to tame Pegasus, but the horse would let no man approach. Finally, the goddess Athena presented Bellerophon with a divine bridle to which Pegasus came willingly. Together, Bellerophon and Pegasus set out on many adventures and battles that ended only when Bellerophon tried to ride Pegasus to heaven and was thrown off.

This digression into Greek mythology is my way of introducing you to the subject of this chapter: the Pegasus Mail program. Pegasus Mail sprang not from the body of a dead

Gorgon, but from the fertile mind of programmer David Harris. So while it may not be divine, it certainly is a powerful program with lots of useful features. (I was going to say that our goal in this chapter will be to tame Pegasus Mail so you can use it to ride out on your Internet e-mail adventures, but even *I* refuse to stoop to such low corniness.)

Corralling a Copy of Pegasus Mail

Pegasus Mail has, as I've said, loads of features, but by far its best feature is its price: free! It's not even one of those try-it-and-if-you-like-it-pay-the-programmer-$25 shareware programs. Nope. Pegasus Mail is a true freebie. To get your mitts on this deal-of-the-century, anonymous FTP to **risc.ua.edu**, switch to the directory **/pub/network/pegasus**, and then download one of the following files:

➤ For the Windows version, grab the file **winpm???.zip**. (The **???** stands for the version number of Pegasus Mail. For example, the current version is 1.2.2, so the file name is **winpm122.zip**.) Once you have the file, create a separate directory for Pegasus Mail (you can call it WINPMAIL, for example), copy WINPM122.ZIP (or whatever) into the directory, and then "unzip" it with the program PKUNZIP by entering the following DOS command:

pkunzip winpm122.zip

(You can get PKUNZIP at umpteen FTP sites on the Net. For example, anonymous FTP to **ftp.psi.com**, head for the **/src/dos** directory, and grab the file **PKUNZIP.EXE**.) Now create a program item for Pegasus Mail in any Program Manager group (the name of the file that starts Pegasus Mail is WINPMAIL.EXE).

➤ For the Mac version, get the file **pmmac???.hqx**. (Again, the **???** will be whatever is the latest version. Right now, it's 2.1.0, so the file name is **pmmac210.hqx**.) You'll need to use a program such as BinHex or StuffIt Expander to decompress the file.

As we discussed back in Chapter 3, in the "A Quick Peek Under the Hood" section programs like Pegasus Mail do their thing by having your computer interact, via modem, with your access provider in two ways:

➤ To get incoming messages, Pegasus Mail talks to a host computer that has been set up as a POP (Post Office Protocol) server.

➤ When sending outgoing messages, Pegasus Mail uses SMTP (Simple Mail Transport Protocol) to pass the messages to a computer that the access provider has designated as the *relay host*.

Both kinds of interaction are controlled with either SLIP (Serial Line Interface Protocol) or PPP (Point-to-Point Protocol), which are just fancy-schmancy terms for the software that lets the two machines understand what the heck the other is talking about.

So, to get to the point, before you can use Pegasus Mail to receive or send e-mail, you need to dial up your access provider and establish either a SLIP or PPP connection. How you go about this will depend on the way your Internet connection is set up:

➤ Some of the better access providers supply their customers with simple "dialer" programs that are set up to dial in and make the SLIP or PPP connection automatically.

➤ If such a dialing program is nowhere in sight, then things get a lot trickier. In this case, you'll have to use a TCP/IP program to establish the connection. For Windows, use *WinSock* (which you can get via anonymous FTP from **wuarchive.wustl.edu**; the file is **/pub/MSDOS_UPLOADS/winsock/twsck???.zip**; the ??? stands for the current version of Trumpet WinSock—as I write this the current version is 2.0b, so the filename is **twsck20b.zip**). Use the program TCPMAN.EXE to connect. For the Mac, you can use MacTCP (available from Apple). The catch, however, is that setting up either program is no day at the beach. My suggestion would be to find a nearby networking guru and have her configure things for you. (I'm sure your access provider's technical support department would also be only too glad to help.)

If you pay by the hour for your connection, or if you pay a monthly fee that limits the number of hours you can spend online, you may consider working "offline" until you're ready to send or receive mail. Working offline means you load Pegasus Mail *before* establishing a connection to your service provider. This way, you can configure the program, perform mail maintenance chores, and compose messages without running up your connection costs. Then, when you're ready for action, you can connect and send your messages or get your incoming mail.

Getting Pegasus Mail Off to a Flying Start

Well, things are looking good so far. You have your copy of Pegasus Mail, it's installed and ready to go, and you have a connection to your access provider humming along nicely. What's next on the agenda? Ah, now we get the ball rolling by actually starting the program, and to do that, you just double-click on the **Pegasus Mail** icon. If you're starting Pegasus Mail for the first time, you'll see the Setup Information dialog box. In the Your **u**ser name text box enter the username that you used to log in to you access provider. Also, activate the **S**ave your username in WIN.INI for future use check box. When you're done, select OK. Our setup chores aren't complete just yet, however. The next couple of sections take you through the rigmarole of configuring Pegasus Mail and setting a few options.

Some Relatively Painless Network Stuff

The first thing you need to do is pull down the File menu, select Preferences, and then select Advanced settings. In the Advanced settings dialog box that appears, look for the section named If WINSOCK.DLL is available, load it-, activate the Always option, and then select OK. To put this option into effect, you need to exit Pegasus Mail (by pulling down the File menu and selecting the Exit command) and then restart the program.

As I've said, Pegasus Mail needs to contact both a POP server and a relay host to get your incoming and send your outgoing messages. So the first order of business is to tell Pegasus Mail where it can find these computers. Begin by pulling down the File menu and selecting the **Network configuration** command. You'll see a TCP/IP Network Configuration dialog box, similar to the one shown in the following figure.

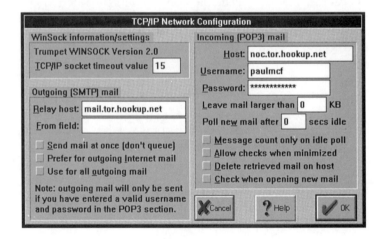

Use this dialog box to let Pegasus Mail in on your network secrets.

This dialog box is kind of scary at first glance, but you'll only have to fill in a few of the options to get started. For the **Incoming (POP3) mail** section, try these on for size:

Host   The name of the computer that's handling the POP server duties at your access provider, generally the same one you log on to.

Username   The username you use to login to your POP account (it's usually the same as your login name).

Password   The password you use to login. (Don't worry, though: the password appears as a series of asterisks so no one else can figure it out.)

Delete retrieved mail on host   When this check box is activated, Pegasus Mail deletes the messages on the POP host computer after it has transferred them to your computer. You should activate this option because it prevents mail from accumulating irresponsibly on the host machine, and it prevents Pegasus Mail from mindlessly retrieving the same messages day after day.

In the **Outgoing (SMTP) mail** section, you have only two options to worry about:

Relay host   The name of the computer at your access provider that relays your messages to the Internet.

Send mail at once (don't queue)   When this check box is activated, Pegasus Mail will send your messages as soon as you click on the **Send** button (as explained in the "Composing a New Message" section of this chapter). When this box is unchecked, Pegasus places the message in a queue for you to send later.

Is it better to send messages right away, or queue them up? Well, certainly, if you're working offline, then you have no choice but to queue your messages. Otherwise, it depends on how prolific an e-mail writer you are. If you're cranking out a bunch of messages, you'd be better off queuing them up and then sending the whole kit and caboodle before, say, heading out to lunch. On the other hand, if you write only the occasional epistle, you should send it right away so you don't forget.

Playing with Some Pegasus Mail Preferences

Just so you can get Pegasus Mail working the way you want, the program offers a number of customization options. To check them out, pull down the File menu, select Preferences, and then select General settings (or you can press **Shift+F10**). Pegasus Mail displays the General Preferences dialog box, as shown in the following figure. Here's the lowdown on the most important of the options:

Personal **n**ame (shown in your address)   The name that appears alongside your e-mail address in the From line of messages you send. For example, my e-mail address is **paulmcf@hookup.net**, so my From lines look like this:

paulmcf@hookup.net (Paul McFedries)

Open new **m**ail folder at startup   Activate this check box to have Pegasus Mail display the **New mail folder** window each time you start the program.

Preserve deleted messages until exit If you check this check box, Pegasus Mail keeps any messages you delete in a special "Deleted Messages" area. (See the "Deleting Unneeded Messages" section to learn how to delete messages.) This way, if you delete a message accidentally, you can rescue it from the Deleted Messages window and breathe a sigh of relief. The deleted messages are blown away for good, though, when you exit Pegasus Mail.

Ask for confirmation before deleting Activating this check box is another safeguard for preventing accidental deletions. In this case, Pegasus Mail displays a dialog box to ask you to confirm the deletion.

Save desktop state between sessions If you activate this option, Pegasus Mail will remember which windows were open and where they were each time you exit the program. When you load Pegasus Mail the next time, it will display all the windows exactly as they were before. A real time-saver.

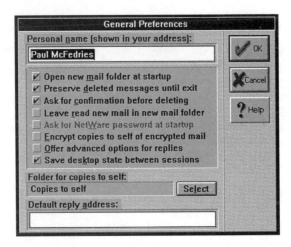

Use the options in the General Preferences dialog box to customize Pegasus Mail to your heart's content.

Dealing with New Mail

Okay, we're finally ready to actually make Pegasus Mail do something constructive. The next two sections show you how to check for new incoming mail and how to read it once you get it.

Checking for Incoming Mail

We'll begin by getting Pegasus Mail to contact your POP server and check to see if there's any mail waiting for you. To do that, pull down the File menu and select the **Check host for new mail** command. Pegasus Mail taps your access provider on the shoulder and asks if any new mail has arrived. If there's mail a-waiting, the program copies the messages to your computer. (This may take a minute or two depending on how many messages there are.)

If you've been working offline, remember to establish a connection to your access provider before attempting to retrieve your mail.

When that chore is complete, you'll need to display the New mail folder to see your messages. If you don't already see the New mail folder window on your screen (the next figure shows you what it looks like), pull down the File menu and select the Read **new** mail command. (For faster service, press **Ctrl+W** in Windows or **Command-R** on the Mac).

Click on these buttons to sort.

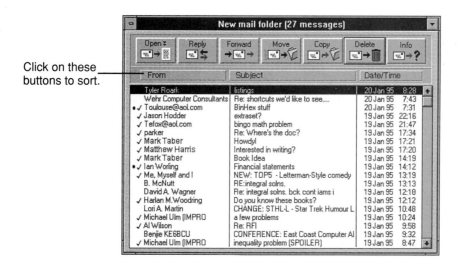

Your incoming messages appear inside the New mail folder.

The new mail folder displays a summary of each message in three columns:

From   This column shows the name of the sender. It also displays a check mark beside those messages you've read, and a black dot beside messages that have attachments. If you'd like to sort the messages by the sender's names, select the Folder menu's Sort by sender command, or click on the **From** button at the top of the column.

141

Subject   This column shows the Subject line of the message. To sort the messages by subject, pull down the Folder menu, and select the Sort by subject command, or click on the **Subject** button at the top of the column.

Date/Time   This column shows the date and time the message was sent. If you'd like to sort the messages by date with the latest at the top (this is the default sort order), select the Folder menu's Sort by date command, or click on the **Date/Time** button at the top of the column. To sort by date with the *earliest* messages at the top, select the Folder menu's Sort by reverse date command, or hold down **Ctrl** (or **Command** on the Mac) and click on the **Date/Time** button.

Opening a Message

To read what your correspondents have to say, you can either highlight a message and then click on the Open button, or you can just double-click on the message.

Pegasus Mail loads the message and displays it in all its glory in a separate window, as shown here. When you're done with the message, you can move to the next message by clicking on the **Next** button or by pressing plus (+). If you need to head back to the previous message, click on **Prev** or press minus (-).

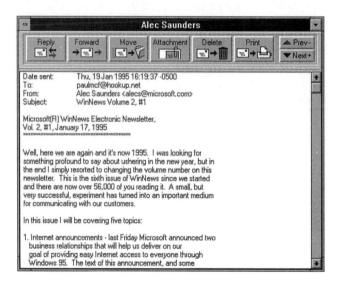

Pegasus Mail displays messages in a separate window.

Dealing with Attachments

Remember all that business about encoding and decoding nontext files I made you sit through back in Chapter 4, in the "Sending Sounds, Graphics, and Other Nontext Files" section? Well, you'll be happy to know that Pegasus Mail eats MIME, Uuencode, *and* BinHex for breakfast. I'll tell you how to send encoded attachments later on in the chapter, but for now, let's see what happens if you receive a message where an attachment piggy-backed a ride.

When you open a message that has an attached file, Pegasus Mail displays the following note in the message body:

```
This message has attachments; click on 'Attachment' to see them.
```

Go ahead and click on the **Attachment** button. The Message Attachments dialog box shows you the name of the file and its file type, if known. To save the attachment to a file, click on **Save**, use the Save As dialog box to select a location for the file (you can also change the file name, if you like), and then click on **OK**. When you're back in the Message Attachments dialog box, click on **Done**.

Replying to a Message

If the author of a message is expecting some kind of response from you, or if you've thought of a witty retort to a message, you need to use Pegasus Mail's Reply feature to compose and send a reply. You'll need to follow these steps:

1. Highlight the message in the New mail folder, or open the message.

2. Click on the **Reply** button. Pegasus Mail displays the Reply Options dialog box with the following options:

    Copy original CC field into reply   Activate this check box to send the reply to any addresses that were listed in the Cc field of the original message.

    Reply to all original addressees   Check this box to send the reply to all the addresses listed in the To and Cc fields of the original message. (As you'll see in a second, Pegasus Mail designates this by entering @REPLYALL.PML in the To field of the reply.)

    Include original message in reply   If you activate this check box, Pegasus Mail inserts the header and text of the original message into your reply.

    'Comment out' original message   If you're including the original message text in the reply, then you should also check this box to make Pegasus Mail add a greater-than sign (>) and a space to the beginning of each line of original text.

3. When you've selected your options, click on **OK**. Pegasus Mail displays a Reply window similar to the one shown in the following figure.

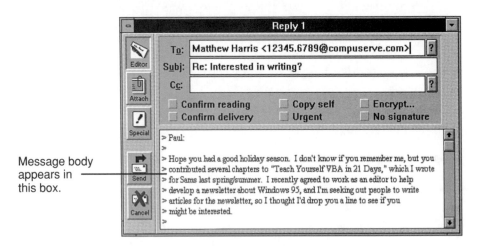

Message body appears in this box.

You use the Reply window to compose your response.

4. Edit the To:, Subj:, and Cc: fields, as needed.

5. If you included the original text, delete any lines that aren't necessary.

6. Add in your own text.

7. Click on the **Send** button. Pegasus Mail sends the message on its merry way.

Forwarding a Message to Another Address

You may occasionally receive a message that you think a colleague or friend would get some use out of, or you may get a message delivered to your address that should have been sent to a different locale. Either way, Pegasus Mail can easily forward the message to another e-mail address. Here are the steps to follow to get this done:

1. Highlight the message in the New mail folder, or open the message.

2. Click on the **Forward** button. The Forward message to dialog box appears with the following options:

   Forward **to**   Enter the forwarding e-mail address you want to use.

   Edit the message before forwarding   If you'd like to add something to the message before passing it on (for example, "Bob: Thought you might get a kick out of this!"), activate this check box.

Forward **a**ttachments as well   If the message came with attachments, check this box
to send them along for the ride.

3. When you're done, click on **OK**. If you chose to edit the message, Pegasus Mail
   displays the text inside a Message window so you can make your changes. Otherwise, it just sends the message.

4. Make your changes as necessary and then click on the **Send** button to forward the
   message.

Working with Folders

As you've seen, Pegasus Mail places all incoming correspondence inside the New mail
folder. In Pegasus Mail parlance, a *folder* is a storage area for messages. The New mail
folder, then, is the storage area for all your incoming mail. Pegasus Mail actually comes
with a second folder that you probably haven't seen yet: the Main folder. Whenever you
close the New mail folder, or exit Pegasus Mail, the program actually moves all the
messages you've read into the Main folder. To prove it for yourself, follow these steps:

1. Read a message or two, if you haven't done so already.

2. Close the New mail folder. (In Windows, you close the folder by double-clicking on
   the Control-menu box in the upper left corner; on the Mac, you close the window
   by clicking on the close box in the upper left corner.)

3. If you're using the Windows version, pull down the File menu and select the **Mail
   folders** command (or press **Ctrl+L**). If you're using Pegasus Mail for the Mac, pull
   down the **File** menu and select the **Open mailbox** command (or press **Command-
   O**). Pegasus Mail displays the Select a folder dialog box.

4. Click on **Main folder** and then click on **Open**. Voilà! The Main folder window
   appears and lists the messages you've read.

Creating New Folders

Moving your read messages to the Main folder is a nice convenience because it keeps your
New mail folder lean and mean. However, what about the Main folder itself? Believe me,
it doesn't take long before it becomes bloated with messages; finding the missive you
need becomes a real needle-in-a-haystack exercise. You could delete some of the detritus
(which I'll show you how to do in the next section), but that's really only a short-term
solution. No, what you really need is a way to organize your mail by, say, correspondent,
or mailing list, or whatever.

The good news is that you can easily achieve this kind of organization just by creating more folders. So you could, for example, create a folder to handle the dispatches that come your way from the mailing lists you subscribe to, or you could create a folder for all your regular e-mail buddies. Here's how you go about creating a new folder:

1. Pull down the File menu and select the **Mail folders** command (or press **Ctrl+L** in Windows or **Command-O** on the Macintosh).

2. In the Select a folder dialog box, click on the **New** button. Pegasus Mail displays the Enter folder long name and file name dialog box.

3. Use the **Long name for folder or tray** to enter a name for the folder.

4. Make sure the **Message folder** option is selected.

5. Click on **OK**. Pegasus Mail creates the folder and returns you to the Select a folder dialog box.

6. Click on **Cancel**.

Moving a Message to a Different Folder

With the folders you need set up and ready to go, you can now start moving messages into these folders. It's easy, too. Just click on the message you want to move (or you can open the message), and then click on the **Move** button to display the Select a folder dialog box. Click on the folder where you want the message moved, and then click on **Open**. Pegasus Mail doesn't open the folder, as you might expect; it just moves the message inside it.

Deleting Unneeded Messages

If you've read a message and know you won't need it again in the future, you should delete it to save some disk space and keep your folders free of debris. To delete a message, click on it and then click on the **Delete** button. Pegasus Mail displays a dialog box asking you to confirm the deletion. Click on **Yes** to get rid of the message.

If you have a whole whack of messages you want to clear out, you can select multiple messages in any folder by using either of the following techniques:

➤ If the messages are consecutive, click on the first message you want to delete, hold down the **Shift** key, and then click on the last message you want to delete.

➤ If the messages are scattered willy-nilly, click on the first message you want to expunge, hold down the **Ctrl** key (or the Mac's **Command** key), and then click on the other messages that are expendable.

When you delete a message, Pegasus Mail actually moves it to a folder called Deleted Messages. This is a precaution just in case you change your mind about deleting a message, or if you accidentally delete a crucial message. To recover a message, select the File menu's **Mail folders** command, and then open the Deleted Messages folder when the Select a folder dialog box appears. Now, click on the message you want to undelete, and move it to the appropriate folder (as described in the last section).

> Pegasus Mail cleans out the Deleted Messages folder every time you quit the program. So if you're going to undelete a message, make sure you do it before ending your Pegasus Mail session.

Composing a New Message

Of course, you won't be spending all your time in Pegasus Mail reading and replying to incoming correspondence and performing message-maintenance chores. You'll also be doing your share of composing and sending out original messages to the Internet community. Here's how you put together a new message in Pegasus Mail:

1. Pull down the File menu and select the New Message command (or press **Ctrl+N** in Windows or **Command-N** on the Mac). Pegasus Mail displays a Message window.

2. Fill in the To:, Subj:, and Cc: fields, as needed. (If you like, you can enter multiple addresses in the To: and Cc: fields. Just be sure to put a comma between each address.)

3. Type in your message text.

4. Click on the **Send** button. Pegasus Mail sends the message.

> If you click on the question mark (?) buttons to the right of the To: and Cc: fields, Pegasus Mail will display a list of e-mail addresses you've used recently. If you want to re-use one of them, click on it and then click on **Paste**. (Click **Cancel** to close the dialog box.)

Adding a Signature to an Outgoing Message

You'll recall, from the "Message Anatomy" section in Chapter 3, that a signature is a few lines of text at the bottom of a message that tells your readers a bit more about yourself. To create a signature in Pegasus Mail, pull down the File menu, select Preferences, select **Signature**, and then select For Internet messages. In the Signatures dialog box that appears, enter your signature and then click on **Save**.

To add your signature to an outgoing message, all you have to do is make sure the Message (or Reply) window's **No signature** check box is deactivated.

Attaching a File to an Outgoing Message

As I explained earlier, Pegasus Mail can handle encoded files that are attached to your incoming messages. So, not surprisingly, it's equally adept at attaching encoded files to outgoing missives. When you're composing a message, click on the **Attach** button, highlight the file you want to attach, and then click on **Add**.

Quitting Pegasus Mail

When you've completed your e-mail chores for the day, you can quit Pegasus Mail by pulling down the File menu and selecting the Exit command (or by pressing **Alt+F4** in Windows or **Command-Q** on the Mac).

There's a Usenet newsgroup that caters to Pegasus Mail users: **bit.listserv.pmail**. You'll see posts from fellow Pegasus Mail proponents concerning technical help, troubleshooting, and announcements of new versions.

The Least You Need to Know

This chapter took a look at the legendary e-mail program Pegasus Mail. To finish, here's a recap of some true myths about Pegasus Mail:

➤ To start Pegasus Mail, double-click on the **Pegasus Mail** icon. If you're starting the program for the first time, you'll need to configure the program by pulling down the File menu and selecting **Network Configuration**.

➤ To download your messages from the POP server, select the File menu's **Check host for new mail** command. When you get your mail, you can read a message by double-clicking on it.

➤ To reply to the current message, click on the **Reply** button, fill out the Reply Options, edit the message, and then click on **Send**.

➤ To forward the current message, click on the **Forward** button, enter the forwarding address, and then click on **Send**.

➤ To delete the current message, click on the **Delete** button.

➤ When you need to compose a new message, use the File menu's New Message command.

Chapter 13

The Karma of Chameleon Mail

In This Chapter

➤ Retrieving and reading incoming mail

➤ Forwarding, deleting, and responding to an e-mail message

➤ Organizing your mail with folders

➤ Composing and sending new e-mail messages

➤ Exposing the true colors of Chameleon Mail

As I explained back in Chapter 2, "An Introduction to the Internet," the Internet began its life as an experiment to see if several computers could be connected together. Along the way, various Jolt-cola-and-pizza-fueled programmers began creating services that would run on this network. So over the years, we ended up with FTP so we could get files, telnet so we could log in to other computers, Usenet so we could exchange news and announcements, and, of course, this e-mail deal we've been trying to figure out. In other words, the historical perspective of the Net is that it's a multifaceted creation that requires a variety of tools.

But now many newcomers are making their way online, and they're bringing with them an entirely new point of view: the Net as a monolithic, uniform whole. To them it seems ridiculous that you should have to crank up all kinds of completely different programs to access the Net's resources. In response to these complaints (and, naturally, smelling a buck or two to be made), several companies have developed their own "suite" of Internet applications. You get all the software you need to deal with the Net, *and* you get a reasonably consistent look and feel among the programs, to boot.

One of the first and one of the most popular of these sets of matching Net furniture is *Internet Chameleon* from NetManage, Inc. (You can contact NetManage at (408) 973-7171.) Internet Chameleon comes not only with Windows-based tools for connecting to the Net, but also for accessing services, such as FTP, Gopher, and the World Wide Web. Most importantly for our purposes, you also get a full-featured Mail program that gives you everything you need to do the e-mail thing. This chapter explores Mail and takes you through the basics of getting and reading e-mail, sending out your own dispatches, and lots more.

Setting Sail with Mail

To keep things focused, I'm going to assume that you (or your friendly neighborhood Internet guru) have installed Internet Chameleon and that you have an account set up at a service provider that includes access to Internet e-mail via SLIP (Serial Line Interface Protocol) or PPP (Point-to-Point Protocol). So, your first order of business is to establish a connection through your modem to the service provider so you can receive and send e-mail. You use either Chameleon's Instant Internet program (if you signed up with one of the preconfigured providers, such as CERFnet or InterRamp) or Chameleon's Custom Connect utility to get the connection happening.

If you pay by the hour for your connection, or if you pay a monthly fee that limits the number of hours you can spend online, you may consider working "offline" until you're ready to send or receive mail. Working offline means you load Mail *before* establishing a connection to your service provider. This way, you can configure the program, perform mail-maintenance chores, and compose messages without running up your connection costs. Then, when you're ready for action, you can get connected and send your messages or get your incoming mail.

When that's done and your SLIP or PPP connection is humming along nicely, go ahead and start Mail by double-clicking on the **Mail** icon in your Internet Chameleon program group. You'll eventually see the Mail - Login dialog box, as shown in the following figure. Select **OK** to load the Mail - Postmaster window.

Use the Mail - Login dialog box to log in to Mail.

What's all this about a *Postmaster*? Well, one of Mail's nice touches is that you can set it up to handle any one of the following three scenarios:

➤ A single user accessing a single Internet e-mail account.

➤ A single user accessing multiple Internet e-mail accounts.

➤ Multiple users accessing separate Internet e-mail accounts.

The idea is that, for each user and each account, you create corresponding "mailboxes" inside Chameleon Mail. This lets you configure Mail to suit each person, and it means the incoming mail won't get mixed together willy-nilly.

Okay, but what about the Postmaster? Ah, the Postmaster, in the Mail scheme of things, is a sort of "super-user" who sets up and configures everyone else's mailboxes. Once the Postmaster sets up a mailbox for a user, that person would start Mail by following these steps:

1. Double-click on the **Mail** icon to display the Mail - Login dialog box.

2. Use the Username drop-down box to select the username that the Postmaster assigned to his mailbox.

3. Type in his password in the **Password** box (again, the Postmaster assigns the person a password to access his mailbox).

4. Select **OK**. Mail starts up and loads the configuration and messages for that person.

Setting up a mailbox is actually a two-step process: first you create the mailbox (this is covered in the next section, "Setting Up a Mailbox"), and then you configure the mailbox so it can properly send and receive mail (see the "Configuring a Mailbox to Send and Receive E-Mail" section). Here's how the Postmaster would set things up for the three scenarios we looked at earlier:

➤ If you're a single user with a single e-mail account, log in as the Postmaster, create a single mailbox for yourself, and then exit Mail. Start Mail again, log in under the mailbox you created (that is, your username), and then configure the mailbox for sending and receiving mail.

151

➤ If you're a single user with multiple e-mail accounts, first log in as the Postmaster, create separate mailboxes for each account, and then exit Mail. Then, for each mailbox, start Mail, select the appropriate mailbox (that is, username) from the Mail - Login dialog box, and then configure the mailbox for sending and receiving mail.

➤ If there are multiple users with separate e-mail accounts, first log in as the Postmaster, create separate mailboxes for each person, and then exit Mail. Then, for each person's mailbox, start Mail, select the appropriate username from the Mail - Login dialog box, and then configure the person's mailbox for sending and receiving mail.

Whew! That's a lot of work (I hope they're paying you well). The next two sections fill in the details for creating mailboxes and configuring them.

Setting Up a Mailbox

To create a new mailbox, log in as the Postmaster and then follow these instructions:

1. Pull down the Services menu and select the Mailboxes command (this command is only available when you log in as the Postmaster). The Mailboxes dialog box appears.

2. In the User field, type in the username that you use (or the other person uses) to log in to the service provider.

3. Select the Add button. Mail displays a dialog box for the user (see figure below).

Use this dialog box to fill in the mailbox details.

4. Use the Password text box to enter a password for the mailbox.

5. Use the In real life text box to enter the person's full name.

6. In the Mail Directory text box, enter a directory to hold the messages and other files for the mailbox. Your best bet here is to create a subdirectory of the C:\NETMANAGE\EMAIL directory using the person's username. (I'm assuming you installed Internet Chameleon in the default C:\NETMANAGE directory.) For example, my username is "paulmcf," so I'd enter the directory **c:\netmanage\email\paulmcf.**

7. Select **OK**. Mail will likely need to create the mail directory, so a dialog box will appear to ask if that's okay with you.

8. Select Yes to return to the Mailboxes dialog box.

9. Select Save to save the mailbox, and then select **Cancel**.

Configuring a Mailbox to Send and Receive E-Mail

To send messages in Mail, you need to tell the program about the computer at your access provider that relays your outgoing messages to the Internet at large. Mail calls this computer the *mail gateway*.

To give Mail the goods on the mail gateway info, pull down the Settings menu, select Network, and then select Mail Gateway. The Mail Gateway dialog box appears, as shown in the figure below. In the Host text box, enter the name (technically, the *domain name*) of the computer at your service provider that handles your outgoing mail.

Use the Mail Gateway dialog box to tell Mail the name of the computer that handles your outgoing messages.

To receive messages in Mail, you need to let the program know about the computer that your access provider has set up as a POP (Post Office Protocol) server and the details of your POP account. (If you need to refresh your memory on this POP poop, trudge back to Chapter 3, and check out the "A Quick Peek Under the Hood" section.) Mail calls this computer the *mail server*, and you can give it the scoop by selecting Network from the Settings menu and then selecting Mail Server. This displays the Mail Server dialog box, as shown on the following page.

Use the Mail Server dialog box to give Mail the info it needs about the computer that stores your incoming mail.

Here a rundown of the fields you need to fill out:

Host The name (that is, the *domain name*) of the service provider computer that handles your POP account.

User The username you use to log in to your POP account on the mail server.

Password The password you use to gain access to your POP account.

Mail dir The directory on the mail server where your mail is stored. You normally don't have to bother with this field because the mail server knows where your mail is stored.

Delete retrieved mail from server If you activate this check box, Mail will delete your messages on the server after it has copied them to your computer. It's a good idea to turn this option on because it prevents you from receiving duplicate copies of your messages (and it frees up disk space on the server).

When you're done, select **OK**.

Saving Your Settings

Now that you've gone through all this rigmarole, you should save your settings. Pull down the File menu and select Save to display the Save Configuration File As dialog box. Enter a name in the File Name text box (it should be the username followed by .CFG; for example, PAULMCF.CFG), and then select **OK**.

Retrieving and Viewing Your Mail

Sheesh, what a load just to be able to do a little e-mail! Ah, well, you'll be happy to know the hard part's over and you can finally get down to work. For starters, the next couple of sections show you how to retrieve messages from the mail server and how to read them once they're safely on your computer.

Retrieving Messages from the Mail Server

As I mentioned earlier, messages sent to your e-mail address actually end up hanging around inside your service provider's mail server. To get at them, you have to tell Mail to retrieve them for you. This means that Mail contacts the server, asks if any new messages are present, and copies any that are in the mail directory on your computer. To set all this in motion, you need only pull down the Message menu and select the Retrieve Mail command (you can also press **Ctrl+T**).

If you've been working offline, remember to establish a connection to your service provider before attempting to retrieve your mail.

As Mail retrieves the messages, it displays information about each one on-screen and keeps you apprised of its progress in the bottom right corner (such as, **Retrieving message 10 of 21**). When all is said and done, your screen will look something like the one shown in the following figure. (This screen is called the *Inbox folder*. I'll talk more about what a folder is later on.)

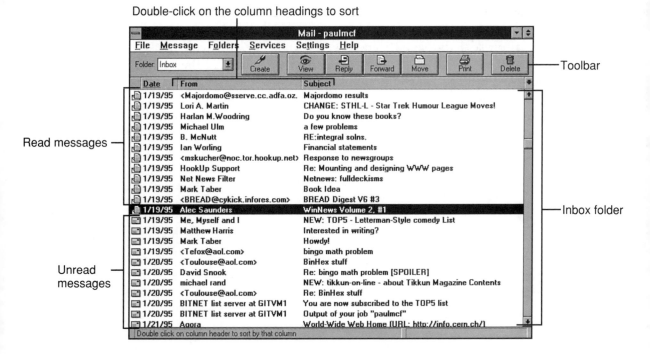

Mail displays info about each of your received messages.

Each line presents summary info about an individual message. The first column shows an envelope icon that represents an unread message. When you've read a message, Mail adds a document on top of the envelope. The **Date** column shows the date the message was sent. (It also shows the time, but you can't see it. To make more room in the **Date** column, use your mouse to drag the right edge of the **Date** heading to the right. You can do this for any column to adjust its width.) The **From** column shows the name of the sender, and the **Subject** column shows the Subject line of the message. (Note: you can sort the messages by date, sender, or subject by double-clicking on the appropriate column heading.)

Viewing a Message

Mail gives you a fistful of ways to read a particular message. The easiest way is probably to just double-click on it. Alternatively, you can highlight the message (by clicking on it, or by using the up and down arrow keys) and then select the Message menu's View command, or press **Ctrl+W**, or click on the **View** button in the toolbar. (By the way, you may be wondering how I was able to get my toolbar buttons to show both pictures and text in the above figure. Easy: just pull down the Settings menu and activate the Smart Buttons command.)

Mail loads up the message and displays it in a view window like the one shown in the following figure. If the full text of the message doesn't fit inside the window, you can use the arrow keys, the **Page Up** and **Page Down** keys, or the scroll bar to scroll through the text. When you're ready to move on to the next message, either select the Message menu's Next message command, click on **Next** in the toolbar, or press **Ctrl+N**. If you'd prefer to go back to the previous message, you can select Previous message from the Message menu, click on the **Previous** button, or press **Ctrl+P**. To get back to the main Mail window, select the File menu's Exit command.

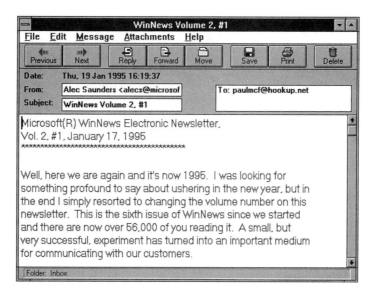

Mail displays your messages in a view window like this one.

Basic Mail Maintenance Chores

When you get snail mail at the office, your assistant or somebody from the mailroom probably places it in your "In" basket. You then sort through and read the mail and farm out each message accordingly: some need to be responded to; some need to be forwarded; some get filed; and some get tossed in the garbage. Chameleon Mail gives you a similar range of choices after you've perused a message:

➤ You can send a reply to the author of the message.

➤ You can forward the message to someone else's e-mail address.

➤ You can save the message to a different folder.

➤ You can delete the message.

The next few sections give you the details for each task.

Sending a Reply

A lot of the messages that come your way—especially those from mailing lists and those
that are FYI-only—won't require any kind of response from you. You can just read them
and then do with them what you will. However, there'll still be all kinds of missives
where a reply to the original author is in order. Here's how you reply to a message in
Mail:

1. Highlight the message in the Inbox folder, or view the message.

2. If you want to reply only to the author of the message (and not to anyone listed
    on the Cc line), pull down the **Message** window, select **Reply to**, and then select
    Sender. (You can also click on the **Reply** button in the toolbar or press **Ctrl+R**.)
    Alternatively, you can reply to the author and all the Cc line addresses by pulling
    down the Message menu, selecting Reply to, and then selecting **All**. In either case,
    Mail displays a window similar to the one shown below.

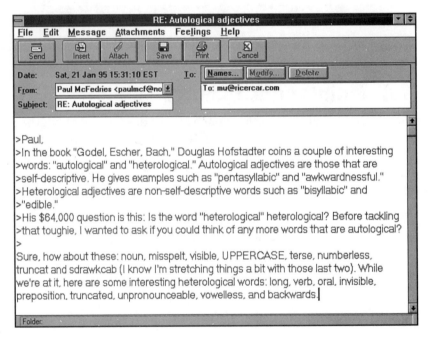

Use this window to set up your reply.

3. If you want to include the original message in your reply, pull down the **Edit** menu,
    select Include Original, and then select **Indented** (don't bother with the **Bracketed**
    command). Mail inserts the original text and adds a greater-than sign (>) to the
    beginning of each line.

4. Delete any unneeded lines from the original message text.

5. Type in your own message.

6. Send the message by pulling down the Message menu and selecting Send, or by clicking on the **Send** button.

Forwarding a Message to Another Address

Some messages just cry out to be shared with others. It could be a good joke, a brilliant argument, or some howler committed by a clueless correspondent. Whatever the reason, when you need to forward a message, follow these Mail steps:

1. Either view the message or highlight it in the Inbox folder.

2. Pull down the Message menu and select Forward. (You can also try clicking on the **Forward** button in the toolbar or pressing **Ctrl+F**.) Mail displays the message in a window.

3. In the To box, select the Names button. The Names dialog box appears.

> You can force Mail to include the original message text automatically in all your replies. Pull down the Settings menu and select **Preferences**. In the Preferences dialog box, activate both the **Include original in reply** and **Indent included message** check boxes, and then select **OK**.

4. Type in the forwarding address and then select **To**. You can also add an address to the Cc line by entering it and selecting the Cc button. Similarly, to add an address to the Bcc line, type the address and select **Bcc**. When you're done, select **OK**.

5. Add whatever extra text you need to the message (such as, "Sandy: Here's another Pentium joke, but this one's *funny*").

6. Send the message by pulling down the Message menu and selecting Send, or by clicking on the **Send** button.

Deleting a Message

Some of the messages you'll receive will be the electronic equivalent of junk mail and you won't want to bother with them again after you've read them. To keep the Inbox folder tidy, you should delete this detritus by highlighting the message and selecting the Message menu's Delete command. (Your other choices are to click on the **Delete** button or to press **Ctrl+D**.)

To make your heavy-duty deletion chores easier, Mail lets you highlight multiple messages and delete them in one fell swoop. Here's how you select multiple messages:

➤ If the messages are consecutive, click on the first message you want to delete, hold down the **Shift** key, and then click on the last message you want to delete.

➤ If the messages are distributed randomly about the folder, click on the first message you want to expunge, hold down the **Ctrl** key, and then click on the other messages that are expendable.

Moving a Message to a Different Folder

Once you've completed all your replying, forwarding, and deleting, the messages left in your Inbox folder will be ones you intend to keep, just in case you need to refer to them later on. But, just as you wouldn't keep all your opened snail mail in the your office In basket, it doesn't make sense to have all those read messages cluttering Mail's Inbox folder.

The solution is to create new folders to hold related types of messages. For example, if you and your boss exchange frequent e-mail notes, you could set up a folder just to hold her correspondence. Similarly, if you subscribe to a mailing list, you could set up a folder to keep the regular mailings you get.

To create a folder in Mail, make sure you have the Inbox folder displayed, and then select the Create command from the Folders menu. In the Create Folder dialog box that appears, type in the name of the folder, and then select **OK**.

To move a message (or messages; see the last section to learn how to select multiple messages), highlight it, pull down the Message menu, and select the Move to Folder command. (The shortcuts: click on the **Move** button or press **Ctrl+M**.) In the Move to Folder dialog box that comes your way, highlight the folder you want to move the messages to, and then select **OK**.

To display a particular folder, use either of the following techniques:

➤ Pull down the Folders menu and select Open to display the Open Folder dialog box. Highlight the folder you want to open and select **OK**.

➤ Use the **Folder** drop-down list on the left side of the toolbar to select the folder you want to display.

Creating a New Message

You certainly won't be spending all your time in Mail reading and replying to incoming correspondence and performing mail maintenance tasks. You'll also be doing your share of creating and sending original messages to friends and colleagues around the Net. Here's how it's done in Mail:

1. Pull down the Message menu and select the Create command. (There are, of course, short-cuts available: you can click on the **Create** button, or you can press **Ctrl+E**.) Mail displays a New Mail window (it's identical to the reply window you used earlier for sending replies).

2. Use the Subject box to enter a subject for the message.

3. In the To box, select the Names button. The Names dialog box appears.

4. Type in the e-mail address of your recipient and then select To. You can also add an address to the Cc line by entering it and selecting the Cc button. Similarly, to add an address to the Bcc line, type the address and select **Bcc**. When you're done, select **OK**.

5. Type in your text.

6. If you've created a signature (see the next section), move the cursor to the end of the message and then select the Edit menu's **Signature** command. Mail inserts your signature.

7. Send the message by pulling down the **Message** menu and selecting Send, or by clicking on the **Send** button.

If you deleted some messages, you may have noticed that Mail also has a folder called *Trash*. When you delete a message, Mail actually moves it to the Trash folder. This is a precaution just in case you change your mind about deleting a message, or if you delete a crucial message by accident. To recover a message, display the Trash folder, highlight the message, and then move it back to its original folder. Keep in mind, however, that Mail cleans out the Trash folder every time you quit the program. So if you're going to undelete a message, make sure you do it before ending your Mail session.

Creating a Signature

Way back in Chapter 3, in the "Message Anatomy" section, I told you that a signature was a block of text that appears at the end of a message to tell the reader a little bit about the author of the message. Rather than typing in your signature each time your create a message, you can create one and save it in Mail. To try this feature on for size, pull down the Settings menu and select the Signature command. In the Mail Signature dialog box that appears, enter your mini-bio in the **Signature** box. (Note that Mail will already have created a basic signature for you. You can edit this text to suit your style.) If you'd like Mail to append your signature automatically to every message you send, activate the **Attach to outgoing mail** check box. When you're done, select **OK**.

Closing Chameleon Mail

When you've completed your e-mail chores for the day, you can quit Mail by pulling the File menu and selecting the Exit command (or by pressing **Alt+F4**).

The Least You Need to Know

This chapter took you through the basics of the Mail program that comes with the Internet Chameleon suite of applications. Just to make sure you leave this chapter with some good karma, here's a quick review of some of the chapter's high points:

➤ To start Mail, double-click on the **Mail** icon in the **Internet Chameleon** program group.

➤ When you first start Mail, log in as Postmaster and create the mailboxes you need. Then log in as a user and configure Mail for sending and receiving messages.

➤ To get your incoming mail, select the Message menu's Retrieve Mail command (or press **Ctrl+T**). To view a message, double-click on it.

➤ To reply to the current message, select the Message menu's Reply to command, and then select either Sender (or press **Ctrl+R** or click on the **Reply** button), or All.

➤ Deleting the current message is a matter of pulling down the Message menu and selecting the Delete command. (The alternatives are pressing **Ctrl+D** or clicking on **Delete**.)

➤ To create a new message, pull down the Message and select Create (clicking on **Create** or pressing **Ctrl+E** will also work).

Chapter 14

Taking Flight with AIR Mail

In This Chapter

➤ Getting incoming messages and reading them

➤ Responding to an e-mail message

➤ Forwarding, saving, and deleting messages

➤ Composing new mail and sending it

➤ Some spectacular AIRial maneuvers designed to help you earn your e-mail wings

Back in Chapter 5, "Learning the Lingo: E-Mail Jargon and Acronyms," I defined a *newbie* as someone new to the Internet. So, for the purposes of this introduction, let's define an *oldbie* as a veteran of the Internet. There are many distinctions we can make between newbies and oldbies, but one important one is how they approach the various tools (such as FTP, Gopher, and e-mail) surfers must use to access the Internet's resources.

To an oldbie, having multiple Net services is analogous to having multiple applications on your computer: when it's time to write, you crank up your word processor; when it's time to crunch numbers, you load a spreadsheet program, and so on. In their minds, the Internet's services are distinct, so they require distinct tools to access them.

To a newbie, however, having multiple Net services is analogous to having separate features inside a *single* application: in a word processor, for example, when you want to check your spelling you select the Spell Check command; when you want to format your characters you run the Font command, and so on. In their minds, the Internet's services are part of a whole (the Internet itself), so you should only need a single program to access them.

The newbie ideal of a sort of "Swiss Army knife" of Internet applications isn't here just yet. (Although some World Wide Web browsers—particularly Netscape from Netscape Communications—are getting there.) The closest we've come so far are *suites* of Internet programs that boast, at least, a consistent interface between the various tools. One such suite is the *Internet In A Box* package from SPRY, Inc. (You can contact SPRY at (206) 447-0958.) This collection includes applications for FTP, Usenet, Gopher, the World Wide Web, and an e-mail program called *AIR Mail* that's the subject of this chapter.

Getting AIR Mail off the Ground

We'll only be dealing with the AIR Mail application in this chapter, so I'm going to make a big leap and assume that you have (or some nearby Net guru has) installed and—with one exception—configured the Internet In A Box package. The exception is that I'll take you through the steps required to configure AIR Mail. Here's how it's done:

1. Open the **Internet In A Box** program group, and double-click on the **Configuration** icon to display the Configuration Utility window.

2. Select the Default Hosts button. The Default Hosts dialog box appears, as shown in the figure on the next page.

3. In the **AIR Mail** box, fill in the following fields:

   Email Username   This is the name you use to log in to your e-mail account. It's usually the same as the login name you use to connect to your service provider.

   Email Password   This is the password assigned to your username.

   POP3 Email   This is the domain name of your service provider's POP (Post Office Protocol) computer.

   SMTP Relay Host   Use this field to enter the domain name of your service provider's SMTP (Simple Mail Transport Protocol) computer.

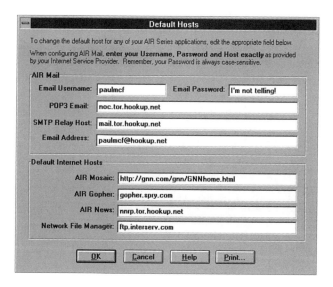

Use the Default Hosts dialog box to specify some AIR Mail options in advance.

A little foggy on this POP and SMTP flummery? Hey, who can blame you? Certainly not I, which is why I've explained everything you need to know in Chapter 3, in the "A Quick Peek Under the Hood" section.

Email Address   This is your Internet e-mail address.

4. Select OK to return to the Configuration Utility window, and then select Exit to return to Program Manager.

With that out of the way, you're ready to get started with AIR Mail. In the **Internet In A Box** program group, double-click on the **AIR Mail** icon. When you run AIR Mail for the first time, you'll see a dialog box called Mail Folder Directory that asks you to enter a "Folder Directory Name." As you'll see later, AIR Mail uses *folders* to store your messages. This dialog box just wants to know which directory to use to store the folder info. Your best bet is just to accept the recommended directory by selecting **OK**.

165

After a few seconds, you'll see the AIR Mail dialog box, as shown in the following figure. The **Host** and **Username** fields should already be filled in for you (AIR Mail gets these values from the **POP3 Email** and **Email Username** fields you saw in the Default Hosts dialog box), so you just need to type your password in the **Password** text box.

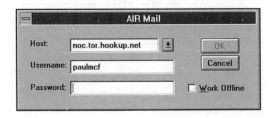

Use the AIR Mail dialog box to login to AIR Mail and your service provider.

You'll also notice the AIR Mail dialog box has a **W**ork Offline check box. If you pay by the hour for your connection, or if you pay a monthly fee that limits the number of hours you can spend online, you may consider working "offline" until you're ready to send or receive mail. Working offline means AIR Mail doesn't establish a connection to your service provider. This way, you can configure the program, perform mail mainte-nance chores, and compose messages without running up your connection costs. Then, when you're ready for action, you can connect (I'll explain how later) and send your messages or get your incoming mail.

When you're ready, select **OK** to continue. If you elected to work online, AIR Mail wakes the Internet In A Box Dialer program and tells it to establish a connection to your service provider. (I'm also assuming you have an account set up at a service provider that includes access to Internet e-mail via PPP—Point-to-Point Protocol.) When that's done, AIR Mail logs in to the mail host computer (again, only if you're working online), checks for incoming messages, and grabs any that are waiting in your mailbox.

A Tour Around the MAILBOX Window

If there were any messages waiting for you when you started AIR Mail, the program displays them in the MAILBOX window, as shown in the following figure. The MAILBOX window is divided into two sections: the *folder pane* and the *message pane*.

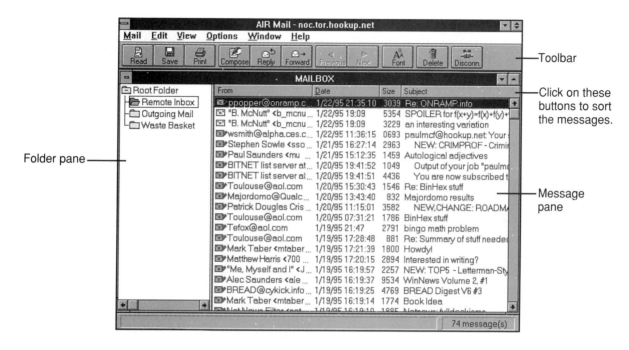

Your received messages appear in the MAILBOX window.

The folder pane is the left side of the window. AIR Mail, as I've said, organizes your messages into storage areas called *folders*. You start out with three folders:

Remote Inbox   This folder stores info about the messages you've received. It's called the "remote" inbox because it doesn't transfer your messages to your computer; instead, it works with them on the service provider's mail computer.

If you'd prefer that AIR Mail transfers your messages to your computer, pull down the Options menu and select Preferences. In the Preferences dialog box, find the **Inbox Location** section and select the Change button. When the Choose Inbox dialog box appears, activate the Local Inbox option and then select **OK**. When you're back in the Preferences dialog box, select **OK**. Exit and restart AIR Mail to put the change into effect. You'll see that AIR Mail has created a new *Inbox* folder that it will use to store the messages transferred to your computer.

Outgoing Mail This folder stores messages that you attempt to send while you're working offline. AIR Mail keeps them in this folder temporarily until such time as you get back online. You can then run a command to send them all at once.

Waste Basket This folder stores messages that you delete (provided, that is, you're working with your messages locally—i.e., on your computer and not with the remote inbox). This allows you to recover an accidentally deleted message.

The message pane displays some vital statistics about the messages contained in the current folder. (You select different folders by clicking on them in the folder pane.) The message pane is divided into four columns:

From This column shows the name of the sender and displays an icon to the left of the author that tells you the status of the message. An envelope icon tells you the message is unread; an envelope icon torn on the right tells you the message has been read (as though you tore open the envelope to read the message). To sort the messages by sender, either select the View menu's Sort by Sender command, or click on the **From** button at the top of the column.

Date This column displays the date and time the message was sent. To sort the messages by date, either select the View menu's Sort by Date command, or click on the **Date** button at the top of the column.

Size This column shows the size (in bytes) of the message. To sort the messages by size, either select the View menu's Sort by Size command, or click on the **Size** button at the top of the column.

Subject This column gives you the Subject line of the message. You can sort the messages by subject either by selecting the View menu's Sort by Subject command, or by clicking on the **Subject** button at the top of the column.

Reading Your Received Mail

Okay, we are, at long last, finally ready to make AIR Mail do something useful. To read one of your messages, you can double-click on it in the message pane, or you can highlight it (by clicking on it or using the arrow keys) and then use any of the following methods:

➤ Select the Mail menu's Read command.

➤ Click on the **Read** button in the toolbar.

➤ Press **Enter**.

If you've been working offline until now, you'll need to connect to your service provider and then download the message data. To connect to the mail host, either click on the **Connect** button, or select the Mail menu's Connec**t** command. Once you're logged in, you can get your new messages by selecting the View menu's New Messages command (or you can press **F10**).

Whichever method you use, AIR Mail loads the article and displays it in a message window like the one shown below. When you've finished with the message, you can move on to the next one by clicking on the **Next** button, selecting the View menu's Next command, or pressing **Ctrl+Page Down**. To return to the previous message, click on the **Previous** button, select Previous from the View menu, or press **Ctrl+Page Up**.

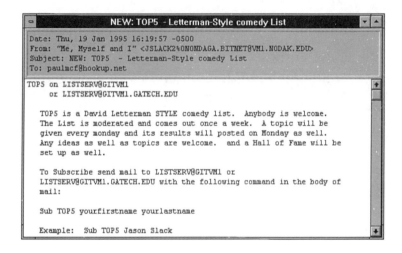

AIR Mail displays your correspondence in a message window like this one.

Basic Mail Maintenance Chores

Once you've read a message, you need to decide what next to do with it. AIR Mail gives you four choices:

➤ You can forward the message to someone else's e-mail address.

➤ You can send a reply to the author of the message.

➤ You can save the message to a different folder.

➤ You can delete the message.

The next few sections run you through the specifics for each task.

Forwarding a Message to Another Address

If a message has some info you want to share with someone, or if a message was sent to your address accidentally, you can forward the message to another person's e-mail address. Follow these steps:

1. Either read the message or highlight it in the message pane.

2. Pull down the Mail window and select the Forward command (you can also click on the **Forward** button or press **Ctrl+F**). AIR Mail displays the Forward Mail window.

3. In the To box, enter the forwarding address of the person you want to receive the message. You can also use the Cc and Bcc boxes to enter other addresses.

4. When AIR Mail displays the Forward Mail window, it includes the original message text in the message body and denotes it with the following line:

   ```
   <---- Begin Included Message ---->
   ```

   Feel free to add some extra text before this line (see figure below).

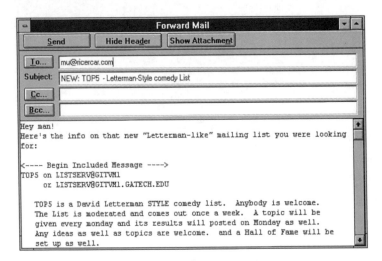

You can add some explanatory text to your forwarded message.

5. Send the message by pulling down the Mail menu and selecting the Send Now command or by clicking on the Send button.

Replying to a Message

If the author of a message is expecting some kind of response from you, or if you've thought of a witty rejoinder to a message, you need to compose a reply and then send it back to the author's e-mail address. Here's how it's done in AIR Mail:

1. Highlight the message in the message pane, or read the message.

2. Pull down the **Mail** window and select the Reply command (you can also click on the **Reply** button or press **Ctrl+Y**). AIR Mail displays the Reply Method dialog box.

3. Select one of the following options and then select **OK**:

   To **Sender**   Activate this option to address the reply only to the author of the message.

   To **All**   Use this option if you want to send the reply to the author *and* to everyone listed in the message's Cc line.

   To **Sender Include**   Select this option to send the reply to the author and include the original message as part of the reply.

   To **All Include**   This option addresses the reply to the author and the people in the Cc line, and it includes the original message in the reply.

4. If you included the original message text, use the Reply Mail window that appears (it looks just like the Forward Mail window you saw earlier) to delete any unneeded lines.

5. Type in your own message.

6. Send the message by pulling down the Mail menu and selecting the Send Now command or by clicking on the Send button.

Moving a Message to a Different Folder

One of the problems with working in the Remote Inbox folder is that you can't access your messages when you're working offline. You can get around this by having AIR Mail transfer your messages to your computer. The simplest way to do that is to switch to the local Inbox folder, as I described earlier. This forces AIR Mail to bring all your messages to your computer, but you'll soon run into another problem: congestion. Even if you only receive a few messages a day, this can still add up to dozens of messages cluttering the Inbox folder.

The solution is to create new folders to hold related types of messages. For example, if you and your boss exchange frequent e-mail notes, you could set up a folder just to hold her correspondence. Similarly, if you subscribe to a mailing list, you could set up a folder to store the regular mailings you get.

To create a folder in AIR Mail, follow these steps:

1. Pull down the **Mail** menu and select the New Folder command. AIR Mail displays the Create New Folder dialog box.

2. In the **New Folder Name** text box, enter a name for the folder.

3. In the **Sub Folder of** box, click on the folder that will contain the folder you're creating. You'll usually select the Root Folder. However, you're free to create folders within the folders you create yourself. For example, you could create a Mailing Lists folder and then, inside it, create subfolders for each mailing list you subscribe to (the following figure shows an example).

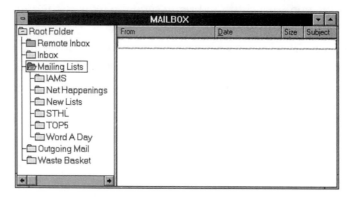

A folder pane showing folders within folders.

4. Select **OK** to create the folder.

To move a message to a different folder, use either of the following techniques:

➤ Highlight the message and select the **Mail** menu's Move command (you can also press **F7**). In the Move Message dialog box that appears, select the folder you want to move the message to and then select **OK**.

➤ Use your mouse to drag the message from the message pane and drop it on the folder in the folder pane.

Deleting a Message

Some of the messages you'll receive will be the electronic equivalent of junk mail, and you won't want to bother with them again after you've read them. To keep your folders tidy, you should delete this detritus by highlighting the message and selecting the **Mail** menu's **Delete** command. (Your other choices are to click on the **Delete** button or to press **Ctrl+D**.) If you're deleting a message from the Remote Inbox folder, a dialog box will appear to ask you for confirmation. If you're sure, select Yes (or, if you're deleting multiple messages, Yes to All).

If you're working with the Remote Inbox folder, your deleted messages are gone for all time, so you should be extra careful about which messages you decide to nuke. If you're working with any other folder, however, AIR Mail transfers deleted messages to the Waste Basket folder. So if you expunge the wrong message by accident, you can recover it by selecting the Waste Basket folder and moving the message back to where it belongs. Of course, you don't want messages piling up in the Waste Basket folder forever, so AIR Mail gives you two ways to take out the trash, so to speak:

> If AIR Mail doesn't ask for confirmation when you get rid of a message from the Remote Inbox folder, you can soon change that. Pull down the Options menu and select the Confirmation command to display the Confirmation dialog box. Activate the Remote Message **Delete** check box and then select **OK**.

➤ To get rid of specific messages in the Waste Basket folder, highlight them and the delete them again.

➤ To clean out the entire Waste Basket folder every time you exit AIR Mail, pull down the **Options** menu and activate the Empty Wastebasket on Exit command.

Composing a New Message

When it's time to foist some of your unmatched prose on certain lucky members of the Internet community, you'll need to compose a message in AIR Mail and then send it off. Here are the steps to follow:

1. Pull down the **Mail** menu and select the Compose New Message command. (Type-A types can also press **Ctrl+N** or click on the **Compose** button.) AIR Mail displays a new Compose Mail window.

173

2. Define the header of your message by filling in the To, **Subject**, Cc, and Bcc fields.

3. Type in your message.

4. Send the message by pulling down the Mail menu and selecting the Send Now command or by clicking on the Send button.

Working with AIR Mail's Address Book

To make it easier to enter addresses in the To, Cc, and Bcc header fields of the Compose Mail window (as well as the Forward Mail and Reply Mail windows), AIR Mail lets you set up an *address book* of commonly used e-mail addresses.

For starters, let's see how you add an e-mail address to the address book. In the Compose Mail window, select the To button to display the Address Book dialog box, and then select the Add button to display the Address Book Detail dialog box. Enter a descriptive name for the address in the **Alias Name** text box, enter the actual e-mail address in the **Internet Address** text box, and then select **OK**. AIR Mail displays the new address in the Address Book dialog box.

To include the address in the To field, just highlight it and then select **OK**. Pasting addresses in the Cc and Bcc fields is just as easy: click on either the Cc or **Bcc** buttons, highlight the address you need, and then select **OK**.

Adding a Signature to a Message

If you like the idea of adding a signature to your outgoing messages, but you dread the idea of adding one by hand to all your messages, AIR Mail can help automate the process.

Your first task is to crank up a text editor, such as the Notepad program that comes with Windows. Type in the signature you want to use, remembering to use a maximum of four lines. Exit the editor and save the file with a name like SIG.TXT. (Also, remember which directory you save the file in, because you'll need it in a sec.)

Return to AIR Mail, pull down the Options menu, and select the Preferences command. In the Preferences dialog box that appears, use the **Auto Attach File** text box to enter the name and location of the signature file you created. For example, if the file is named SIG.TXT and you saved it in the C:\WINDOWS directory, you'd enter **c:\windows\sig.txt**. Select **OK** to return to AIR Mail. Now, with every message you send, AIR Mail will append the signature file to the end of your messages—automatically!

Adding an Attachment to a Message

AIR Mail can send nontext files using the uuencoding we looked at back in Chapter 4, in the "Sending Sounds, Graphics, and Other Nontext Files" section. To add an attachment to an outgoing message, select the Show Attachment button in either the Compose Mail, Reply Mail, or Forward Mail window. A box called the *attachment pane* appears at the bottom of the window. Select the Attach button, pick out the file from the Attach File dialog box that appears, and then select **OK**. An icon for the file appears inside the attachment pane.

Quitting AIR Mail

To bail out of AIR Mail, pull down the Mail menu and select the Exit command, or press **Alt+F4**.

The Least You Need to Know

This chapter showed you the basics of AIR Mail, the mail program that comes with the Internet In A Box suite of applications. Here's a bird's-eye view of the terrain we covered:

➤ Before starting AIR Mail, be sure to use the Internet In A Box Configuration utility to enter your service provider's e-mail details.

➤ To start AIR Mail, double-click on the **AIR Mail** icon in the **Internet In A Box** program group.

➤ To read your mail, highlight a message in the message pane, and then either select the Mail menu's Read command, or click on the **Read** button.

➤ To reply to the current message, select the Mail menu's Reply command, or click on the **Reply** button.

➤ You can move the current message to a different folder by selecting the Mail menu's Move command, or by pressing **F7**.

➤ You can handle your message-deleting chores by either pulling down the Mail menu and selecting the Delete command, or by clicking on the **Delete** button.

➤ To compose a new message, select Compose New Message from the Mail menu, or click on the **Compose** button.

Mail Bonding with America Online

If you access the Net through America Online (AOL), your mail machinations will be a lot easier than most people's. Why? Well, two reasons:

➤ You don't have to bother with all the usual rigmarole those other poor saps on the Internet have to put up with: locating an access provider, configuring protocols, finding software. As you'll see, doing the e-mail thing on America Online is a simple matter of dialing in, jumping to the Post Office area, and getting down to business.

➤ Compared to the other online services, AOL's e-mail system is a pleasure to use. It's well thought out, the interface makes sense, and it has some nice features that make e-mail easy.

Yeah, sure, there are some problems: AOL chokes on file attachments from the Net, you can't organize your mail into folders, and you can't get original message text inserted automatically into a reply. These quibbles aside, however, if all you need is basic e-mail, there are worse ways to go about it. This chapter takes you through the basics of the AOL Post Office.

A Trip to the America Online Post Office

You can find all of America Online's e-mail features, appropriately enough, in an area called the *Post Office*. Once you sign in to America Online, you can get to the Post Office using any of the following methods:

➤ Click on the **Post Office** button in the Main Menu window.

➤ Pull down the **Mail** menu and select the Post Office command.

➤ Select the Go To menu's **Keyword** command (or press **Ctrl+K** in Windows or **Command-K** on the Mac), type **post office** in the Keyword dialog box, and then select **Go**.

Whichever method you use, you'll eventually see the Post Office window as shown in the figure below.

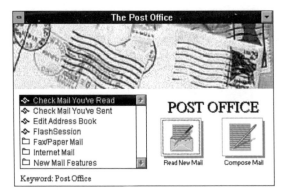

The AOL Post Office is where you'll be doing your e-mail duty.

Once your monthly five hours are up, you'll be paying by the hour for your AOL connection. So you should consider working "offline" until you're ready to send or receive mail. Working offline means you handle some of your AOL e-mail toil *before* establishing a connection to the service. This way, you can do things, such as composing messages and performing address book maintenance, without running up your connection costs. America Online even gives you a way to read your incoming mail offline. For all the offline details, see the "FlashSessions: A Cheaper Way to Work" section later in this chapter.

Reading Your Mail

Our first order of Post Office business will be to read any messages that have been sent your way either by fellow America Onliners or by denizens of the Internet. America Online divides your mail into two categories: new mail that you haven't seen yet and old mail that you've read before.

Checking Out Your New Mail

If you've received any new missives since your last session (or if there are still some unread messages you didn't get to last time), America Online will let you know when you first login. In this case, you can click on the **YOU HAVE MAIL** button in the Welcome window to see a list of your new correspondence.

Otherwise, you can get to your new mail from the Post Office by clicking on the **Read New Mail** button. (There's also a keyboard shortcut you can use: **Ctrl+R** in Windows or **Command-R** on the Mac.) America Online displays a list of your fresh e-mail missives in the New Mail window shown in the next figure. The first column shows the date the message was sent. (If you received a dispatch from a fellow America Online subscriber that has a file attached, you'll see a disk icon beside the date to let you know.) The second column shows the screen name or e-mail address of the author, and the third column shows the message subject.

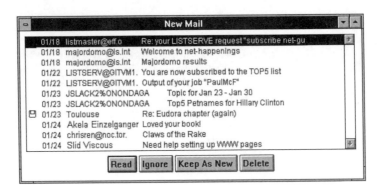

*America Online displays your new mail in a window called—
you guessed it—New Mail.*

The New Mail window gives you four ways to proceed with each message:

➤ To read a message, either double-click on it, or highlight it and click on the **Read**
button. America Online loads up the message text and displays it in a message
window like the one shown in the following figure. When you're done with the
current message, you can move onto the next one by clicking on the **Next** button.
(Note that once you've read a message, America Online won't include the message
in the New Mail window the next time you check your new mail. However, the
message is safely tucked away in the Old Mail window, as described in the next
section.)

➤ If you don't want to read a message, but you'd like America Online to remove it
from the New Mail window, click on the **Ignore** button and then click on **OK** when
AOL tells you the message has been ignored. The message doesn't get chucked out
of the New Mail window right away, but it'll be gone (trust me) the next time you
check your new mail. (If you want to read an ignored message later on, you'll find it
in the Old Mail window; see the next section for details.)

➤ If you've read (or ignored) a message, but you decide you'd like to keep it in the
New Mail window, click on the **Keep As New** button, and then click on **OK** when
AOL tells you the message has been kept as new.

➤ If you'd like to get rid of a message for good, click on the **Delete** button, and then
click on **OK** when AOL tells you the message has been deleted.

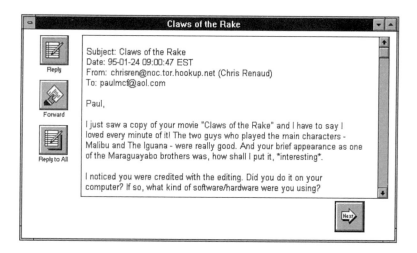

America Online uses a message window like this one to display your messages.

Rereading Your Old Mail

As I mentioned in the last section, once you've read a message (or selected the **Ignore** option in the New Mail window), America Online considers the message to be old news and not worthy of appearing in the New Mail window. So if you'd like to reread a message, you need to double-click on the **Check Mail You've Read** command in the Post Office window. (Alternatively, you can select the **M**ail menu's Check Mail You've **R**ead command.) America Online displays the Old Mail window, which works just like the New Mail window we looked at in the last section. (Except, of course, there's no **Ignore** button.)

Keeping the Conversation Going: Replying to a Message

E-mail messages generally arrive at their appointed destinations so quickly that it's almost possible to use it for conversations. No, you won't get the immediate give-and-take of a face-to-face or telephone confab, but it's close. Since a conversation, by definition, requires an *exchange* of ideas, you'll need to keep up your end of things by replying to a message sent your way. Here's how it's done the America Online way:

1. Read the message you want to reply to.

2. In the message window, highlight the text you want to include in your reply, and select the Edit menu's Copy command (or press **Ctrl+C** in Windows or **Command-C** on the Mac).

3. If you just want to reply to the author of the message, click on the **Reply** button. If you want to reply to all the addressees listed in the To and Cc fields, click on the **Reply to All** button. America Online displays a send window that's addressed accordingly.

4. In the message box, place the cursor where you want the original text to appear, and then select the Edit menu's **Paste** command (or press **Ctrl+V** in Windows or **Command-V** on the Mac) to paste the original message text.

5. To differentiate the original text from your new text, add a greater-than sign (>) and a space at the beginning of each line of original text (as shown in the following figure).

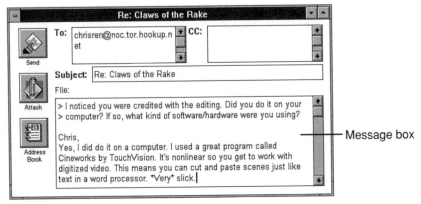

You use a send window like this one to respond to a message.

6. Add in your own text.

7. Click on the **Send** button. America Online sends the message, closes the send window, and displays a dialog box letting you know the message is on its way.

8. Click on **OK**.

Psst! Pass It on: Forwarding a Message

What do you do if someone sends an e-mail message to you by mistake or if you want a colleague or friend to take a look at a message you've received? The easiest thing to do is just forward the message to the appropriate e-mail address.

To forward a message in America Online, first read it, and then click on the **Forward** button in the message window. When the send window appears, enter the forwarding address or AOL screen name in the **To** field (and any other addresses you can think of in the Cc field), and then click on **Send**. When America Online confirms that the message has been sent, click on **OK**.

Saving Messages for Posterity

If someone sends you a particularly memorable message, you'll probably want to preserve it for the ages. The best way to do this is to save the message to its own file by following these easy steps:

1. Read the message you want to save.

2. Pull down the File menu and select the Save command (or you can press **Ctrl+S** in Windows or **Command-S** on the Mac). America Online displays the Save Text As dialog box.

3. Use the File Name text box to enter a name for the file and the Directories list box to select a location.

4. Click on **OK**. America Online saves the message to your computer.

Working with the America Online Address Book

If you send lots of messages, it's a pain trying to remember everyone's address (especially some of those absurdly lengthy Internet addresses). The solution is to fill up your America Online *address book* with the e-mail addresses you use the most. Then, when you're composing a dispatch (as explained in the next section), you can simply look up the appropriate address in the book and paste it. We're talking big-time convenience here. Follow these steps to add one or more addresses to the address book:

1. Display the address book using any of the following methods:

   ➤ From the Post Office, double-click on the **Edit Address Book** command.

   ➤ Select the Mail menu's Edit Address Book command.

   ➤ In any send window, click on the **Address Book** button. (In the Mac version, you first have to place the cursor inside either the **To** or Cc box.)

2. Click on the **Create** button. America Online displays the Address Group dialog box.

3. You can use this dialog box in either of two ways:

➤ If you'll be sending messages to a single address, enter a description (usually the person's name) in the **Group Name** text box, and enter their AOL screen name or their Internet address in the **Screen Names** text box.

➤ If you'll be sending messages to a group of addresses (as part of a Cc line for example), enter a description for the group in the **Group Name** text box, and use the **Screen Names** text box to enter each AOL screen name or Internet address (separated by commas).

4. Click on **OK** to return to the Address Book window.

5. Repeat steps 2–4 to add other addresses to the book.

6. When you're done, click on **OK**.

Composing a New Message

Of course, you won't be spending all your time in the America Online Post Office reading, forwarding, and replying to incoming correspondence. You'll also be doing your share of composing and sending out original messages to not only your AOL pals, but on the Net as well. Here are the steps to plow through to compose and send a message:

Here's where you can put your address book to good use. Instead of typing in an address, select the **Address Book** button to display the Address Book dialog box. Highlight the address you want to use, and then click on the **To** button (or the **Cc** button). When you're done, select **OK**.

1. In the Post Office, click on the **Compose Mail** button. (You can also select the **Mail** menu's Compose Mail command, or you can press **Ctrl+M** in Windows or **Command-M** on the Mac). America Online displays the Compose Mail window (which is identical to the Send windows you saw earlier).

2. Use the **To** and Cc boxes to enter the screen names or e-mail addresses of the recipients.

3. Type in the message subject in the **Subject** box.

4. Use the message box to enter the text of your message.

5. If you're sending the message to a fellow AOL subscriber, you can attach a file by selecting the **Attach** button. Use the Attach File dialog box that appears to select the file, and then click on **OK**.

6. If you're working offline, select the **Send Later** button to queue the message (I'll tell you how to send your queued messages in the next section). Otherwise, click on the **Send** button to send the message on its electronic journey. When the send operation is complete, America Online displays a dialog box to let you know.

7. Click on **OK**.

FlashSessions: A Cheaper Way to Work

One of America Online's nicest features is the ability to work offline without running up your monthly bill for connection time. For example, you can compose messages and add or edit names in your address book while you're offline.

To get the most out of your offline time (and, so, to save the most money), you need to use what America Online calls *FlashSessions*. A FlashSession is an America Online session that's controlled entirely by the AOL software. The FlashSession signs you in to America Online automatically and then performs one or more of the following tasks:

➤ It sends any outgoing messages you composed offline.

➤ It retrieves any new incoming messages that have arrived since your last session. This allows you to read your new messages offline.

➤ It downloads any files you placed in the Download Manager during your last America Online session.

When those chores are complete, the FlashSession signs off America Online automatically. It really is quite slick, and I'll tell you everything you need to know in the next few sections.

Setting Up Your FlashSessions

The only drawback to FlashSessions is that they take a bit of work to set up. Nothing difficult, mind you, but it does take a while. The good news is you only have to go through the whole thing once by following these steps:

1. Pull down the **Mail** menu and select the **FlashSessions** command. If you're using the Windows version, the FlashSessions Walk-Through dialog box appears; if you're using the Mac version, the FlashSessions dialog box appears, as shown in the next figure. (The rest of these steps show Windows users how to navigate the Walk-Through; Mac users can come along for the ride so they know what each of the options in the FlashSessions dialog box means.)

2. Click on **Continue**. America Online asks if you want to retrieve your unread mail during the FlashSessions.

3. If you do, click on **Yes**; otherwise, click on **No**. Now America Online asks if you want your FlashSessions to automatically download files that are attached to your messages.

4. Click on **Yes** or **No**, as appropriate. America Online asks if you want to send your outgoing mail during your FlashSessions.

5. Once again, click on **Yes** or **No** to answer. Now America Online asks if you want your FlashSessions to automatically retrieve the files you placed in the Download Manager during any previous (regular) AOL sessions.

185

6. You know the drill by now: click on **Yes** or **No**. The next window wants to know which screen names (nicknames) you'd like to use for your FlashSessions.

7. Activate the check box for each screen name you want to use, and enter the appropriate password that's associated with each name. When you're done, click on **Continue**. America Online asks if you want to schedule your FlashSessions.

8. If you'd prefer to crank up your FlashSessions any time you want, click on **No** and skip to step 12. However, if you'd like to have your FlashSessions run at a specific time (say, hourly or while you're on lunch), click on **Yes**.

9. If you elected to schedule your FlashSessions, first select the days of the week you want it to run, and then click on **Continue**. The next window wants to know how often to run the FlashSessions.

10. Click on the option you want and then click on **Continue**. The next window asks you to enter a starting time for the FlashSessions.

11. The spinner on the left is the hour and the one of the right is the minutes. Select a time and then click on **Continue**. America Online—quite rightly—congratulates you for surviving the procedure.

12. Click on **OK**.

If you ever need to make changes to your FlashSession settings, you'll be happy to know that you don't need to plow through all those steps again. Instead, just select the **Mail** menu's **FlashSessions** command, and you'll see the FlashSessions dialog box shown in the following figure. You can use the check boxes and buttons to change specific FlashSession settings. (For example to change the time you've scheduled for your FlashSessions, you'd select the **Schedule FlashSession** button.) The gluttons for punishment in the crowd who'd prefer to go through the whole walk-through again can do so by clicking on the **Walk Me Through** button.

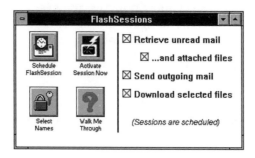

Use the FlashSessions dialog box to make changes to your FlashSession options.

Starting a FlashSession

If you didn't schedule your FlashSessions, then you'll need to fire them up by hand. You do this by pulling down the Mail menu, selecting the **FlashSessions** command, and then clicking on the **Activate Session Now** button in the FlashSessions dialog box. America Online then displays the Activate FlashSession Now dialog box. If you'd like to stay online once the FlashSession has completed its dirty work, activate the **Stay online when finished** check box. To get the FlashSession started, click on the **Begin** button. Keep your eyes peeled on the FlashSession Status window to watch the FlashSession in action.

When You're Back Offline

If you set up the FlashSession to retrieve your new mail, the messages will be sitting inside your computer waiting to be read. All you have to do is pull down the Mail menu and select the Read Incoming Mail command. America Online displays the Incoming FlashMail window that lists all your new messages. To read one of these messages, highlight it and click on **Open**.

 America Online has a feature that lets you send e-mail to a fax machine or snail mail postal address. To learn more about this feature, check out Chapter 22, "Stacks of Fax Hacks: Faxing Via E-Mail."

The Least You Need to Know

This chapter took you on a tour of the America Online Post Office facilities. Here's a review of some of the sights we saw along the way:

➤ To get to the Post Office, click on **Post Office** in the Main Menu, or select the **Mail** menu's **Post Office** command.

➤ To read your mail, either click on the **Read New Mail** button in the Post Office (for new mail), or select the **Mail** menu's **Check Mail You've Read** command (for old mail), and then double-click on the message you want to read.

➤ When you need to reply to the current message, click on the **Reply** button.

➤ To forward the current message, click on the **Forward** button.

➤ The America Online address book can store your most frequently used e-mail addresses. Double-click on the **Edit Address Book** command in the Post Office, click on **Create**, and then enter a descriptive name and an e-mail address.

➤ To compose a new message, click on the **Compose Mail** button in the Post Office.

➤ FlashSessions are automatic America Online sessions that can send queued messages that were written offline and retrieve new messages so they can be read offline. Select the Mail menu's **FlashSessions** command to set up and start your FlashSessions.

Chapter 16

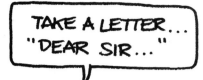

E-Mail Correspondence the CompuServe Way

In This Chapter

➤ Composing and sending e-mail messages

➤ Working with the Address Book

➤ Reading mail you've received

➤ Saving messages to the Filing Cabinet

➤ Sending a reply to an e-mail message

➤ A complete look at CompuServe's e-mail regalia

As a member of the CompuServe community, you can send e-mail to your fellow subscribers as well as the Internet without having to bother with the hassle of tracking down an access provider, endlessly configuring your computer to understand Netspeak, and scouring cyberspace for e-mail software. It's true that CompuServe's e-mail facilities are a bit clumsy, but they have everything you need to get through all your day-to-day e-mail travails. And, hey, with your trusty *Complete Idiot's Guide* at your side, you'll get through without a hitch.

There are seemingly billions of different ways to access CompuServe, and I just don't have the space in a single chapter to cover them all. So our trip through CompuServe's e-mail territory will use just the CompuServe Information Manager (CIM) in its two most common guises: WinCIM and DOSCIM. Either version lets you bypass the text-based CompuServe menus and work in a graphical environment. If you'd like to get your paws on a copy of either program (they cost a mere $10 and you also get a $10 usage credit), type **GO WINCIM** or **GO DOSCIM**, press **Enter**, and then follow the instructions.

By the way, WinCIM and DOSCIM are very similar, and many of the commands and procedures we'll look at will be identical in both versions. So, to save a bit of verbiage in this chapter, I'll often use just "CIM" to refer to both WinCIM and DOSCIM.

A Note About CompuServe's Mail Rates

Before you start firing off dispatches left, right, and center, you should know what kind of usurious rates you'll be charged for the privilege.

Things are simplest for those on the Alternative Pricing Plan: your e-mail messages are included in the price you pay for your connect time.

If you're on the Standard Pricing Plan, though, CompuServe checks out each message you send, counts the number of characters it contains, and then charges you accordingly:

➤ The first 7,500 characters (about three letter-sized pages) in a message cost you 15 cents.

➤ Each additional 2,500 characters (about one letter-sized page) cost you 5 cents.

➤ CompuServe only charges these rates for messages you *send* to fellow CompuServe subscribers; there's no charge for messages you receive. For Internet messages, however, CompuServe charges these rates for missives you send *and* receive.

➤ You get a $9 e-mail credit as part of your monthly fee.

Most of your e-mail messages will weigh in at less than 7,500 characters, so you can figure that each message you send will cost you about 15 cents. If these short notes are all you send, then your $9 allowance will let you send up to 60 messages a month, which is only about two a day.

Things can start to get expensive if you do a lot of Internet mailing (especially if you subscribe to a busy Net mailing list), or if you start sending things such as graphics files. For example, suppose you send a file that's 100K in size (100K = 100,000 characters). The first 7,500 characters cost you 15 cents, and the remaining 92,500 characters cost you 5 cents for each 2,500. 2,500 goes into 92,500 a total of 37 times, so your extra cost is 37 times 5 cents, or $1.85. So your total charge for sending that "Beavis and Butthead" graphic is 15 cents plus $1.85, or $2.00 even.

Kicking Off the CompuServe Information Manager

Now that you know what kind of hit your pocketbook will take, let's start running up those bills. The various incarnations of the CompuServe Information Manager give you an easy, menu-driven interface to all of CompuServe's features. E-mail—especially reading and composing messages—is *way* easier using either WinCIM or DOSCIM than the ugly command line. With that plug aside, your first task is to get the software up and running:

➤ For WinCIM, double-click on the **WinCIM** icon in the WinCIM Program Group.

➤ For DOSCIM, use the DOS CD command to change to the directory where you installed DOSCIM. For example, if you selected the default directory (C:\CSERVE\DOSCIM), you type **cd\cserve\doscim** and press **Enter**. Now type **cim** and press **Enter** to get the party started. When DOSCIM asks whether you want to connect to CompuServe, select Continue to stay offline for now.

Composing a New Message

To get started with CompuServe's e-mail system, let's go through the procedure for sending a message. Here are the basic steps, from go to whoa:

1. Pull down the **Mail** menu and select the Create Mail command. CIM displays the Recipient List dialog box, as shown in the following figure.

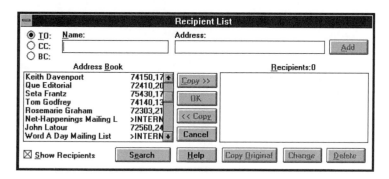

Use the Recipient List to enter the addressees for your message.

If you add a recipient by mistake, highlight it in the Recipients list and then select the Delete button in WinCIM, or the **Remove** button in DOSCIM.

2. Activate the **TO**, **CC**, or **BC** option.

3. Add a recipient by following one of these procedures:

   ➤ If the recipient isn't in your Address Book (see the "Adding Addresses to Your Address Book" section a little later in this chapter), type his name in the Name field, type his e-mail address in the **Address** field, and then select Add. CIM adds the recipient to the Recipients list.

   ➤ If the addressee can be found in your Address Book, highlight the name in the Address Book list and then select the Copy >> button. CIM adds the recipient to the Recipients list.

4. Repeat steps 2 and 3 to add any other recipients you need.

5. Select **OK**. CIM closes the Recipient List and displays the Create Mail window, as shown below.

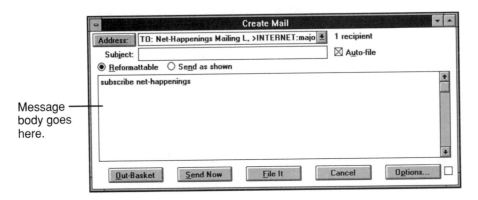

Use the Create Mail window to enter a subject and the message text.

6. Use the **Subject** text box to enter the subject of the message. (Note that CIM won't let you send a message unless you enter something in both the **Subject** and message boxes. If you're sending a note to a mailing list where you don't have to fill in one of these fields, just enter a space.)

7. Enter the message body in the large text box.

8. Finish up by doing one of the following:

   ➤ To send the file right away, select the Send Now button in WinCIM or the Send button in DOSCIM. The program connects to CompuServe (if you weren't connected already) and fires off the message.

➤ If you'd prefer to send the file later, select the **Out-Basket** button. This stores the message in a special area called the Out-Basket. (See the next section to learn how to send messages from the Out-Basket.) Why wouldn't you just send the message now? Well, if you have a bunch of messages, you could compose them all while you're offline (that is, not connected to CompuServe), save each one in the Out-Basket, and then send them all later while you head off to lunch.

Sending Messages from the Out-Basket

If you created some outgoing messages and stored them in your Out-Basket, CIM gives you two ways to send them on their electronic journey:

➤ Pull down the **Mail** menu and select the **Out-Basket** command in WinCIM, or the **Send Mail in Out-Basket** command in DOSCIM. In the Out Basket window that appears, you can send a single message by highlighting it and selecting the **Send** button. If you'd like to send everything in the Out Basket, just select the Send All button. (Note that, in this case, DOSCIM displays a Send All Mail dialog box. Activate the **Disconnect after operation** check box and then select **Proceed.**)

➤ Pull down the **Mail** menu and select the **Send/Receive All Mail** command. In the Send and Receive All Mail dialog box that appears, activate the **Disconnect when Done** check box and then select **OK**. CIM connects to CompuServe, sends everything that's sitting in the Out-Basket, and then disconnects automatically.

Adding Addresses to Your Address Book

As you saw earlier, CIM has an Address Book that lets you store e-mail addresses. This is real handy for storing addresses of your online buddies and colleagues because you don't have to remember their CompuServe numbers or their Net locations. Even if you *can* remember such things, the Address Book is still a time-saver because you don't have to type in a name and address each time you want to specify a recipient.

Both WinCIM and DOSCIM give you three ways to add new entries to your Address Book:

When you're composing a message. In the Recipient List dialog box, once you've added a name and address to the Recipients list, you can copy it to the Address Book by highlighting it and selecting the << Copy button in WinCIM, or the << **New** button in DOSCIM.

When you're reading a message. If a message you received is open (I'll tell you how to do that later in this chapter), select the From button. CIM displays the Add to Address Book dialog box showing the name and address of the person who sent you the message. Make any necessary adjustments and then select **OK** in WinCIM, or **Save** in DOSCIM.

Using the Address Book dialog box. Pull down the **Mail** menu and select Address Book (or press **Ctrl+A** in WinCIM). In the Address Book dialog box that appears, select Add in WinCIM or **New** in DOSCIM, fill in the **Name** and **Address** fields in the Add to Address Book dialog box, and then select **OK** in WinCIM, or **Save** in DOSCIM. You can also use the Address Book dialog box to modify an address (highlight it and select Change in WinCIM or **Edit** in DOSCIM) or to delete an address (highlight it and select Delete). When you're done, select **OK**.

Sending a File

If you need to send a file to someone (and if the exorbitant rates CompuServe charges for sending e-mail haven't scared you off), CIM makes it easy. Here's how it's done:

1. Select the Mail menu's **S**end File command. CIM displays the Recipient List dialog box.

2. Fill in the addressees as described earlier, and then select **OK**. The Send File Message dialog box appears.

3. Use the **Subject** text box to enter the subject of the message (such as the name of the file).

4. Select the File button to display the Open dialog box, pick out the file you want to send, and then select **OK**. CIM enters the name of the file in the File text box.

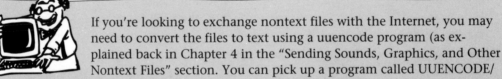

If you're looking to exchange nontext files with the Internet, you may need to convert the files to text using a uuencode program (as explained back in Chapter 4 in the "Sending Sounds, Graphics, and Other Nontext Files" section. You can pick up a program called UUENCODE/ UUDECODE in CompuServe's PC Communications Forum (GO PCCOM). Look for the file UU522.ZIP.

5. Select the type of file you're sending: **B**inary, **T**ext, **G**IF, or **J**PEG.

6. If you want to add any extra info about the file (such as a description), use the Additional information text box.

7. Select either **O**ut-Basket or **S**end Now.

Getting Your New Mail

Any mail that's sent to your CompuServe address is stored in a special mailbox set aside just for you. So, the next of your CompuServe e-mail labors will be to connect to the service to get any new mail that has arrived in your mailbox. CompuServe gives you two ways to do this:

➤ You can read your mail while you're online (connected to CompuServe).

➤ You can retrieve your messages to your computer where CIM stores them in a special area called the *In-Basket*. This allows you to read your mail while you're offline (disconnected from CompuServe).

The next couple of sections show you how to swing both ways.

Reading Your Mail Online

To read your e-mail messages while connected to CompuServe, pull down the **M**ail menu and select the **G**et New Mail command. If you're not already online, CIM dials your modem and establishes a connection. The program then heads for your mailbox, grabs any messages waiting there, and displays some info about them inside the Get New Mail window, as shown in the following figure (in DOSCIM, the window is called New Mail).

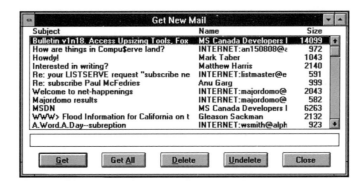

CIM displays info about your messages in the Get New Mail window.

The Get New Mail window shows you three chunks of information for each message: the first column is the subject of the message, the second column gives you the name or Internet address of the author, and the third column shows the size of messages in characters.

To read a message, either double-click on it in the Get New Mail window, or highlight it and select the **G**et button in WinCIM, or the **R**ead button in DOSCIM. CIM loads the message text and displays it in a new window, as shown here. Notice that, for dispatches sent from Internet country, the first part of the message contains a lot of header gobbledygook, most of which can be safely ignored. When you're done with the message, select the **Cancel** button to return to the Get New Mail window.

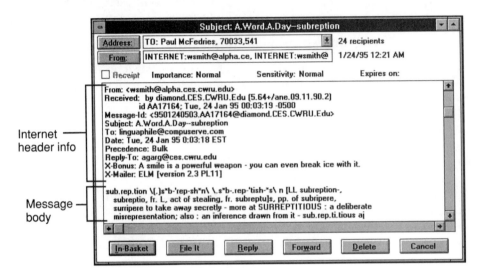

Internet header info

Message body

CIM displays your messages in a separate window like this one.

Reading Mail from Your In-Basket

If you'd prefer to retrieve your mail to your computer and read it offline from there, you need to tell CIM to download some or all of your messages to the In-Basket. CIM gives you no less than three ways to get the job done:

➤ If you're online and you've opened a message, you can send it to your In-Basket by selecting the In-Basket button.

➤ If you're online, you can send all the messages listed in the Get New Mail window to the In-Basket by selecting the Get All button in WinCIM, or the All button in DOSCIM.

➤ If you're not yet connected to CompuServe, pull down the Mail menu and select the Send/Receive All Mail command. In the Send and Receive All Mail dialog box that appears, activate the Disconnect when Done check box and then select **OK**. CIM connects to CompuServe, retrieves your messages, and then disconnects automatically.

196

Now you need to open your In-Basket to read the mail. (If you're still online, you can disconnect because, as I've said, the In-Basket lets you read your messages while offline.) Pull down the **M**ail menu and select the In-Basket command. CIM displays the In Basket window, as shown in the following figure. In the first column, an envelope icon and the word **Mail** tell you the message arrived via the CompuServe mail system. Also, you'll see a small, right-pointing arrow » for messages you haven't read yet (in DOSCIM, it's a small dot). The second column tells you the message subject, the third column gives you the author's name or address, and the fourth column shows the date the message was sent.

DOSCIM also gives you a way to retrieve specific messages. For each message, highlight it in the New Mail window and select the Mark button. When the ones you want are marked, select the Retrieve button.

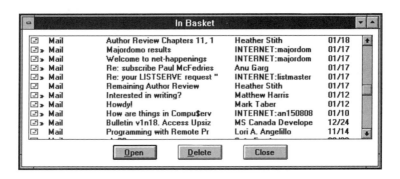

The In Basket window lets you read your correspondence offline.

To read a message, double-click on it, or highlight it and select the **O**pen button in WinCIM, or the **R**ead button in DOSCIM. As before, CIM displays the message in a separate window. (Note, though, that the window the In-Basket displays has one extra perk: there's a Next button you can select to take you to the next message in the list.)

Handling Your Messages

Whether you're reading your messages from the Get New Mail window or from the In-Basket, CIM gives you no less than four different ways to handle a piece of mail once you've read it:

➤ You can save the message to a special storage area called the *filing cabinet*.

➤ You can send out a reply to the author of the message.

➤ You can forward a message to a different address.

➤ You can delete the message.

The next few sections give you the nitty-gritty on all four tasks.

Filing Messages in CIM's Filing Cabinet

At your office, you probably have a filing cabinet or two set up to store at least some of the snail mail correspondence that comes your way each day. When you're done with a message that you want to keep, it's a simple matter of filing it in the appropriate folder just in case you need to reread it later.

CIM lets you work with your e-mail the same way. CIM has a storage area called the *Filing Cabinet* that you can use to hold related types of correspondence. For example, if you exchange regular e-mail letters with the employees of a particular company, you can set up a folder inside the Filing Cabinet to hold only messages from that company. Similarly, you can create folders for mailing lists, ongoing projects, play-by-mail games, friends, colleagues, you name it.

To get you started, let's see how you go about adding folders to the Filing Cabinet. Here's what you do:

1. Pull down the Mail menu and select the Filing Cabinet command, or press **Ctrl+F**. CIM displays the Filing Cabinet dialog box.

2. Select the New button to display the Add New Folder dialog box.

3. Type the name of the folder in the Folder Name text box (up to 20 characters) and then select **OK**. CIM returns you to the Filing Cabinet dialog box.

4. Repeat steps 2 and 3 to add more folders to the Filing Cabinet.

5. When you're done, select **Close** in WinCIM, or **Cancel** in DOSCIM.

Now that you've created a folder or two, you can save a message to a folder by opening the message and selecting the File It button. In the Store Message dialog box that appears, highlight the folder you want to use, and then select Store in WinCIM, or **Save** in DOSCIM.

How do you read a message stored in a folder? Easy: just select the Mail menu's Filing Cabinet command to display the Filing Cabinet dialog box, highlight the folder that contains the message, and then select the Open button. The window that appears lists the messages in the folder, and you can work with them just as though you were using the In-Basket.

Responding to a Message

Some of your correspondents will ask you for information or pose a question or two in their messages. A reply is, of course, in order (you don't want to be rude) and CIM makes this easy, as you'll see in the following steps:

1. Open the message you want to respond to.

2. In the message window, highlight the text you want to include in your reply, and select the Edit menu's Copy command (or press **Ctrl+C**).

3. Select the Reply button. CIM displays a Reply to window with the appropriate address and subject already filled in for you.

4. In the message box, place the cursor where you want the original text to appear, and then select the Edit menu's Paste command (or press **Ctrl+V**) to paste the original message text.

5. To differentiate the original text from your new text, add a greater-than sign (>) and a space at the beginning of each line of original text.

6. Add in your own text.

7. Select either **Out-Basket** or **Send Now**, as described earlier in this chapter.

Forwarding a Message to Someone Else

What do you do if someone sends an e-mail message to you by mistake or if you want a colleague or friend to take a look at a message you've received? The easiest thing to do is just forward the message to the appropriate e-mail address.

To forward a message in CompuServe, first open it and then select the Forward button. When CIM displays the Recipient List dialog box, select the forwarding address you want to use and then select **OK**. In the Forward window that appears, add any extra text you need, and then select either **Out-Basket** or **Send Now**.

Deleting a Message

Lots of the messages you get won't be worth a second look. To keep your folders neat and tidy, you should delete these useless messages by highlighting them and selecting the **Delete** button. When CIM asks if you're sure, select **Yes** in WinCIM, or **OK** in DOSCIM.

CompuServe has a feature that lets you send e-mail to a fax machine. To learn more about how this works, check out Chapter 22, "Stacks of Fax Hacks: Faxing Via E-Mail."

The Least You Need to Know

This chapter gave you the goods on CompuServe's e-mail connection. Just to help things sink in, here's a quick review of what you need to know:

➤ You start WinCIM by double-clicking on the **WinCIM** icon in Program Manager. To start DOSCIM, switch to the DOSCIM directory (usually C:\CSERVE\DOSCIM), type **cim**, and press **Enter**.

➤ To compose a new message, select the **Mail** menu's Create Mail command, enter your recipients, and then enter a subject and message body.

➤ To work with the Address Book, select the **Mail** menu's Address Book command, or press **Ctrl+A**.

➤ You can send files to your e-mail correspondents by pulling down the **Mail** menu and selecting the Send File command.

➤ To read your mail while you're online with CompuServe, select the **Mail** menu's Get New Mail command. If you prefer to read your mail offline using the In-Basket, select the **Mail** menu's Send/Receive All Mail command. (You can also choose the Get All button from the Get New Mail window.)

➤ The Filing Cabinet is a great way to organize your mail into folders. To create a folder, pull down the **Mail** menu, select the Filing Cabinet command, and then select New. To move an opened message into a folder, select the File It button.

➤ When you need to reply to the current message, select the **Reply** button.

➤ To forward the current message, select the Forward button.

Chapter 17

Perusing the E-Mail Connection for Prodigy

In This Chapter

➤ Downloading the E-Mail Connection for Prodigy

➤ Working with the Address Book

➤ Composing e-mail messages

➤ Reading your mail

➤ Forwarding and replying to messages

➤ A complete E-Mail Connection correspondence course

Prodigy is one of the largest of the online services, but they've only recently recognized the existence of the Internet. As a result, their Net services lack a certain polish and elegance. This is especially evident in the Prodigy e-mail system, which, in its basic guise, wouldn't know what the Internet was if it fell over it! As you'll see in this chapter, however, there's a way to bring the Prodigy mail system into the 90s, and it's this beefed up version of Prodigy e-mail that we'll examine in this chapter.

Making the Prodigy Mail System Usable

If all you'll be doing is sending e-mail to fellow Prodigy patrons, then why the heck did you buy this book! Seriously, though, the basic Prodigy e-mail system is only set up to handle exchanges between Prodigy subscribers. If you want to send and receive dispatches from other services—especially the Internet—you need to download some extra software. Why, yes, this extra software *does* cost extra bucks! (And, yes, anger *is* the appropriate reaction for having to fork out more money just to get features that are standard issue on other online services. And while *you* may use terms like "gouge" and "scam," I, as a responsible author, couldn't possibly say such things.)

The software you need is called *E-Mail Connection for Prodigy*. It's actually a separate Windows application that knows how to interact with the Prodigy mail system. (If you use the DOS version of Prodigy, you'll have to get a different program called *Mail Manager*. However, I won't cover Mail Manager in this chapter. As I write this, there is, unfortunately, no software available to improve the Prodigy mail experience of Mac users.)

Here's a short list of the extra features that E-Mail Connection brings to the Prodigy table (all of which, to belabor the point, are standard fare in services such as America Online and CompuServe):

➤ Exchanging mail with other online services and the Internet.

➤ Composing and reading e-mail offline (that is, when you're not connected to Prodigy).

➤ An Address Book to store frequently used e-mail addresses.

➤ Having e-mail messages delivered to fax machines and regular postal addresses.

Keep in mind, as well, that Prodigy charges you 1 cent per 1,000 characters for *each* addressee in your outgoing correspondence. So if you're sending a message to 10 people, your real cost is 10 cents per 1,000 characters.

To make things worse, not only will you be charged $14.95 for these "privileges," but Prodigy also charges you for the messages you send from E-Mail Connection *and* the ones you receive! Now, admittedly, the cost is only 1 cent for every 1,000 characters in a message. However, it can quickly add up to some serious cash if you send and receive lots of e-mail (especially if you subscribe to one of the active Net mailing lists).

If you still think all this is worth it, then follow these steps to get your mitts on the program (keep in mind, however, that the whole process will take 30 minutes or more):

1. Log on to Prodigy, select the **Jump** button to display the Jump dialog box, type **about mail manager**, and then select **OK**. Prodigy displays the About Mail Manager screen, which lets you know what you're about to get yourself into.

2. Page through the About Mail Manager screens until you get to the screen shown in the following figure.

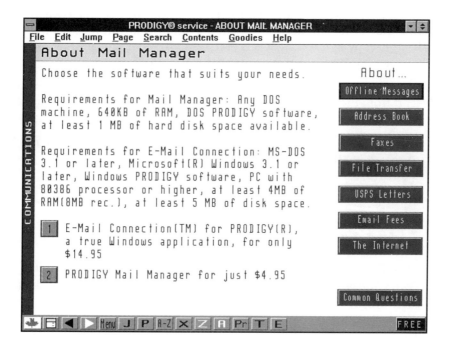

Use this screen to select the E-Mail Connection software.

3. Select **1** to download E-Mail Connection for Prodigy. Prodigy displays more info about E-Mail Connection.

4. To get things started, select **1** to display the Download window.

5. Change the displayed directory, if necessary (it shouldn't be), and then select **AUTHORIZE PURCHASE AND BEGIN DOWNLOAD.** The Download in Progress window appears to let you know how things are going. When the download is complete, another dialog box will appear to let you know.

6. Select **OK** and then select **Continue**. The How to Install screen appears. You can either read this screen or you can read the next section to learn how to install your new software.

Installing E-Mail Connection for Prodigy

Here are the steps to follow to install E-Mail Connection on your system:

1. Start File Manager and select the PRODIGY directory (or whatever directory you used to download E-Mail Connection).

203

2. Double-click on the **EMCSETUP.EXE** file. The E-Mail Connection Setup dialog box appears.

3. Select Continue. The Destination Directory dialog box appears to ask where you want E-Mail Connection installed. Enter a different directory, if necessary (I installed my copy in C:\PRODIGY\PEMC), and then select Continue. Now Setup asks which program group to use for the E-Mail Connection icons.

4. If you want to use a group other than the default **PRODIGY<R> Software** group, select it from the list, and then select Continue when you're ready. Now Setup asks you about something called "Mail Enabling."

5. If you don't know what mail enabling is, select No; otherwise, select Yes. Setup starts extracting the E-Mail Connection files and then displays a dialog box when it's done.

6. Select **OK**.

Starting E-Mail Connection for the First Time

You start E-Mail Connection by double-clicking on the **E-Mail Connection** icon in the **PRODIGY<R> Software** program group. When you load the program for the first time, it takes you through the following brief setup routine:

1. First, the E-Mail Connection User License Agreement dialog box appears. Select the **I agree, continue** button (you can read the legalese first, if you're brave enough). Now you'll see the New User Information dialog box.

2. Fill in the various fields (Name, Title, and so on) and then select **Ok**. E-Mail Connection searches for the PRODIGY directory and lets you know when it finds it.

3. Select Yes to assure the program that the directory is okay. The program now displays the PRODIGY Service Settings dialog box so you can enter your Prodigy data.

4. Type in your PRODIGY ID and Autologon Nickname.

5. Select **Ok** to display the main E-Mail Connection window.

The following figure shows the screen you'll see once you've finished the previous setup steps (and each subsequent time you start E-Mail Connection).

Tool Bar

Window Bar

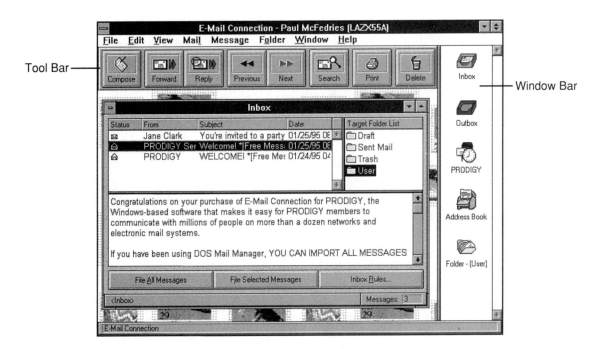

The E-Mail Connection window with the Inbox folder displayed.

The E-Mail Connection window is a bit confusing at first, so let's see if we can knock some sense into things. The most unusual feature is the Window Bar on the right side of the screen. Each icon you see represents a window that you can open in E-Mail Connection. There are, for starters, five in all:

Inbox   This is one of E-Mail Connection's *folders*. A folder is a storage area for messages, and the Inbox folder holds the messages you retrieve from Prodigy. In the preceding figure, the Inbox folder is open (I'll talk more about it later on).

Outbox   This is another folder. You can use Outbox to store the messages you compose in E-Mail Connection.

PRODIGY   This window lets you connect to Prodigy. When the connection is established, E-Mail Connection retrieves your incoming messages and stores them in the Inbox folder, and it takes all your composed messages from the Outbox folder and sends them off to their destinations.

Address Book   This window stores the e-mail addresses you use to send the messages you compose.

Folder - (User) This is another folder that you can use to save incoming messages and keep the Inbox folder uncluttered.

The rest of this chapter gives you the details on using each of these windows.

Populating Your Address Book

Before you can send any messages through E-Mail Connection, you have to enter the addresses you'll be using in the Address Book. I'm not sure why E-Mail Connection insists on this strange way of doing things. I mean every other e-mail program on the planet lets you enter *ad hoc* addresses and save only those you use most frequently. Ah, well, when in Rome....

One interesting, but potentially cumbersome, feature of E-Mail Connection is that it automatically saves to the Address Book the sender's address for all your incoming mail. If you'd like to change this behavior, select the Mail menu's Mail Preferences command to display the Mail Preferences dialog box, deactivate the Auto add to address book check box, and then select Ok.

Here are the steps required to add an address to the E-Mail Connection Address Book:

1. Open the Address Book by either double-clicking on the **Address Book** icon in the Window Bar, or by pulling down the **Window** menu and selecting **Address Book**.

2. Select the Add button. The Add Address dialog box appears.

3. Make sure the Individual Address check box is activated and then select Ok. E-Mail Connection displays the Address Book Entry dialog box. The next figure shows this dialog box with an example entry.

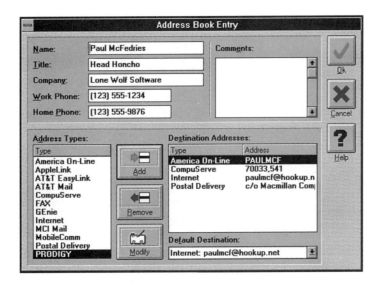

Use the Address Book Entry to add a person's various addresses to the Address Book.

4. Fill in the Name, Title, Company, Work Phone, and Home Phone fields.

5. In the Address Types list, select the type of address you want to use, and then select Add. E-Mail Connection displays a dialog box suitable for the address type. For example, if you select **Internet**, the Internet Address dialog box that appears gives you fields for entering the User ID and Domain name of the person's e-mail address.

6. Enter the required info and then select Ok. The address appears in the Destination Addresses list.

7. Repeat step 5 and 6 to add more addresses for this person.

8. If you'll be sending e-mail to one of the person's addresses more than the others, select it from the Default Destination drop-down list.

9. When you're done, select Ok to return to the Address Book window, and then close the window by minimizing it, or by double-clicking on the **Control-menu** box in the top left corner.

Composing a New Message

Okay, now that you have an address or two in the Address Book, you're ready to start composing messages. Remember: the messages you create in E-Mail Connection are stored in the Outbox folder and sent all at once later on. You don't need to be connected

In the **To** and CC boxes, you don't have to type in the person's entire name. For example, if you're addressing the message to "Sebastian Cabot," you could just type, say, **seb** and press **Enter**.

to Prodigy for any of this. To compose a message in E-Mail Connection, follow these steps:

1. Select the Message menu's New (Compose) command. (You can also click on the **Compose** button in the Tool Bar, or press **F2**.) E-Mail Connection displays the Draft window.

2. In the **To** box, type in the name of the recipient and then press **Enter**. The person's name and default address type are entered into the box below (see the following figure). To change the person's address type, double-click on his name and then select a new Destination from the dialog box that appears.

Double-click on name to change address type.

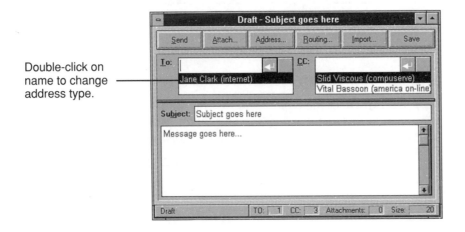

Use the Draft window to compose your outgoing messages.

3. If you want to include an address in the Cc line, type the person's name in the CC box and press **Enter**.

4. Use the Subject box to enter the message subject.

5. Type in your text in the box below the Subject field.

6. To run a spell check on the message text, select the Edit menu's **Spell Check** command, or press **Ctrl+S**. If the spell checker finds a word it doesn't like, you'll see the

Spelling Error dialog box appear. Select Change to accept the recommended correction; select Ignore to move on; or select Add to add the word to the spell checker's vocabulary.

7. Select the Send button. The Send Confirmation dialog box appears to tell you the message has been "queued" (which means it's now in the Outbox).

8. Select Ok.

Connecting to Prodigy to Send and Retrieve Mail

Once you've composed all your messages, it's time to get E-Mail Connection to send them via Prodigy. At the same time, the program will also retrieve any messages that are waiting for you. To get started, display the PRODIGY window by either selecting the Window menu's **PRODIGY** command, or by double-clicking on the **PRODIGY** icon in the Window Bar.

Setting Some Logon Options

Before proceeding, let's take a look at the various logon options you can choose from. Select the **Configure** button to display the PRODIGY Service Settings dialog box, and then select the Options button to get to the Default Logon Options dialog box.

In the Signon Method box, select one of the following options:

Auto Mail/Log Off   This option logs you on to Prodigy, sends and retrieves your e-mail, and then logs off. This is the most convenient option and the one you'll likely use the most.

Auto Mail/Highlights   This option logs you on to Prodigy, sends and retrieves your e-mail, displays Prodigy's Highlights page, and then leaves you logged on.

Auto Mail/Stay Online   This option logs you on to Prodigy, sends and retrieves your e-mail, and then leaves you logged on at the Mail page.

Auto Logon/Manual   This option logs you on to Prodigy, displays Prodigy's Mail page, and then leaves you logged on. Messages are *not* sent or retrieved.

Manual Logon   This option displays the Prodigy software only. You have to logon manually.

In the **Download Options** box, activate one or more of the following check boxes:

Get Prodigy Messages   Activate this check box to retrieve all the Prodigy messages in your mailbox.

209

Get Internet Messages   Activate this check box to retrieve all the Internet messages in your mailbox.

Get Files   Activate this check box to retrieve all the files in your mailbox.

When you're done, select **Ok** to return to the PRODIGY Service Settings dialog box, and then select **Ok** to return to the PRODIGY window.

Logging On to Prodigy

Now you're ready for the fun to begin. Here are the steps to follow to logon to Prodigy:

1. Select the **Connect** button in the PRODIGY window. The E-Mail Connection dialog box appears.

2. If you don't want E-Mail Connection to retrieve your mail, deactivate the **Receive Incoming Messages** check box. If you don't want E-Mail Connection to send your queued messages, deactivate the **Send Outgoing Messages** check box.

3. Select **Ok**. E-Mail Connection loads the Prodigy software. Depending on how you've set up your Prodigy Autologon, you may need to enter your Prodigy user ID or your password, in the SIGN-ON window. If so, enter the required data and logon as usual.

4. When E-Mail Connection logs off (or you log off yourself), the program checks for new messages and, if it finds any, displays a dialog box to let you know. In this case, you can select **Yes** to display the Inbox folder and see your new mail.

Reading Mail from the Inbox Folder

If E-Mail Connection picks up any stray missives in its travels, it displays them inside the Inbox folder (see the figure earlier in this chapter). If the Inbox isn't on your screen now, you can bring it out of hiding by selecting the **Window** menu's **Inbox** command, or by double-clicking on the **Inbox** icon in the Window Bar.

The top left portion of the Inbox displays a summary list of all your incoming messages. The **Status** column shows a closed envelope icon for messages that haven't been read, and an opened envelope icon for messages you have read. The **From** column shows the name of the sender, the **Subject** column shows the message's Subject line, and the **Date** column shows the date and time the message was sent.

When you highlight one of these summaries, the message text appears in the pane below. If you'd prefer to work in a bigger window that also shows the header, pull down the Message menu and select **Open**, or else double-click on the message summary. E-Mail Connection displays the message in a Message window, such as the one shown in the following figure. To move onto the next message, pull down the Folder menu and select the Next Message command. (You can also click on the **Next** button or press **F6**.) To head back to the previous message, select the Folder menu's Previous message command. (Those in a hurry can also either click on the **Previous** button or press **F5**.)

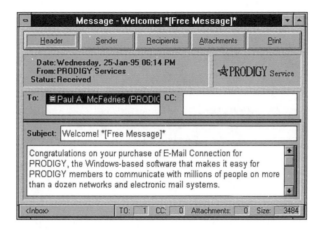

Double-click on a message in the Inbox to display this Message window.

Message Maintenance

Once you've read a message, E-Mail Connection gives your a fistful of message maintenance options. Here's the rundown:

➤ You can forward a message to a different address.

➤ You can send out a reply to the author of a message.

➤ You can delete a message.

➤ You can save a message to a different folder.

The next few sections give you the nitty-gritty on all four tasks.

Forwarding a Message to Someone Else

What do you do if someone sends an e-mail message to you by mistake, or if you want a co-worker or friend to take a look at a message you've received? E-Mail Connection lets you pass on a message by forwarding it to the appropriate e-mail address.

To forward a message in E-Mail Connection, highlight it in the Inbox or open the message, and then select the Message menu's Forward command. (Shortcut-happy types may prefer clicking on the **Forward** button in the Tool Bar or pressing **F3**.) You'll see a Forward dialog box with a **Prefix message text** check box activated. This is fine, so select Ok to move on. E-Mail Connection displays the Draft (Forward) window so you can enter the e-mail addresses of the forwardees, and maybe some explanatory text in the message body.

When you're done, select the Send button to queue up the message for later sending. (This is covered in the "Connecting to Prodigy to Send and Retrieve Mail" section earlier in this chapter.)

Responding to a Message

Responding to a question someone has posed or to a request for information is no sweat. Here's how it's done in E-Mail Connection:

1. Either highlight the message you want to respond to in the Inbox, or open the message.

2. Pull down the Message menu and select the Reply command. (Speed freaks can click on the **Reply** button or press **F4**.) The Reply dialog box appears.

3. If the original message had multiple recipients, activate either **Sender Only** (to address the reply only to the author), or **All Recipients** (to address the reply to everyone who received the original). In the **Reply Message** section, you should leave both the **Include original message** and **Prefix message text** check boxes activated.

4. Select Ok. E-Mail Connection displays the Draft (Reply) window with the To, CC, and Subject fields filled in for you.

5. Remove any lines from the original text that you don't need for your reply.

6. Type in your own text.

7. Select the Send button to add the reply to the Outbox. (See the "Connecting to Prodigy to Send and Retrieve Mail" section earlier in this chapter, for instructions on sending the message.)

Deleting a Message

Many of the missives that'll come your way would be more properly called "dis-missives" because they're not worth the electrons they rode in on. To place this e-junk in E-Mail Connection's equivalent of the ol' circular file, highlight the message in the Inbox, and select the Message menu's Delete command. (If you're in a hurry to get rid of a message, click on the **Delete** button or press **F9**.) E-Mail Connection displays the Confirm Delete dialog box with two options:

Move to Trash If you activate this option, E-Mail Connection moves the message out of the Inbox folder and into another folder called, appropriately, *Trash*. Why would you want to do that? To guard against accidental deletions. There's no worse feeling than deleting some crucial memo or note by mistake. If you place the message in the Trash folder, however, it's a simple matter of displaying the Trash and moving the message back to its original folder. (All this stuff about displaying folders and moving messages between them is covered in the next section.)

Keep in mind, however, that E-Mail Connection cleans out the Trash folder each time you exit the program. So if you're going to undelete a message, make sure you do it before ending the current E-Mail Connection session.

Delete from database Only select this option if you're absolutely sure you want to delete the message because once it's gone, no amount of verbal abuse or wild gesticulation will bring it back.

When you've made your choice, select **Ok** to perform the expulsion.

Understanding Folders

Besides the Inbox and the Outbox folders that you've seen, E-Mail Connection actually comes with four other folders:

Draft Use this folder to save messages that you're in the middle of composing. If you close the Draft window before sending a message, E-Mail Connection will ask if you want to save or delete the message. If you select the **Save** button, the message is moved to the Draft folder where you can resume your composition later on. (I'll tell you how to open different folders in a second.)

Sent Mail This folder holds a copy of each outgoing message you send.

Trash As you saw in the last section, this folder holds your deleted mail just in case you need to undelete it.

User This folder is yours to do with what you will.

To display any of these folders, you can use the following techniques:

➤ Pull down the Folder menu, select **Open Folder**, and then select the folder you want from the cascade menu that appears.

➤ In the Inbox folder's **Target Folder List**, double-click on the folder you want to display.

Creating New Folders

As I've said, the User folder is your territory to use as you see fit. You'll probably find that you use it mostly to store your incoming messages and keep the Inbox uncluttered. (I'll let you know how to move messages between folders in the next section.) However, it won't take long before the User folder itself becomes an untidy mess with messages from disparate authors scattered willy-nilly.

The solution is to create "subfolders" to organize your related correspondence. You could create folders for friends, colleagues, customers, projects, mailing lists—the sky (or your hard disk size) is the limit.

To create a subfolder of the User folder, select the Folder menu's Create User Folder command. In the Create User Folder dialog box that appears, enter the name of the folder in the New User Folder Name text box, and then select Ok. E-Mail Connection shows the new folder branching off the User folder, as shown in the following figure. (You may need to click on the User folder to see your new subfolder.)

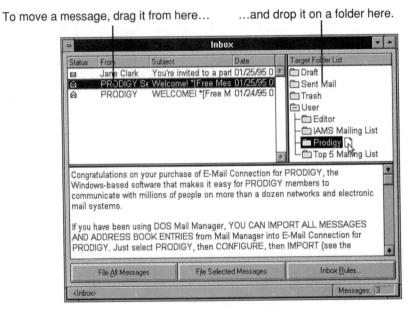

You can create all kinds of subfolders to hold related correspondence.

Moving a Message to a Different Folder

There will be lots of times when you'll need to move a message from one folder to another. For example, you may want to clean out your Inbox folder by moving your messages to the User folder. Or if you accidentally delete a precious message, you can recover it by moving it from the Trash folder to its original folder.

To move a message, highlight it, and then select the Message menu's **Move** command. In the Move Message dialog box that appears, highlight the folder you want to move the message to and then select **Ok**.

An even easier way to move a message is to drag its summary and drop it on the destination folder (see the preceding figure).

As I mentioned earlier, E-Mail Connection allows you to send e-mail to a fax machine or snail mail address. If you'd like to use these features, check out Chapter 22, "Stacks of Fax Hacks: Faxing Via E-Mail." (Be forewarned, however: faxing and postal delivery will cost you even *more* money!)

The Least You Need to Know

This chapter showed you how to work with E-Mail Connection for Prodigy. Here's the highlight film:

➤ To download a copy of E-Mail Connection, jump to **about mail manager**, page through the screens, and follow the instructions to download the program.

➤ Before you can compose a message, you need to add the addressee to the Address Book by double-clicking on the **Address Book** icon.

➤ To compose a new message, select the Message menu's New (Compose) command, or click on the **Compose** button.

➤ To connect to Prodigy and send your queued message and retrieve your mail, double-click on the **PRODIGY** icon.

➤ You can read your mail either by highlighting a message in the Inbox, or by selecting the Message menu's Open command.

➤ Select the Message menu's Forward or Reply commands to forward or reply to a message.

Chapter 18

Delphi's Mail Delivery

In This Chapter

➤ Composing e-mail messages

➤ Working with InterNav's Address Book

➤ Reading your mail

➤ Forwarding and replying to messages

➤ A (not so) definitive look at Delphi's mail drudgery

Delphi is not only one of the oldest online services (it started up in 1981—which is eons ago in computer years), it's also the only online service that has had a complete menu of Internet connections for a number of years. (Most of the other big-time services have managed only just recently to carve out a spot on the bandwagon.) So it will come as no surprise that Delphi can handle e-mail traffic to and from the Internet without complaint (and, more importantly, without charging you any extra fees). This chapter shows you how to use the Delphi e-mail system both from the command line and by using the slick, new InterNav application that adds a graphical touch to Delphi. (If you'd like to download InterNav, log on to Delphi, type **go using internav** and press **Enter**, and follow the instructions on the screen.)

Entering the Delphi Mail System

Let's get right down to the proverbial brass tacks by seeing how you enter the Delphi mail system. Get yourself logged on to Delphi, and do one of the following:

➤ From the command line, type **mail** and press **Enter** to display the MAIL Menu; then type **mail** again and press **Enter** to select the **Mail (electronic)** command. Delphi tells you how many new messages are waiting for you and displays the MAIL> prompt.

➤ From InterNav, click on the **E-Mail** button or pull down the View menu and select the **Mail** command. The Mail screen appears and Delphi displays the Folders window, as shown in the following figure. I'll tell you more about the Folders window when we talk about reading your mail later in this chapter.

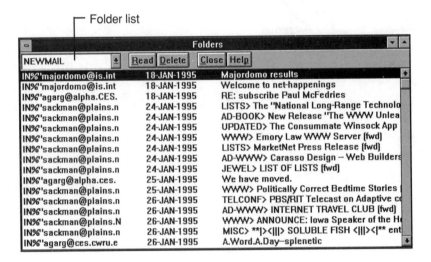

InterNav displays the Folders window when you first enter the mail system.

Composing a New E-Mail Message

Now that you're in the Delphi mail system, let's begin by learning how to compose and send a message. (Note: If you plan to send a message to someone with an Internet e-mail address, refer to the "Exchanging Mail with Delphi" section in Chapter 4, to learn the proper way to do it in Delphi.) The next two sections show you the command line and InterNav steps.

Composing from the Command Line

To compose a message from the MAIL> prompt, you need to following these steps:

1. Type **send** and press **Enter**. Delphi displays the **To:** prompt.

 If you need to specify a Cc line for your message, use the command **send / cc_prompt**, instead. After you enter an address at the **To:** prompt, Delphi will display a CC: prompt so you can enter your Cc addresses (put a space between each address).

2. Enter the recipient's e-mail address and press **Enter**. Delphi prompts you to enter the Subject line.

3. Type in the subject of the message and press **Enter**. Now Delphi displays the following prompt:

   ```
   Enter your message below. Press CTRL/Z when complete, or Ctrl/C to quit:
   ```

4. Type in your message text. Make sure you press **Enter** when you get to the end of a line. Keep in mind, though, that once you press **Enter**, you can't go back and change the line (by using the Backspace key, for example).

5. When you're done, press **Ctrl+Z**. Delphi sends the message and returns you to the MAIL> prompt.

Composing from InterNav

If you use InterNav, you begin a new message by clicking on the **Send New Mail** button, or by selecting the Mail menu's **S**end Message command. InterNav displays the Send window, as shown in the following figure. Enter the recipient's e-mail address in the To text box, and use the CC box to enter the addresses of anybody else you think ought to receive the message. (If you enter multiple addresses in the CC box, make sure you leave a space between them.) Now use the **S**ubject text box to enter the Subject line of the message, and then use the message box (the large area below the **S**ubject box) to type in your precious prose.

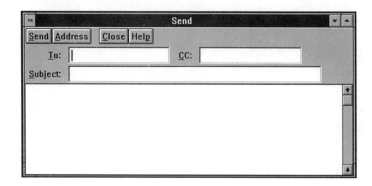

Use the Send window to compose your messages with InterNav.

When you're done, either select the Send button, or pull down the Mail menu and select the Send Message command. Once the message is winging its way Netward, InterNav will display a dialog box to let you know. Select **OK** to remove the dialog box and then select Close to get rid of the Send window.

Working with the InterNav Address Book

Besides giving Delphi's non-too-attractive command line a much-needed makeover, the InterNav application brings a few new features to the Delphi table. For example, InterNav comes with an *Address Book* that you can use to hold the e-mail addresses you use the most. Just think: no more having to memorize arcane Net addresses; no more sticky notes plastered all over your monitor with the e-mail locales of friends and colleagues; and no more forgetting the proper way to address an Internet missive from Delphi. The next couple of sections give you the goods on using the Address Book.

Getting Addresses Into the Address Book

For starters, let's see how you add new e-mail addresses to the Address Book. Here are the steps to follow:

1. Pull down the File menu and select the Address Book command. (If you're not currently in Delphi's e-mail system, you can also click on the **AddrBook** button.) The E-Mail Address Book dialog box appears, as shown in the following figure.

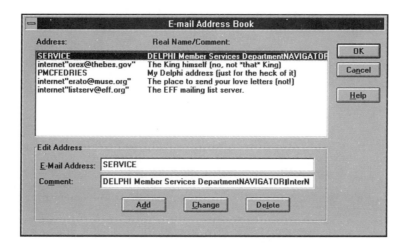

Use InterNav's Address Book to hold the e-mail addresses you use most often.

2. In the E-Mail Address text box, enter the person's e-mail address or Delphi username.

3. Use the Comment text box to enter the person's real name or some other description.

4. Select the Add button. InterNav adds the info to the list. If you entered an Internet address, InterNav gives it the proper Delphi format.

5. Repeat steps 2–4 to add more addresses.

6. Select OK. When InterNav asks if you want to save your changes, select Yes.

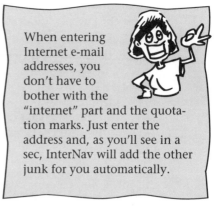

When entering Internet e-mail addresses, you don't have to bother with the "internet" part and the quotation marks. Just enter the address and, as you'll see in a sec, InterNav will add the other junk for you automatically.

Putting the Address Book to Good Use

Now that you've populated your Address Book with all your favorite e-mail sites, actually using the thing is a breeze. When you're in the Send window, instead of entering addresses by hand in the To or CC fields, you can simply pluck them right from the Address Book. Just place the cursor in either the To or CC field and select the Address button. When the E-Mail Address Book dialog box appears, highlight the address you need and then select OK.

Reading Your Mail

If it's publication day for any of the mailing lists you subscribe to, or if any of your Net friends have sent some notes your way, you'll have a few messages waiting in your Delphi mailbox. To be more precise, the messages are waiting in a special folder called *NEWMAIL*. In Delphi lingo, a *folder* is a storage area for messages. There are three folders in all:

> **NEWMAIL**   Delphi uses this folder, as I've said, to hold your new messages.

> **MAIL**   This folder holds the messages you've read.

> **WASTEBASKET**   This folders holds the messages you've deleted.

The next couple of sections show you how to read the messages in any folder.

Reading Mail from the Command Line

If Delphi detects new messages when you enter the mail system, it makes the NEWMAIL folder the current folder. Otherwise, it makes the MAIL folder the current one. To see a list of the messages in the current folder, type **directory** and press **Enter**. Delphi will display the name of the current folder in the upper-right corner of the screen, as well as info about each message, like so:

```
# From                   Date         Subject
1 IN%"orex@thebes.gov"   18-APR-1995  Need help with riddle!
2 IN%"athena@olympia.com" 18-APR-1995 Father needs headache remedy
3 APOLLO                 19-APR-1995  Re: Request for stock trends
```

The first column is the message number, the second column is the Delphi username or Internet address of the sender (Internet addresses begin with **IN%**), the third column tells you the date the message was sent, and the last column shows the subject of the message.

Delphi gives you two ways to read your messages:

➤ If you want to read all your messages starting with the first one, press **Enter** to display the first page of the first message. Keep pressing **Enter** to read the rest of the message and to move on to the next message.

➤ If you'd prefer to read a specific message, type **read**, a space, and the message number, and then press **Enter**. For example, to read the third message, you'd type **read 3** and press **Enter**.

222

While you're reading a message, you can also enter the following commands:

Enter	To
CURRENT	Move back to the beginning of the message.
FIRST	Display the first message in the current folder.
LAST	Display the last message in the current folder.
NEXT	Skip to the next message.

If you want to read a message from a different folder, use the SELECT *folder* command, where *folder* is the name of the folder you want to work with. For example, to switch to the MAIL folder, you'd type **select mail** and press **Enter**.

When you've read a message, Delphi will move it automatically to the MAIL folder, but it only does this *after* you exit the mail system (by typing **exit** and pressing **Enter**).

Reading Mail with InterNav

As you saw earlier, when you enter the e-mail system using InterNav, the program displays the Folders window. The drop-down list in the upper-left corner of this window tells you which folder you're currently looking at. If you have any new messages, InterNav automatically displays the NEWMAIL folder; if you don't have any new mail, you'll see the MAIL folder instead. (You can easily switch between folders by selecting them from this drop-down list.)

Whichever folder you're looking at, it shows summary info for each of its messages. The first column tells you the Delphi username or Internet e-mail address of the author (Internet addresses begin with **IN%**), the second column tells you the date the message was sent, and the third column shows the Subject line of the message.

To read a message in any folder, highlight it, and select the **M**ail menu's **R**ead Message command (you can also just double-click on the message). InterNav gathers the message text and displays it in a separate window like the one shown in the following figure.

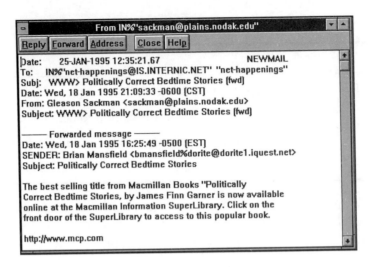

InterNav uses a window like this to display your messages.

I'll show you how to do things like forward and reply to a message in the next section. For now though, when you've finished reading the message, select the Close button. InterNav displays a dialog box asking if you want to delete the message. If you select **No**, InterNav moves the message into the MAIL folder; if you select **Yes**, InterNav sends the message to your WASTEBASKET folder. (Note, however, that InterNav doesn't move the message right away. It waits until you either exit the mail system—by selecting the **Go Back** button—or you close the Folders window.)

Message Replying, Forwarding, Deleting, and More

Reading messages, of course, is only part of our jobs as responsible e-mail users. We'll also have to reply to some messages, forward others, and perform basic message maintenance, such as deleting messages and saving them to other folders. The next few sections show you how to perform these chores using both the command line and InterNav.

Sending Out a Reply

One of the few negative consequences about e-mail's ease-of-use is that people aren't shy about asking you to send them info or to respond "ASAP" about one crisis or another. Hey, it was no sweat for them to send the message in the first place, so it should require even less sweat for you to respond, right? Well, luckily for them, that's usually the case, as you'll see in the next couple of sections.

Replying from the Command Line

To send a reply from the command line, first read the message you want to reply to. Then type **reply** and press **Enter**. Delphi shows the To and Subject lines, and then displays the following prompt:

```
Enter your message below. Press CTRL/Z when complete, or Ctrl/C to quit:
```

Type in your message. (Again, press **Enter** at the end of each line, but check the line for mistakes before doing so.) When you're done, press **Ctrl+Z** to send the reply.

Replying with InterNav

To reply to a message using the InterNav application, follow these steps:

1. Read the message to which you're replying.

2. Highlight the message text you want to quote in your reply, and then select the **Edit** menu's Copy command (or press **Ctrl+C**).

3. Select the Current menu's Reply command, or else select the Reply button. InterNav displays the Reply window. This window is similar to the Send window you saw earlier, except InterNav fills in the **To** and **Subject** fields for you automatically.

4. Use the CC text box to add other recipients, if necessary.

5. Move the cursor into the message box, and then select the Edit menu's Paste Quoted command. InterNav pastes the original message text with greater-than signs (>) as quote markers.

6. Enter your own text.

7. Select the Send button. When InterNav lets you know the message was sent, select **OK** and then select Close to shut down the Reply window.

Forwarding a Message

Have you ever been stuck in one of those bureaucratic phone mazes where you keep getting sent to different departments? This would be the human equivalent of "forwarding," and it's not pleasant when you're in the middle of it. E-mail forwarding, however, can be quite useful if you get a message that should've gone to someone else, or even if you just want to share a particularly enlightening message with your cohorts.

Forwarding from the Command Line

To forward a message from the MAIL> prompt, you first have to read the message you want to forward. Then type **forward** and press **Enter**. (If you want to specify a Cc line, use the command **forward /cc_prompt** instead.) At the **To:** prompt, enter the e-mail address of the forwardee and then press **Enter**. At the **Subj:** prompt, type in a subject and press **Enter**. Delphi forwards the message, no (more) questions asked.

Forwarding with InterNav

Here are the steps required to use InterNav to forward a message:

1. Read the message you want to forward.

2. Select the Current menu's Forward command, or select the Forward button. InterNav displays a dialog box that tells you only the original message will be forwarded. Any changes you may have made to the message will not be forwarded.

3. That sounds fair, so select **OK**. Now, you'll see the Forward Message dialog box, as shown in the following figure.

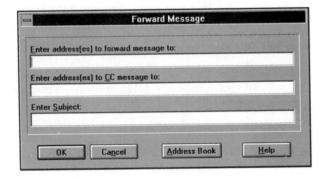

Use the Forward Message dialog box to fill in the details of your forwarded message.

4. Fill in the following fields:

   Enter address(es) to forward message to—Use this field to enter the e-mail addresses of the people you want to forward the message to directly. If you like, you can use the Address Book button to select entries from your Address Book.

   Enter address(es) to CC message to—Use this field to enter the addresses of the people you want to forward courtesy copies to. (Again, you can use your Address Book to make this easier.)

   Enter Subject—Use this field to enter a subject for the forwarded message.

5. Select **OK**. InterNav dutifully forwards the message.

Deleting a Message

Have a message you no longer need? Receive some e-junk-mail that you'd like to see filed under "G"? No problemo. Delphi lets you transfer messages to your WASTEBASKET folder with a few simple commands. Why doesn't it just delete a message for good and be done with it? Well, because *you* may decide you aren't done with it. For example, you may delete an important message by accident. Since the missive is sitting patiently in your WASTEBASKET, you can easily fish it out. (See the "Working with Delphi's Folders" section to learn how to do this.)

Bear in mind, though, that Delphi cleans out the WASTEBASKET folder each time you exit the e-mail system. So if you have a message you want to undelete, make sure you do it before you leave the mail system.

Deleting from the Command Line

Deleting messages from the command line is as easy as shooting fish in a barrel (and somewhat similar). Here's a rundown of the various methods you can use:

➤ If you want to delete the message you're reading, type **delete** and press **Enter**.

➤ To delete any message, type **delete**, a space, the message number, and then press **Enter**. For example, to delete message 10, you'd enter the command **delete 10**.

➤ To delete multiple messages, use the DELETE command with a *message list*. A message list just specifies which message numbers you want to work with. For example, the list **5–10** specifies message numbers 5 through 10. To delete these messages, you'd enter the command **delete 5–10**.

Deleting from InterNav

As you've seen already, when you close one of InterNav's message windows, the program asks if you want to delete the message. Selecting Yes will send it to the WASTEBASKET folder. But InterNav also gives you two other ways to expunge an unneeded message:

➤ In the Folders window, highlight the message you want to delete, and then select the Delete button.

➤ When you're reading a message, pull down the Current menu, and select the Delete command.

In either case, InterNav will display a dialog box asking you to confirm the deletion. Select **Yes** to put the kibosh on the message. Note, however, that the message won't appear in the WASTEBASKET folder until you close the Folders window (by selecting the **Close** button) and then reopen it (by selecting the **Mail** menu's View Folders command, or by clicking on the **View Folders** button).

Working with Delphi's Folders

As I mentioned earlier, Delphi sets up three folders for you: one to hold your unread messages (NEWMAIL), one for your read messages (MAIL), and another for your deleted messages (WASTEBASKET). Delphi automatically moves deleted messages to the WASTE-BASKET folder and read messages to the MAIL folder, but what if you want to move messages around by hand? For example, you may want to recover an accidentally trashed message from the WASTEBASKET folder.

You can do this, but you have to be at the command line (sorry, InterNav users). Here's how it works:

1. At the MAIL> prompt, use the SELECT command (as described earlier in the "Reading Mail from the Command Line" section) to select the folder that has the message you want to move.

2. Use the READ command to read the message you want to move.

3. Move the message by using the MOVE *folder* command, where *folder* is the name of the destination folder. For example, to move the current message to the MAIL folder, you'd type **move mail** and press **Enter**.

You can also use the MOVE command to create new folders. Why on earth would you want to do such a thing? Well, you'll probably find after a while that your MAIL folder is getting a bit unruly with all those messages piling up. You can take some of the pressure off by creating new folders to hold related messages. You could set up folders for, say, your e-mail buddies, your office coworkers, your customers, current projects, mailing lists you subscribe to, and whatever else you can think of.

To create a new folder, use the MOVE folder command, but this time *folder* is the name of the new folder. For example, if you want to create a folder called PERSONAL, you'd type **move personal** and press **Enter**. (I'm assuming here, of course, that the current message is one you want to move into the new folder. If not, you'll need to read a suitable message before entering the MOVE command.) Delphi will then display the following prompt:

```
Folder PERSONAL does not exist.
Do you want to create it (Y/N, default is N)?
```

Type **y** and press **Enter** to create the folder and move the current message into it.

The Least You Need to Know

This chapter showed you how to wield Delphi's e-mail system from both the command line and from InterNav. Here's the condensed version of what happened:

➤ To invoke the Delphi mail system, type **mail**, press **Enter**, and type **mail** again at the command line; or select InterNav's **E-Mail** button.

➤ To compose a new message from the command line, type **send**, press **Enter**, and then follow the prompts. If you use InterNav, click on the **Send New Mail** button, or select the Mail menu's **S**end Message command.

➤ You can read your mail from the MAIL> prompt either by repeatedly pressing **Enter**, or by specifying a message number in the READ command. For InterNav, highlight a message and select Read, or double-click on a message.

➤ Command-line replies are started with the **reply** command. In InterNav, select the Reply button.

➤ To forward the current message, enter the **forward** command at the MAIL> prompt, or select the Forward button in InterNav.

➤ To delete the current message, enter the **delete** command at the command line, or select the Current menu's Delete command in InterNav.

Part 3
E-Surfing: Accessing the Internet Via E-Mail

Until now, most of your e-mail travail has probably been devoted to composing notes, letters, dispatches, and bulletins of one form or another, and shipping them out to one or more recipients. However, Internet e-mail can handle more than just swapping notes between cronies, colleagues, and complete strangers. In fact, many of the Net's vast resources are available via the e-mail system. Things like files, Gopher documents, Usenet newsgroups, and even World Wide Web pages can all be delivered to your electronic mailbox through the magic of e-mail. The last six chapters of this book let you in on the secrets for using e-mail to tap into this rich source of info and entertainment.

Messing Around with Mailing Lists

This chapter leads off our coverage of accessing the Net via e-mail with one of the most popular of Net pastimes: mailing lists. I'll tell you what mailing lists are, how to subscribe and send articles to them, and how to get a list of lists. If you're keen enough, I'll also show you how to start up your own mailing list.

What Are These Mailing List Things All About?

Mailing lists are pretty simple, but I'll set up an analogy anyway, just for the heck of it. Think of the snail mail you get each day and think, in particular, of the magazines and newsletters you subscribe to. How is a magazine put together? Well, it all starts, of course, with a theme: computers, business, music, biker babes, whatever. Then, each month, authors write articles, columnists write columns, editors write editorials, and various people send in rambling tirades masquerading as letters to the editor. All this verbiage is gathered together, lots of ads and maybe a crossword puzzle or two are tossed in, and then the whole package is shipped out to those people who've paid good money either to subscribe to the magazine or to distribute it to stores.

Mailing lists are quite similar. Each list has a particular theme, people send in electronic mail messages to the person who runs the list (this is called *posting* to the list), that person gathers these messages together and then sends them out, again via e-mail, to those people who are subscribed to the list. It's sort of like getting a magazine, except for two, not insignificant, things: there are no ads and you don't have to pay a cent for your subscription.

What kinds of themes are available? Perhaps a better question to ask would be what kinds of themes *aren't* available! There are, in fact, thousands of mailing lists covering everything from airplane clubs to Led Zeppelin, from AI (artificial intelligence) to Z-cars (such as the Nissan 300ZX). You're bound to find at least a couple of lists that turn your crank and, if a particular subject near and dear to your heart doesn't have its own list, you can start your own.

Besides their subject matter, mailing lists also differ according to how you subscribe to them (which I'll talk about in the next section), and how their messages get sent to you. For the latter, you'll come across three kinds of lists:

Moderated　Many lists have a *moderator* who scans the incoming messages, filters out the dreck, and then passes along the good stuff to the list's subscribers. So, as you can imagine, these tend to be low-volume lists generating maybe only a few messages a day.

Unmoderated　In this type of list, any and all messages tendered to the list are sent out to the subscribers. Since there's much less work for the list administrator, this is the most common type of list and many of them generate dozens of messages a day. (The *list administrator*, by the way, is the person who organizes the list and maintains the list of subscribers. They're also sometimes called the *list owner* or the *list manager*.)

Digest　In most mailing lists, the messages submitted to the list are immediately sent out to the subscribers (unless, of course, the list moderator has to take a crack at them first). As a result, you'll often get messages dribbling in all day long, which can be annoying. To solve this problem, many busy lists offer *digest* versions that combine all their messages and send them in one fell swoop, usually at the end of the day or week.

 If you've participated in any Usenet newsgroups, you may be thinking that mailing lists and Usenet sound a lot alike. Well, that's because they are. Some mailing lists are, in fact, moderated digests of Usenet newsgroups. The major difference, of course, is that the articles in a mailing list are sent directly to your e-mail address where you can read them at your leisure. Also, many mailing lists (especially the moderated ones) are a more pleasurable read because they boast a higher signal-to-noise ratio than most Usenet newsgroups. (*Signal-to-noise ratio* is a rough comparison between the number of interesting, well-written, useful messages—the signal—and the number of dull, badly written, useless drivel—the noise.)

How Do I Subscribe to a List and Join in on the Fun?

Unlike a Usenet newsgroup where you can just use your newsreader software to dial in to the group and see what's going on, you can't eyeball any mailing list messages until you tell the list administrator that you want to join the list. This is called *subscribing* to the list and, since it can be confusing, we'll take a close look at it in this section. In particular, we'll break down the subscription process into the following three steps:

1. Determine the subscription address of the list.

2. Figure out whether you're dealing with a person or a software program.

3. Using the info from step 2, compose the request and send it to the subscription address.

The next three sections discuss each step in detail. Before moving on, a quick caveat is in order. Instead of going off half-cocked and subscribing to every mailing list in sight, you may want to start with just two or three until you get your feet wet. As I've said, some lists can generate dozens of messages a day, so there's no point biting off more than you can chew.

Step 1: Determine the List's Subscription Address

Most mailing lists have two e-mail addresses: a *subscription address* and a *posting address*. The subscription address (it's also called the *administrative address*) is the one you use to subscribe (or unsubscribe) to the list. The posting address (it's also called the *distribution address* or just simply the *list address*) is the one you use to post messages that you want distributed to the list's readers.

This is an important distinction to keep in mind because one of the grossest violations of mailing list netiquette is to send a subscription request to the distribution address. What's so bad about that? Because it means that (unless the list has a moderator)
your subscription request gets farmed out to the thousands of people who are already
subscribers to the list (and haven't the faintest desire to see your request).

Later in this chapter, I'll tell you about some Net resources that can supply you with
lists of the available mailing lists. These lists will often give you a "contact" name that
serves as the list's subscription address. For example, here's an entry for the Bagpipe
mailing list:

```
bagpipe
    Contact: bagpipe-request@cs.dartmouth.edu

    Purpose: Any topic related to bagpipes, most generally defined as
    any instrument where air is forced manually from a bellows or bag
    through drones and/or over reeds.  All manner of Scottish, Irish,
    English, and other instruments are discussed.  Anyone with an
    interest is welcome.
```

So the subscription address for this list is **bagpipe-request@cs.dartmouth.edu**.

In other cases, you'll only get the posting address, which always takes the following
general form:

```
listname@some_domain
```

Here, `listname` is the name of the list and `some_domain` is the domain name of the
computer where the list is located. For example, the posting address of the *Uma* list (the
Uma Thurman Appreciation Society's mailing list) is **uma@arastar.com**. To get the
subscription address, you usually just add **-request** to the list name. So the subscription
address for the *Uma* list is **uma-request@arastar.com**.

Step 2: Are You Dealing with a Person or a Program?

The administrivia associated with mailing lists is quite time-consuming, so many list
administrators use a program called a *list server* to handle subscriptions and other day-to-
day chores. (In fact, these programs have become so popular that many people now refer
to mailing lists as "listservs.")

So the next step in the subscription process is to figure out whether you'll be
sending your request to a person or a program. What's the diff? Well, as you'll see in the
next section, subscription requests to a list server program use cryptic commands that the

program understands. However, most humans (especially busy list administrators), don't respond well to cryptic commands and prefer, instead, friendly, polite notes.

How can you tell if you'll be dealing with software? Your only clue will come from the list's subscription address. If it includes the word *listserv* or the word *majordomo*, then the list uses an automated program. (The word *listserv* refers to a program called *Listserv* and *majordomo* refers to a program called *Majordomo*.)

For example, the *Mayberry* mailing list (for devotees of the old TV show *Mayberry, R.F.D*) uses the subscription address **listserv@bolis.sf-bay.org**. Similarly, if you want to subscribe to *Police* (the mailing list for fans of the rock group *The Police*), you'd use the address **majordomo@xmission.com**.

If you can't tell whether or not you'll be dealing with a program, assume you're dealing with a person. (This is particularly true if, say, you only have the list's posting address and you'll be sending your subscription to the list's "-request" address.)

Step 3: Compose and Send the Subscription Request

Okay, now that you know where you'll be sending your subscription request and to whom (or what), it's time to actually compose and send the message. How you do this will depend on whether you're sending the request to a person, a Listserv list, or a Majordomo list.

If you're sending the request to a person, you don't have to write any long-winded rationales or tome-like descriptions of yourself (unless the list administrator requests these things). Instead, just state your business in a polite, to-the-point missive. For example, here's the message I'd send if I wanted to subscribe to the Bagpipe mailing list I mentioned earlier:

```
To: bagpipe-request@cs.dartmouth.edu
From: paulmcf@hookup.net (Paul McFedries)
Subject: Subscription request


Please subscribe me to the Bagpipe mailing list.
```

Before too long, you'll receive a reply that either tells you you're subscribed to the list or gives you further instructions on how to subscribe.

If you're sending the request to the Listserv program, you need to follow two simple guidelines when composing the request:

➤ Leave the Subject line blank.

➤ In the message body, type only the following command:

```
sub listname your_name
```

Here, *listname* is the name of the mailing list and *your_name* is your full name.

For example, if I wanted to subscribe to the Mayberry mailing list, my message would look like so:

```
To: listserv@bolis.sf-bay.org
From: paulmcf@hookup.net (Paul McFedries)
Subject:


sub mayberry Paul McFedries
```

Finally, if you're sending the request to the Majordomo program, here are the guidelines to follow:

➤ Leave the Subject line blank.

➤ Type only the following command in the message body:

```
subscribe listname
```

Again, *listname* is the name of the mailing list.

For example, I could subscribe to the Police mailing list by sending the following message:

```
To: majordomo@xmission.com
From: paulmcf@hookup.net (Paul McFedries)
Subject:


subscribe police
```

Once you've sent in your subscription request, you'll likely receive a reply message that lets you know you're subscribed, tells you a bit more about the list, and gives you instructions for things such as posting to the list and unsubscribing. Be sure to save this message so you'll have access to these instructions down the road.

How Do I Unsubscribe to a List?

Not all mailing lists are created equal. Many lists are quite useful and become an indispensable part of their subscribers' online lives. Other lists, however, are decidedly dispensable. Whether it's the sheer volume of messages that's intolerably high, or a signal-to-noise ratio that's intolerably low, some lists just aren't worth the effort. In these cases, you'll want to cancel your subscription (unsubscribe) as soon as possible before brain rot sets in.

If the list is controlled by a person, you'll need to send a message to that person asking to be unsubscribed from the list, like so:

```
To: bagpipe-request@cs.dartmouth.edu
From: paulmcf@hookup.net (Paul McFedries)
Subject: Subscription cancellation request


Please unsubscribe me to the Bagpipe mailing list.
```

If the list's administration is controlled by the Listserv program, send a message to the *listserv* address with a blank Subject line and the following command in the message body:

```
signoff listname
```

As before, `listname` is the name of the mailing list. For example, to unsubscribe to the Mayberry mailing list, I'd send the following note:

```
To: listserv@bolis.sf-bay.org
From: paulmcf@hookup.net (Paul McFedries)
Subject:


signoff mayberry
```

If the list uses the Majordomo program, you'd send a message with a blank Subject and the following message body:

```
unsubscribe listname
```

Again, `listname` is the name of the mailing list. For example, I could unsubscribe to the Police mailing list with the following message:

```
To: majordomo@xmission.com
From: paulmcf@hookup.net (Paul McFedries)
Subject:

unsubscribe police
```

How Do I Post Messages to a List?

After you've spent some time reading a list's mailings and have gotten a feel for the tone and subject matter of the posts, you may feel like adding your two cent's worth to the discussion. This is easy enough: you just compose your message (don't forget to include a Subject line) and send it to the list's posting address. What if you only have the subscription address? No sweat. You can get the posting address in one of two ways:

➤ The reply message you receive when you subscribe to a list should give you instructions for posting, including the posting address.

➤ If you have the subscription address, the posting address will take the following general form:

```
listname@sub_domain
```

Here, `listname` is the name of the list and `sub_domain` is the domain name used in the subscription address. For example, the subscription address for the Bagpipe list is **bagpipe-request@cs.dartmouth.edu**, so the posting address is **bagpipe@cs.dartmouth.edu**.

Is There a List of Mailing Lists?

There sure is. In fact, there are several so-called *lists-of-lists* that you can use to get started with your mailing list subscriptions. Here's a sampling:

➤ To get a list of mailing lists that use the Listserv program, send a message to **listserv@bitnic.bitnet** and enter the following command in the message body: **list global**. You'll receive the list broken down into several messages (there are, currently, eleven messages in all) that give you, for each mailing list, the list name, the posting address, and a one-line description.

➤ The Massachusetts Institute of Technology (MIT) also maintains a list-of-lists. Anonymous FTP to **rtfm.mit.edu** and head for the following directory

```
/pub/usenet-by-group/news.answers/mail/mailing-lists
```

From there, you'll need to download the files named part01, part02, and so on (there are, for now, 14 files all told).

New mailing lists come online every day, so your list-of-lists will be out of date before you know it. To stay on top of things, you should subscribe to the New List mailing list that sends out announcements of new mailing lists as they're created. To subscribe, send an e-mail message to **listserv@vm1.nodak.edu** and include the following command in the message body (where *your_name* is your full name):

```
sub new-list your name
```

How Can I Start My Own Mailing List?

Did you check out one of the lists-of-lists and then groan in disappointment when you found out there was no mailing list for devotees of Chia Pets? I thought so. Well, why not start your own list? Here's a summary of the steps involved:

1. Ask your system administrator or the postmaster at your service provider if your system can handle mailing lists. Also, ask if there's a list server program such as Listserv or Majordomo available.

2. Write a charter for the mailing list. The charter describes the list and should include the following points:

    ➤ The purpose of the list.

    ➤ Who the list will appeal to.

    ➤ A list of topics that will be appropriate.

    ➤ Whether or not the list is moderated.

    ➤ Whether or not the list uses the digest format.

3. Create a text file that lists the e-mail addresses of the initial list subscribers. At first, this will probably only be your own address, but if you do have multiple addresses, place each one on a separate line like this:

```
nflanders@redeemer.org
mburns@mammon.com
hsimpson@moes.net
```

241

4. Send a message to the system administrator or postmaster asking them to create a new mailing list for you. Tell them the name of the list, give them a brief description, and let them know the name of the file that has the list of original subscribers.

So much for the preliminaries. The reply you get from the system administrator or postmaster ought to give you the details about how to manage the list and use the list server program, if there's one handy.

By the way, I've created a mailing list for readers of *The Complete Idiot's Guide to Internet-E-mail* which I hope we can use to get to know each other better. Feel free to ask questions about the book, e-mail in general, the Net, or whatever you feel like. To subscribe, send a message to **listmanager@hookup.net** with the following command in the message body:

```
subscribe cig-internet-email
```

The Least You Need to Know

This chapter began our look at accessing the Net via e-mail with a quick peek at mailing lists. Here's a rehash of the main events:

➤ A mailing list is a collection of messages that is sent out regularly to a group of subscribers.

➤ There are thousands of mailing lists available and each one covers a specific topic. Lists can be moderated, unmoderated, or in digest form.

➤ To subscribe to a mailing list, get the list's subscription address and then send a message asking to subscribe to the list. If the list's administration is automated by the Listserv program, use the command **sub *listname your_name***. If the Majordomo software is handling the dirty work, use the command **subscribe *listname***.

➤ Sending messages for general distribution to the mailing list's subscribers is called *posting* to the list. When posting, make sure you use the list's posting address.

➤ There are lists-of-lists available from **listserv@bitnic.bitnet** and **rtfm.mit.edu**.

Chapter 20

Using E-Mail to Find and Retrieve Files

In This Chapter

➤ Using FTPmail to do FTP via e-mail
➤ Wielding the MIT mail server
➤ Finding files through e-mail with archie
➤ Full-bore file finagling the e-mail way

When it comes to files, the Net's cup definitely runneth over. You want graphics? The Internet is glutted with GIFs and jam-packed with JPEGs. You want sounds? There are bells, boops, beeps, and belches to beat the band. You want text? The Net has text files out the wazoo covering everything from the Freedom of Information Act to UFO abductions. You want programs? There are terabytes (that's *millions* of megabytes, folks) of games, utilities, and full-blown applications, most of which cost either nothing or next to nothing.

The normal Net gateway to this file extravaganza is FTP (File Transfer Protocol), but what's a surfer to do if he doesn't have access to FTP? Well, the savvy e-mail user can grab just about any file using the Net's version of mail order. This chapter shows you how to use the e-mail system to grab any file you need from any FTP site on the Internet.

Ordering Files with FTPmail

The first system we'll look at is called FTPmail. It works just like FTP except that, instead of logging in anonymously to a computer and typing in FTP commands, you list all the commands you want to run in the body of an e-mail message. You then send this message to a computer called an *FTP gateway*, which handles the nitty-gritty of logging in to the FTP site, running the FTP commands, and sending the file back to your e-mail address.

For starters, here's a list of the FTPmail gateways you can use to send in your FTP orders (for fastest results, use the one closest to you):

Address	Location
ftpmail@sunsite.unc.edu	United States (North Carolina)
ftpmail@doc.ic.ac.uk	United Kingdom
ftpmail@decwrl.dec.com	United States (Massachusetts)
ftpmail@cs.uow.edu.au	Australia

 The following instructions work for the **sunsite.unc.edu** and **doc.ic.ac.uk** gateways. The **decwrl.dec.com** and **cs.uow.edu.au** gateways use slightly different commands. To get a list of their commands, send a message with just **help** in the body and nothing in the subject line.

You can use these gateways to request files from *any* Net computer that supports anonymous FTP sessions. To understand how FTPmail works, let's review the basics of FTP. To get any file via FTP, you need three pieces of information:

➤ The domain name of the FTP site

➤ The directory in which the file resides

➤ The name of the file

For example, if you'd like to get your mitts on a copy of the program PKUNZIP (for decompressing .ZIP files), you'd anonymous FTP to the site **ftp.psi.com**, change the directory to **/src/dos**, and get the file **pkunzip.exe**. Here's an e-mail message that accomplishes the same thing using FTP mail:

```
To: ftpmail@sunsite.unc.edu
Subject:

open ftp.psi.com
cd /src/dos
get pkunzip.exe
quit
```

Let's take a closer look at what's going on here. The message is addressed to the FTPmail server at **sunsite.unc.edu** and the Subject line is blank. The body of the message contains four commands. The first command is **open** and it tells FTPmail which FTP site we want to log in to. In this case, we want to log in to **ftp.psi.com**, so we use the following command (the **open** command assumes we're logging in as "anonymous" and using our e-mail address as the password):

```
open ftp.psi.com
```

The second command is **cd** and you use it to change to a different directory. In the example, we change to the **/scr/dos** directory with the following command:

```
cd /src/dos
```

Now that we're in the proper directory, the next task is to get the file we need using, appropriately enough, the **get** command:

```
get pkunzip.exe
```

The last command is always **quit** which tells FTPmail that it can take five because we don't have any more commands to run. Eventually, FTPmail will start up its own FTP session, run your commands, and then pass along the file to your e-mail address. In the meantime, you'll get a response that confirms your message was received:

```
<FTP EMAIL> response

ftpmail has received the following job from you:
      reply-to paulmcf@noc.tor.hookup.net
      open ftp.psi.com anonymous paulmcf@noc.tor.hookup.net
      cd /src/dos
      get pkunzip.exe

ftpmail has queued your job as 969533.6029
Your priority is 9 (0 = highest, 9 = lowest)
Requests to sunsite.unc.edu will be done before other jobs.
```

The FTPmail response also tells you how many "jobs" (that is, FTPmail requests) are ahead of yours. In the above example there are 70 jobs in the queue, which is typical. What this really means is that it will take a while before you get your file (a few hours or more; FTPmail is not, to say the least, the fastest way to surf the Net).

```
There are 70 jobs ahead of this one in the queue.
2 ftpmail handlers available.

To remove send a message to ftpmail@sunsite.unc.edu
containing just:
delete 969533.6029
```

Notice that FTPmail has added a **reply-to** command to specify the return address of the output. This defaults to your return e-mail address, but you can use the **reply-to** command yourself to specify a different address. Notice, also, that FTPmail added **anonymous** and my return e-mail address to the **open** command. FTPmail uses **anonymous** to log in to the FTP site, and it uses the e-mail address as the password.

Here's a list of some other FTPmail commands you can use when ordering files (to get a complete list, send a message to one of the FTPmail gateways with just the word **help** in the message body):

ls   Gives you a listing of the file names in the current directory.

dir   Gives a more detailed listing of the files in the current directory.

uuencode   Tells FTPmail to uuencode files before sending them. (See the "Sending Sounds, Graphics, and Other Nontext Files" section in Chapter 4 to learn more about uuencode.)

mime   Tells Ftpmail to send files using MIME (again, this is covered in Chapter 4).

For example, suppose you want to obtain PGP (Pretty Good Privacy) from **ftp.csua.berkeley.edu** and you know this site stores its PGP stuff in the directory **/pub/cypherpunks/pgp**. What do you do if you're not sure of the file name? In this case, you'd need to send multiple messages to get the contents of the **/pub/cypherpunks/pgp** directory, determine the file you need, and then have it sent to your mailbox. Here's what the body of the first message would look like:

```
open ftp.csua.berkeley.edu
cd /pub/cypherpunks/pgp
dir
quit
```

When this job is complete, you'll receive two reply messages: one that shows the results of each command, and another that contains the actual directory listing, which will contain, in part, the following lines:

```
drwxrwxr-x  2 hughes     98       512 Sep 13 05:21 pgp25
drwxrwxr-x  2 hughes     98       512 Sep 13 05:22 pgp26
drwxr-xr-x  2 2446       98       512 Sep 23 07:57 pgp261
drwxr-xr-x  2 2446       98       512 Oct 27 10:11 pgp262
-rw-rw-r—  1 hughes     98     26603 Jul  3  1993 pgpdoc1.txt.gz
-rw-rw-r—  1 hughes     98     35990 Jul  4  1993 pgpdoc2.txt.gz
```

Yuck! Fortunately, there are only two things you really have to worry about in this listing:

➤ In the jumble of letters in the first column, if the first letter is "d," it means the entry is a directory. Everything else is a file.

➤ The last column tells you the name of the directory or file.

In this case, you know you want the latest version of PGP (2.6.2), so it must be in the **pgp262** directory (the fourth line, above). We still don't know the name of the file, so this means, unfortunately, that we'll have to send in another request for a listing of the **pgp262** directory. Bummer. Here's what the message body looks like:

```
open ftp.csua.berkeley.edu
cd /pub/cypherpunks/pgp/pgp262
dir
quit
```

When we get the directory listing this time, it will look, in part, like this:

```
-rw-r—r—  1 2446        98    282786 Oct 23 06:39 pgp262.zip
-rw-r—r—  1 2446        98    167102 Oct 23 06:44 pgp262dc.zip
-rw-r—r—  1 2446        98    827006 Oct 23 06:02 pgp262s.tar.Z
-rw-r—r—  1 2446        98    548053 Oct 23 06:03 pgp262s.tar.gz
-rw-r—r—  1 2446        98    658945 Oct 23 06:33 pgpdocs.zip
```

Suppose the file you want is **pgp262.zip**. Then the body of your final message will look like so:

```
open ftp.csua.berkeley.edu
cd /pub/cypherpunks/pgp/pgp262
uuencode
get pgp262.zip
quit
```

Here, I've told FTPmail to use Uuencode to send the file. (If the file arrives in separate chunks, you'll need to combine them and then uudecode the whole thing.)

Getting Files Through the MIT Mail Server

One of the Net's most popular FTP sites is the Usenet archive at MIT: **rtfm.mit.edu**. This site contains FAQ lists for hundreds of Usenet newsgroups, as well as many articles that are posted periodically to one group or another. You could use FTPmail to grab files from this archive, but MIT has set up a program called a *mail server* that makes the job a lot easier (and a bit faster).

In fact, the mail server is so easy that all you need to learn are two simple commands: **send** and **quit**. As with FTPmail, you enter these commands in the body of a message and then fire it off. You use the **send** command to specify both the directory that contains the file you need and the name of the file. For example, I told you in Chapter 19 that there's a list of mailing lists in the directory **/pub/usenet-by-group/ news.answers/mail/mailing-lists**. The list is split into 14 files named **part01**, **part02**, through **part14**. If you wanted, say, just the first three parts, you'd send the following message:

```
To: mail-server@rtfm.mit.edu
Subject:

send /pub/usenet-by-group/news.answers/mail/mailing-lists/part01
send /pub/usenet-by-group/news.answers/mail/mailing-lists/part02
send /pub/usenet-by-group/news.answers/mail/mailing-lists/part03
quit
```

You can enter up to 20 commands in a single message. If you leave out a file name in a **send** command, the mail server will send you a listing of the files in the directory. For example, the command **send /pub/usenet-by-group** will generate a list of all the files (and, in this case, directories) in the **/pub/usenet-by-group** directory.

Finding Files with archie

FTPmail and the MIT mail server work well (albeit slowly) when you know the name of the file you want to get or the name of the directory you want to work with, but what if you're not sure about the correct file or directory name, or even whether a particular file or directory exists? You could try using **dir** or **ls** commands to do a brute force search of an FTP site, but that could take forever. No, the best solution is to take advantage of an Internet service that specializes in finding files: *archie*.

The archie service maintains a database of all the files and directories from thousands of sites that offer anonymous FTP access. The idea is you give archie a particular keyword and it searches its database to see if it finds a match. If the search was successful, archie returns the name of the FTP site, the directory, and the file name; everything you need, in other words, to get the file via FTPmail.

To use archie via e-mail, crank up a new message and address it to one of the following, so-called *archie servers* (for fastest results, use the one closest to you):

Address	Location
archie@archie.ans.net	United States (New York)
archie@archie.internic.net	United States (New Jersey)
archie@archie.rutgers.edu	United States (New Jersey)
archie@archie.sura.net	United States (Maryland)
archie@archie.unl.edu	United States (Nevada)
archie@archie.uqam.ca	Canada (French)
archie@archie.funet.fi	Finland
archie@archie.wide.ad.jp	Japan
archie@archie.doc.ic.ac.uk	United Kingdom
archie@archie.hensa.ac.uk	United Kingdom

Your search is handled by the **find** *keyword* command, where *keyword* is the name of the file or directory you want to locate. For example, if you know you need the file **pkunzip.exe**, but you're not sure where to find it, you'd enter the following commands into the body of your message (beginning at the first line):

```
find pkunzip.exe
quit
```

Most of the time, though, you won't know the exact name of the file you need. For example, suppose you want to get a copy of *VShield*, which is a DOS anti-virus program. You might guess that its file name would be VSHIELD.EXE or VSHIELD.ZIP, but searching for these files will prove fruitless (trust me). The problem is that many programs—including VShield—include their version numbers as part of the distribution file. So, for example, the VShield file might be called VSHIEL20.ZIP or VSHLD114.ZIP, or who knows what.

To find files like these, you have to tell archie to search for only part of the file name (a *substring*) by adding the following command to your message: **set search sub**. So your VShield search message may look like this:

```
set search sub
find vsh
quit
```

When you receive your reply, archie lists the "Host" (the FTP site), the "Location" (the directory), and the file info for every file it found that included the substring *vsh*. Here's a partial listing:

```
Host archive.latrobe.edu.au

    Location: /pub/msdos/virus
        FILE  -r—r—r—   111996  19 Jul 01:00 vsh1205.zip

Host beethoven.cs.colostate.edu

    Location: /pub/msdos/virus
        FILE  -rwxr—r—   151389  01 Feb 23:27 vsh111.zip
etc.
```

So, for example, you could get version 2.05 of VShield via anonymous FTP at **archive.latrobe.edu.au** by looking in the directory **/pub/msdos/virus** and grabbing the file **vsh1205.zip**.

The Least You Need to Know

This chapter gave you the lowdown on using the e-mail system to find and retrieve files. Here's a summary of just a few of the amazing things you learned:

➤ To run some FTP commands, insert them inside an e-mail message and send it to an FTPmail server (such as **ftpmail@sunsite.unc.edu**). The server will run the commands and send you the results.

➤ In FTPmail, use the **open** command to connect to an FTP site, use **cd** to change directories, use **dir** to get a directory listing, and use **get** to download a file. Make sure you end every message with **quit**.

➤ The MIT mail server can send you any file from the **rtfm.mit.edu** site. Place one or more **send** commands in the body of a message and fire it off to **mail-server@rtfm.mit.edu**.

➤ To use archie to find a file, send a message to an archie server (such as **archie@archie.ans.net**) with the command **find** *file*, where *file* is the name of the file you're trying to locate.

➤ If you'd prefer to search for part of a file name, add the command **set search sub** to the beginning of the message.

Chapter 21

Postal Posting: Usenet Through E-Mail

In This Chapter

➤ Newsgroups that have mailing lists

➤ Computers that store newsgroup articles

➤ How to post articles via the e-mail system

➤ A selection of e-mail newsgroups

➤ How to start spreading the news using only your e-mail software!

To read and post Usenet articles, you normally need two things: a service provider that has a computer set up to handle Usenet and a newsreader program. If you lack one or the other, you can still get your Usenet news fix by doing your reading and posting via the e-mail system. This chapter tells you everything you need to know.

Gateways to the News

The easiest way to participate in Usenet is to take advantage of the many *mail-to-news* gateways that exist. These gateways are mechanisms that make certain newsgroups act just like the mailing lists you learned about back in Chapter 19. You use similar methods to subscribe to a newsgroup, and its articles will then be sent automatically to your e-mail address. To post an article to the newsgroup, you just send an e-mail message to the list's posting address, and the message will be kindly forwarded to the group. It's all quite civilized, really.

Getting a List of Mail-to-News Gateways

As I've said, not all Usenet newsgroups boast a mail-to-news gateway, so you won't get full access to the 10,000 or so groups that exist. However, some five hundred groups *do* have a gateway, so there's still lots of fun to be had.

To get a list of these newsgroups and their corresponding mailing list addresses, anonymous FTP to **rtfm.mit.edu** and head for the following directory:

```
/pub/usenet-by-group/news.answers/mail/news-gateways
```

Look for the file named **part1** and download it to your computer. When you check out this file (its official name is "Mailing Lists Available in Usenet"), you'll see a list that looks like the following:

```
Newsgroup     Mailing list     Status
—————  ——————   ———
alt.aquaria.killies killies@mejac.palo-alto.ca.us
alt.cd-rom   cdrom-l@uccvma.ucop.edu
alt.clearing.technology     clear-l@vm.ucs.ualberta.ca
alt.fan.tom-robbins magic-l@american.edu
alt.health.cfids-action     cfids-l@american.edu     M
```

The left column gives you the newsgroup name, the middle column gives you the list's address (which is also the posting address) in the form *listname@domain*, and the right column gives you the status of the group ("M" means the group is moderated; there are other codes and the file tells you what they mean).

Subscribing to a Newsgroup

To subscribe to any one of these newsgroups, you subscribe to its corresponding mailing list. Unfortunately, the "Mailing Lists Available in Usenet" article doesn't give you subscription addresses, so you'll need to make some educated guesses. Here are some things to watch out for:

➤ The mailing lists corresponding to all the **bit.listserv** newsgroups use Listserv programs to handle subscriptions, so the subscription address uses **listserv** in place of the list name. For example, the newsgroup **bit.listserv.catholic** has a mailing address of **catholic@auvm.american.edu**. So you can assume this group's subscription address is **listserv@auvm.american.edu**.

➤ If the list name ends with **-d** or **-l** or **-p** (which stand for digest, list, and publication, respectively), the list probably uses a Listserv program to handle subscriptions.

➤ For all other lists, add **-request** to the list name in the list address. For example, the **alt.aquaria.killies** group has a list address of **killies@mejac.palo-alto.ca.us**. So you could try **killies-request@mejac.palo-alto.ca.us** as the subscription address.

Once you've figured out the subscription address, you can send in the subscription request as described in Chapter 19, in the "How Do I Subscribe to a List and Join In on the Fun?" section.

Reading and Posting to a Newsgroup

Once you're subscribed, the mail-to-news gateway will start sending the newsgroup's articles to your e-mail address where you can read them at your leisure. To post your own articles, compose a new mail message and send it off to the newsgroup's mailing list address. The gateway will automatically pass on the article to the newsgroup where it will appear as a regular article.

The only tricky part about all this comes when you want to reply to an article. If you just slam your e-mail software's **Reply** command, it'll address your reply to the newsgroup/mailing list as a whole (that is, to the list's posting address). If all you want to do is send a response to the author of the article, you'll need to edit the To line of your reply and add in the author's e-mail address by hand.

More Ways to Read and Post to Usenet Via E-Mail

The mail-to-news gateways are an easy way to get your Usenet kicks. The problem, though, is that only about five percent of the available groups sport their own gateway. So if a newsgroup you're dying to subscribe to isn't one of the lucky few, you're out of luck, right? No way, José. The Net's resident geniuses have come up with all kinds of ways to do the Usenet thing through the e-mail system. The next few sections give you the scoop.

Getting Articles the Belgian Way

A server in Belgium keeps track of about 1,100 newsgroups and holds on to articles for between three and seven days, depending on the group. The groups covered include a large number in the **bionet**, **misc**, **news**, **rec**, **sci**, and **soc** hierarchies. However, this site's real forte is the **comp** hierarchy, which it covers in full.

To get articles from this server, you first need to get the full list of newsgroups it carries. You do that by sending a message to **listserv@cc1.kuleuven.ac.be** and typing the following in the message body (leave the Subject line blank):

```
/ NEWSGROUPS
```

When you get the reply, you'll see a list of newsgroups such as this:

```
/GROUP comp.risks 5
/GROUP comp.robotics 5
/GROUP comp.security.announce 5
```

The number after the group name tells you how many days the server keeps the articles for that group. The next step is to get a list of the available articles for a particular group. Start another message, address it to **listserv@cc1.kuleuven.ac.be**, and include the appropriate **/GROUP** line in the message body. For example, to get a list of articles for the **comp.robotics** newsgroup, you'd include the following line:

```
/GROUP comp.robotics
```

The reply you'll get will include a line for each article, like so:

```
/ARTICLE 2122 4536 author@domain comp.robotics Frequently Asked Questions
/ARTICLE 2122 4537 another@elsewhere Microcontroller primer and FAQ
/ARTICLE 2122 4538 dood@doobie.do Fiber optic gyroscopes
```

After the /ARTICLE command, you'll see two numbers that are used internally by the server, then the e-mail address of the article's author, and then the Subject line.

If any of the articles strike your fancy, you can get them by copying the appropriate /ARTICLE lines and pasting them in the body of another message addressed to **listserv@cc1.kuleuven.ac.be**. The server will reply by sending you each article as a separate message.

To get complete instructions for using this server, send a message to **listserv@cc1.kuleuven.ac.be** with only **/NNHELP** in the message body.

Getting Articles the Swiss Way

CERN (the European Laboratory for Particle Physics) has a server that archives Usenet articles for a few days or so. The list of newsgroups covered by the CERN computer is extensive, and the articles stored for each groups are easy to get. The downside is that you get *every* article in the newsgroup, which can add up to a lot of mail if you ask for a busy group.

To avoid getting a bunch of articles you don't want, you can first ask CERN to send you a list of the articles' Subject lines. Address a new message to **listproc@www0.cern.ch** and include the command **send news:***group* in the message body, where *group* is the name of the newsgroup you want to see. For example, to see a list of articles for the newsgroup **comp.society.folklore**, you'd use the following command:

```
send news:comp.society.folklore
```

If the Subject lines look reasonable, you get the articles themselves by sending another message to **listproc@www0.cern.ch**, but this time you include the command **deep news:***group* in the message body (where, again, *group* is the group name). For example, to get all the articles for **comp.society.folklore**, you'd use the following command:

```
deep news:comp.society.folklore
```

As if all this weren't enough, there's even *another* way to get Usenet articles that involves the Net's Gopher system. I'll show you how it works in Chapter 24 (see the "Gopher It with E-Mail" section).

Posting Via E-Mail

Posting articles via e-mail is simplicity itself. For starters, you need to address the message to one of the following locations:

➤ *newsgroup.name*@**news.demon.co.uk**, where *newsgroup.name* is the name of the newsgroup to which you want to send the article.

➤ *newsgroup.name*.**usenet@decwrl.dec.com**, where, once again, *newsgroup.name* is the name of the group you're invading.

➤ *newsgroup-name*@**cs.utexas.edu**, where *newsgroup-name* is the name of the group you're posting to. Make sure, however, that you replace all the periods in the group name with dashes. For example, if you're sending a message to **sci.physics.fusion**, you'd use the e-mail address **sci-physics-fusion@cs.utexas.edu**.

Next, use the Subject line of the e-mail message to enter the subject of your article, and then use the message body to enter the article body and (optionally) your signature.

That's all there is to it. Just send your message and it'll appear in the group like any other post. (It's probably a good idea to try a test post or two before you go off on some e-mail posting rampage. Remember to use one of the dedicated **test** groups, such as **misc.test**.)

Anonymous E-Mail Posting for Clandestine Articles

The vast majority of Usenet articles are fully aboveboard and open to all and sundry. However, there are times when people prefer to post articles and still remain anonymous. For example, someone still "in the closet" may want to post to one of the gay and lesbian newsgroups, or someone who actually *likes* Barney the Dinosaur may want to defend the poor fellow in **alt.barney.dinosaur.die.die.die**.

For those times when Usenetters prefer to travel incognito, an anonymous posting service has been set up in Finland. Sound familiar? It should, because it's the same service we looked at back in Chapter 6, in the "E-Mail Incognito: Anonymous Remailing Services" section. The procedure is basically the same, but I'll take you through the steps, just to be safe:

1. Start a new mail message and address it to **anon@anon.penet.fi**.

2. Use the Subject line of the e-mail message to enter the subject of your article.

3. In the first line of the message, enter X-Anon-To: *newsgroup*, where *newsgroup* is the name of the newsgroup in which you want the article to appear. For example, if you want to post to **alt.sex.fetish.diapers** (yes, it's a real group), you'd enter the following:

   X-Anon-To: **alt.sex.fetish.diapers**

4. Use the message body to enter the article body. (Make sure, of course, that you don't add a real signature to the end of the article.)

5. Send the message.

If you haven't used the service before, you'll receive a response telling you your anonymous "code name." As I explained back in Chapter 6, your next step is to set up a password. When the password has been accepted, you can then post anonymously to **anon@anon.penet.fi**. The top of each message should look something like this:

```
X-Anon-To: put the group name here
X-Anon-Password: put your password here
```

Filtering the News Down to a Dull Roar

The "Usenet Readership Summary Report for Jun 94" tells us that Usenet types are sending an average of over 67,000 messages a day, totaling over 172 megabytes of data! (If you'd like to see this report for yourself, FTP to **rtfm.mit.edu** and look in the **/pub/ usenet-by-group/news.lists** directory.) Adjectives such as mountainous, gargantuan, Herculean, even Brobdingnagian, only begin to describe these eye-popping numbers. Clearly, even the most dedicated of Usenet junkies can monitor only a tiny percentage of this tidal wave of verbiage.

So how in Hades do you make sure you don't miss anything? For example, you may read **alt.cereal** faithfully, but what if an interesting breakfast cereal discussion suddenly breaks out in **rec.music.tori-amos**? (She is, after all, the "Corn Flake girl.") Well, the good folks at Stanford University's Department of Computer Science have come up with a solution. The Stanford Netnews Filtering Service (SNFS) lets you set up a Usenet "profile" consisting of one or more keywords (such as "cereal"). Then, every day, SNFS scours the hoards of news articles and picks out the ones that match your profile. These articles are then e-mailed to you so you can read them at your leisure. Is that handy or what?

Okay, let's see how this thing works. In your mail program, start a new message and address it to **netnews@db.stanford.edu**. In the body of the message, type the following:

subscribe *first-word second-word ...*

Here, *first-word* and *second-word* are the words you want SNFS to watch out for (this is your *profile*). For example, typing **subscribe cereal** tells SNFS to pick out any article that contains the word *cereal*. Here are some things to keep in mind when selecting your profile:

➤ If you enter multiple words, SNFS only matches articles that contain *all* the words. For example, entering **subscribe cereal oats** tells SNFS to send only those articles containing the word *cereal* and the word *oats*. (You can enter as many words as you like.)

➤ If you want SNFS to match articles that *don't* contain a word, preface the word with **not**. For example, to find all articles that contain *cereal* and *oats*, but not the word *Quaker*, you'd enter the following:

subscribe cereal oats not quaker

Make sure, by the way, that you always put the **not** portion of the profile at the end of the line.

➤ Don't make your profile too broad. Entering *sex* will match thousands of articles, whereas *sex kinky* would narrow things down a little.

You can also customize your profile by adding one or more of the following commands:

lines   This command tells SNFS how many lines of the article to send. The default is 20, but you can enter any number between 1 and 60.

period   This is the frequency (measured in days) with which SNFS sends you its articles. The default is 1 (that is, every day), but you can enter whatever number you like.

expire   This is the number of days you want the subscription to remain in effect. The default is 9,999 days.

For example, if you want your subscription to return only 10 lines every 5 days, and to expire in 365 days, your profile would look something like this:

```
subscribe cereal oats not quaker
lines 10
period 5
expire 365
```

When you're done, send the message. In a little while, you'll receive an e-mail reply telling you whether or not the subscription went through okay.

What happens if SNFS sends you only 20 lines of, say, a 50-line article? Well, you have two options: you could use your newsreader to check out the article directly in the newsgroup, or you can have SNFS send you the full article via e-mail. For the latter, send a missive to **netnews@db.stanford.edu**, and enter the following in the message body:

get *article*

Here, ***article*** is the name of the article as given by SNFS (for example, **alt.cereal.1234**). To get more info on this and other features of SNFS, send an e-mail note to **netnews@db.stanford.edu** with the word **help** in the message body.

E-Mail Newsgroups to Check Out

Now that you know how to plug in to Usenet's newsgroups, there are a few e-mail-specific groups you may want to keep an eye on. The next few sections give you the details.

Conversations with Fellow Elm Fans

If you use the Elm e-mail software (which we discussed back in Chapter 10, "Cruising Down Elm Street"), you'll want to subscribe to the newsgroup **comp.mail.elm**. You'll find tips on how to get the most out of Elm, technical help, and lots more.

```
FAQ Info:
      Article:  Elm Mail User Agent FAQ - Frequently Asked Questions
      RTFM.MIT.EDU Directory: /pub/usenet-by-group/comp.mail.elm
```

Meetings with MIME Mavens

MIME (the Multimedia Internet Mail Extensions we talked about in Chapter 4, in the "Sending Sounds, Graphics, and Other Nontext Files" section) is becoming the standard way to foist nontext files on other people through the e-mail system. If you'd like to know more about MIME, or have some questions you'd like to ask, the newsgroup **comp.mail.mime** is the place to be.

```
FAQ Info:
      Articles: comp.mail.mime frequently asked questions list (FAQ) (1/3)
           comp.mail.mime frequently asked questions list (FAQ) (2/3)
           comp.mail.mime frequently asked questions list (FAQ) (3/3)
      RTFM.MIT.EDU Directory: /pub/usenet-by-group/comp.mail.mime
```

General Mail Confabs

For general discussions about electronic mail, mail etiquette, the impact of e-mail on society, and lots more, tune in to the newsgroup **comp.mail.misc**.

```
FAQ Info:
      Articles:      FAQ: How can I send a fax from the Internet?
           FAQ: How to find people's E-mail addresses
           FAQ: International E-mail accessibility
           Filtering Mail FAQ
           Signature and Finger FAQ
           UNIX Email Software Survey FAQ [Part 1 of 3]
           UNIX Email Software Survey FAQ [Part 2 of 3]
           UNIX Email Software Survey FAQ [Part 3 of 3]
           Updated Inter-Network Mail Guide
      RTFM.MIT.EDU Directory: /pub/usenet-by-group/comp.mail.misc
```

A Forum for Pegasus Mail Users

If you use Pegasus Mail, you'll want to read Chapter 12, "Taming Pegasus Mail," *and* you'll want to subscribe to the newsgroup **bit.listserv.pmail** (or to the Pmail mailing list at **pmail@ua1vm.ua.edu**). You can get technical help for Pegasus Mail, learn new techniques, keep abreast of new versions, and more.

Parleys About Pine

We covered the Pine e-mail program back in Chapter 9, "Riding Pine's Pony Express." If you're looking for tips and advice on getting the most out of Pine, you should keep tabs on the newsgroup **comp.mail.pine**.

The MS-DOS Mail Round Table

If you use any MS-DOS mail program, the newsgroup **comp.os.msdos.mail-news** has discussions related to using e-mail software in a DOS or Windows environment. There's also talk about the relative merits of various DOS and Windows e-mail applications, advice for getting connected, and more.

```
FAQ Info:
       Articles: comp.os.msdos.mail-news FAQ (01/02) intro
             comp.os.msdos.mail-news FAQ (02/02) software
     RTFM.MIT.EDU Directory: /pub/usenet-by-group/comp.os.msdos.mail-news
```

Other E-Mail Newsgroups

To round out our look at e-mail newsgroups, here's a list of a few more groups that may be of interest:

comp.mail.list-admin.policy	General discussions about policy issues related to running mailing lists.
comp.mail.list-admin.software	Talk about the various software programs used to run mailing lists.
comp.mail.mh	Discussions about the Unix Message Handling (MH) e-mail system.
comp.mail.mush	Conversations about yet another Unix e-mail program: the Mail User's Shell (MUSH).
comp.mail.sendmail	Configuring and using the **sendmail** daemon.

comp.mail.smail	Administering and using the **smail** daemon.
comp.mail.uucp	Doing the e-mail thing in a UUCP (Unix-to-Unix-Copy) network environment.

The Least You Need to Know

This chapter showed you the ins and outs of using the Internet e-mail system to access Usenet newsgroups. Here's a summary of just a few of the tricks you learned:

➤ A few hundred newsgroups have mail-to-news gateways that make the groups available through mailing lists. You subscribe and post to these groups just like regular mailing lists.

➤ The Net also has a couple of servers that store Usenet articles. The one at **listserv@cc1.kuleuven.ac.be** specializes in the **comp**, **news**, and **sci** hierarchies. The one at **listproc@www0.cern.ch** has an extensive list of newsgroups, but doesn't give you any way to choose selected articles.

➤ To post an article to any newsgroup, send a message to either *newsgroup.name*@**news.demon.co.uk**, *newsgroup.name*.**usenet@decwrl.dec.com**, or *newsgroup-name*@**cs.utexas.edu**.

➤ Use the **anon@anon.penet.fi** service to post articles anonymously.

➤ The Stanford Netnews Filtering Service can track Usenet for you and return articles that contains specific keywords. The address of the service is **netnews@db.stanford.edu**.

➤ In your Usenet travels, don't forget to stop by e-mail-related groups such as **comp.mail.misc** and **comp.mail.mime**.

Stacks of Fax Hacks: Faxing Via E-Mail

Remember, a decade or so ago, when the fax (or the *facsimile* as we called it back then) was the hottest thing around, the new kid on the telecommunications block? How amazing it seemed that we could send a letter or memo or—incredible!—a *picture* through the phone lines and have it emerge seconds later across town or even across the country. Oh sure, the fax that came slithering out the other end was a little fuzzier, and certainly a lot slimier, but, heck, it sure beat the post office.

Nowadays, though, faxing is just another humdrum part of the workaday world. Any business worth its salt has a fax machine and, thanks to the mass marketing of fax/modems, the lives of many individuals have become fax-enhanced, as well. Meanwhile, e-mail is rapidly becoming (if it's not already) *the* preferred way to transmit messages in the wired culture of the '90s. Are fax and e-mail just two communications ships passing in the night and never the twain shall meet? No way. In fact, if you have clients or friends that don't have an e-mail account, you can still keep in touch by sending an e-mail message to their fax machine! This chapter lets you in on this bit of digital voodoo and shows you just how easy it is.

An Experiment in Remote Printing

The most notorious of the Internet's e-mail-to-fax services goes by the unlikely name "An Experiment in Remote Printing" (which I'll shorten to ERP to save my poor, aching fingers). It was started back in June of 1993 by a couple of guys (Carl Malamud and Marshall Rose) who wanted to do some research on how to "integrate the e-mail and facsimile communities." Really. Net folks seem to get a real kick out of doing things like that.

The basic idea behind ERP is simple enough. Using a special Internet location, you send an e-mail message that includes the recipient's name and fax number. ERP extracts the fax area code and then routes the message to one of the participating organizations that covers that particular area code. The organization then uses a plain old fax/modem to fax the message to the recipient. Best of all, the whole thing won't cost you a dime!

What's the catch? Well, it's simply that the system can't offer coverage that's even remotely universal. A few dozen U.S. area codes are supported (mostly in major urban centers), and selected parts of the UK, Japan, Australia, and a few other countries are also in the loop. The problem is that ERP relies on institutions and individuals linked to the Net to farm out the incoming faxes. If no one from a particular area code is willing to participate in the experiment, fax machines in that neck of the woods remain out of touch. On the bright side, though, new organizations are joining the ERP cause all the time, so the coverage is expanding rapidly.

 You can get a list of ERP's current coverage areas by sending an e-mail message to **tpc-coverage@town.hall.org** with a blank Subject line and nothing in the message body. You can also get a FAQ list about ERP by sending a note to **tpc-faq@town.hall.org** (again, sans subject and body).

If you'd like to give the ERP server a whirl, start a new e-mail message and use the following general form for the address:

```
remote-printer.Recipient_Name/Location@p.h.o.n.e.n.u.m.b.e.r.tpc.int
```

Yeah, you're right: that *does* look like a mess. Here's what each bit means, in plain English:

Recipient_Name   This is just the name of the person who'll be receiving the fax. Don't use spaces or any kind of punctuation marks. You can separate names with an underscore (_), and ERP will convert the underscores to spaces when the fax is sent.

Location   Use this part to specify the recipient's department name, floor number, room number, or whatever other info that's needed to make sure they get the fax. Again, use underscores to represent spaces.

p.h.o.n.e.n.u.m.b.e.r   This is the strangest of the hoops ERP makes you jump through. This part is the recipient's fax number, but you have to separate each number with a period (.) and you have to enter the number *backwards*! Hey, I just write about this stuff, I don't make it up. (Technically, I suppose I should have written the general form as *r.e.b.m.u.n.e.n.o.h.p*, but that just seemed too mind-blowing.)

Let's make all this gobbledygook concrete by looking at an example. Suppose you want to send a fax to Herb Tarlek in the Sales Department at the number 1-234-555-6789. Here's how you'd set up the address of your message:

```
remote-printer.Herb_Tarlek/Sales_Dept@9.8.7.6.5.5.5.4.3.2.1.tpc.int
```

Just so you know, here's what the cover sheet of the resulting fax will say:

```
Please deliver this facsimile to:
    Herb Tarlek
    Sales Dept
```

Anyway, back to your e-mail message. Once you have the address sorted out, all that remains is to fill in the body with whatever bulletin you want to send to your correspondent. When that's done, just ship out the message. If, for some reason, the fax can't be sent (which may happen, say, if the area code you entered isn't covered by ERP), you'll get a reply telling you the bad news.

The Net also has a few other e-mail-to-fax services, but they only cover limited geographical areas. For example, the Rabbit fax service covers only local calls from Sacramento, California (area code 916). To get more info, send a message to **request@rabbit.rgm.com** with the Subject line **052**.

Commercial Internet Faxing Services

The Experiment in Remote Printing service is free, which is nice, but it also falls into the you-get-what-you-pay-for category. In this case, what you get is a limit on the number of cities, states, and countries that you can fax. No, if you're looking to fax just about anywhere at just about anytime, then you'll have to go commercial. It means paying a monthly fee (usually) and anywhere from 25 cents to 6 dollars for a fax (depending on how far-flung the destination is), but at least the message will get where you want it to go.

Faxing with the FAXiNet Service

You could call FAXiNET an e-mail-to-fax-and-back-again service because it's one of the few that lets you not only send e-mail as a fax, but also receive a fax as e-mail. The service is quite extensive, as well, with links to some 200 countries around the world.

The rate charged by FAXiNET depends on which plan you choose:

➤ Plan 1 is designed for high-volume faxers. You're charged a one-time "activation fee" of $35.00, and then you fork out $9.95 a month for "account maintenance." Faxes to U.S. and Canadian destinations will cost you only 39 cents each.

➤ Plan 2 is for occasional faxing. The one-time activation fee is $20, and you pay no monthly charge. Instead, FAXiNET hits you up for 65 cents each time you fax to a U.S. or Canadian destination. (Note, too, that Plan 2 users have to prepay $25 dollars worth of fax charges.)

For other countries, FAXiNET's Plan 1 rates range from 56 cents per page for the United Kingdom, to $1.52 for Mexico, to a whopping $5.86 for Madagascar. Plan 2 users add 25 cents to these rates. To get a complete rate schedule and to find out about things such as including logos and letterheads on your faxes, and receiving faxes as e-mail, contact FAXiNET at any of the following locations:

AnyWare Associates FAXiNET,
32 Woodland Road, Boston, MA 02130
Phone: (617) 522-8102
Automated e-mail: **info@awa.com**
Human e-mail: **sales@awa.com**
World Wide Web: **http://www.awa.com/faxinet/**

InterFax Faxing

The InterFax service lets you send faxes to any fax machine in the world. You pay a one-time sign-up fee of $25, and then you shell out $5 per month, which entitles you to send five pages. After that, it'll run you 50 cents a page. Here's how to contact InterFax:

InterFax
PO Box 162, Skippack, PA 19474
Phone: (215) 584-0300
Fax: (215) 584-1038
E-mail: **faxmaster@pan.com**

To keep up with the latest and greatest on Internet e-mail-to-fax services, you'll want to read the article "FAQ: How can I send a fax from the Internet?" by Kevin Savetz. It's posted twice a month to Usenet's **comp.internet.services** newsgroup. It's also available via anonymous FTP from **rtfm.mit.edu**. It's in the following directory (under the name **fax-faq**):

```
/pub/usenet-by-group/news.answers/internet.services
```

Faxing from Online Services

If you're a subscriber with one of the Big Three online services (America Online, Compu-Serve, and Prodigy), your e-mail-to-fax chores are the easiest of all. That's because each of these services has set up a fax system that lets you deliver e-mail to just about any fax machine. (Some even let you send e-mail and have it delivered as snail mail.) The rest of this chapter dials in to each service and shows you how its respective fax systems work.

Online Faxing with America Online

America Online lets you send an e-mail message as a fax to any phone number in the United States or Canada. The cost is quite expensive at $2 per fax, which is billed directly to your AOL account. (Note, however, that AOL lets you send a single message to mul-tiple fax machines, but the service will charge you $2 for *each* destination.)

To send a fax, you create an e-mail message using the same steps I showed you back in Chapter 15, in the "Composing a New Message" section. The only difference is that, in the **To:** box, type the name of the recipient, an "at" sign (@), and then the area code and phone number of the fax machine. For example, if you're sending a fax to Millicent Peeved at 212-555-4321, you'd enter the following:

```
Millicent Peeved@212-555-4321
```

If you want to send the message to multiple fax machines, use the CC box to enter the appropriate names and phone numbers. (You can include e-mail addresses, too, if you also need to send the message to someone online.)

When you're done, select the **Send** button. America Online displays a dialog box to let you know how much the fax will cost and to ask if you accept the charges. Select **Yes** and then select **OK** when AOL lets you know the message was sent.

To get more info about AOL's fax service, including the latest prices and how to send an e-mail message to a snail mail address, pull down the Mail menu and select the Fax/Paper Mail command. The Fax/Paper Mail window that appears contains a bunch of documents that should answer any questions you have.

Sending Faxes from CompuServe

CompuServe's e-mail-to-fax service is one of the better ones because it lets you send a message to any fax machine in the world. This convenience comes at a price, however:

➤ If you're sending the fax to a machine in the U.S. or Canada, it'll set you back 75 cents for the first 1,000 characters, and 25 cents for every 1,000 characters on top of that. (There's a 50,000 character limit(!), so you won't be able to fax, say, your latest novel.)

➤ If your fax has a European destination, you'll have to fork out 90 cents for the first 1,000 characters, and another 90 cents for every other 1,000-character chunk you send.

To send a fax, follow the same steps that I outlined for a regular e-mail message back in Chapter 16, in the "Composing a New Message" section. The only difference is how you specify the address:

➤ In the Name box, enter the name of the person who'll be receiving the fax.

➤ In the **Address** box, type **FAX:** and then the fax phone number. For example, if you're sending the fax to 1-444-555-6666, enter **FAX:1-444-555-6666**.

Now just create the message in the usual way and send it off. If the fax goes through okay, CompuServe will place a system message in your In-Basket letting you know how much the transmission cost you.

If you're feeling spunky, you can also create a custom cover sheet for your CompuServe faxes. Here are the steps to follow:

1. When entering your message, type **\CUSTOM** by itself on the first line of the message.

2. On the second line of the message, type **\BEGIN COVER**.

3. If you'd like to include the CompuServe banner (the words "FACSIMILE COVER PAGE" in 24-point type), type **\BANNER** on a line by itself.

4. Use the following codes to add basic header info to the cover sheet:

Use	To Include
\TO\	The recipient's name
\PHONE\	The recipient's fax number
\FROM\	Your name
\SUBJECT\	The Subject line of the message
\DATE\	The current date

5. Type in any text you want to appear on the cover sheet.

6. Type **\END COVER** on a line by itself to mark the end of the cover sheet.

7. Type in the rest of your message. Everything after the \END COVER\ statement appears on a new page.

The following figure shows an example message that uses all of these codes to create a custom cover sheet.

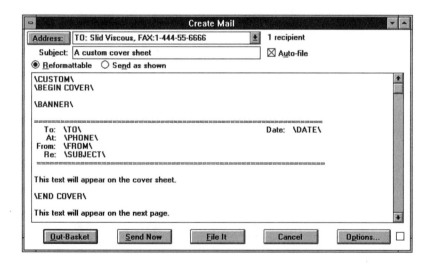

An example of a custom cover sheet in CompuServe.

Faxing from Prodigy's E-Mail Connection

To send faxes from Prodigy, you need to download the E-Mail Connection software I told you about in Chapter 17, in the "Making the Prodigy Mail System Usable" section.

(Prodigy's regular e-mail service can't handle faxes.) Once you have E-Mail Connection, faxing is a piece of cake. (Although it will cost you $1.25 per page, up to a maximum of 20 pages.)

For starters, you need to define a fax "address" for your recipient. Here are the steps to follow:

1. Double-click on the **Address Book** icon in the Window Bar, or pull down the Window menu and select the **Address Book** command. The Address Book window appears.

2. If you're adding the fax number to an existing address, highlight the name and select **M**odify. If you're creating a new address, select the Add button. E-Mail Connection displays the Address Book Entry dialog box.

3. Fill in the address fields, if necessary.

4. In the A**d**dress Types list, select **FAX** and then select Add. This displays the FAX 'Address' dialog box, as shown in the following figure.

Use the FAX 'Address' dialog box to enter the recipient's fax number.

5. In the **Fax Phone** box, use the three text boxes to enter the area code and phone number for the fax machine.

6. If the call isn't a long-distance number, deactivate the **L**ong distance check box.

7. If you don't need to dial an area code to complete the call, deactivate the Requires area code check box.

8. Select **Ok** to return to the Address Book Entry dialog box, and then select **Ok** again to return to the Address Book window.

With that over with, you send a fax by composing a new message (see the "Composing a New Message" section in Chapter 17), and selecting the FAX address in the To box.

The Least You Need to Know

This chapter gave you the scoop on the various services—both free and commercial—that you can use to send an e-mail message to a fax machine. Time now to check out a few reverse-angle replays:

➤ The Experiment on Remote Printing is a free e-mail-to-fax service that covers selected area codes in North America and around the world. Send your message to **remote-printer.*Name/Location@number*.tpc.int**.

➤ Commercial services, such as FAXiNET and InterFax, can fax e-mail messages just about anywhere, but they'll charge you a monthly fee and anything from two bits to two bucks or more per page.

➤ To send a fax from America Online, just compose a normal e-mail message, but address it to ***name@fax_number***.

➤ CompuServe users can send a fax by using the address **FAX:*fax_number*** when they compose the e-mail message.

➤ To send a fax through Prodigy, you need the E-Mail Connection software. Open the Address Book and create a FAX "address" (i.e., the fax number) for your recipient.

Chapter 23

The Way-Out World of Play-by-E-Mail Games

Once you've sent out all your serious e-mail messages, done your replying duty, and performed your mail maintenance, it's time to relax and have a little fun. That means cranking up a copy of *Tetris* or *Doom*, right? Not necessarily. As you'll see in this chapter, there's a whole universe of cool "play-by-e-mail" games that let you get your ya-yas out right from the comfort of your own e-mail program.

What's All This Play-by-E-Mail Stuff About?

The idea behind play-by-e-mail (PBeM) games is simple, at least on the surface. Each game progresses by a series of "turns." In each turn, the players involved in the game (there can be as few as two or as many as two hundred) write down their next "move" in an e-mail message and then send it in to the "gamemaster." The gamemaster processes each move, updates the game, mails the results back to each player, and the whole thing repeats. In most games, the turns happen every 2 to 10 days and, with an average duration of 30 or more turns, they can last for months at a time.

The type of move you make depends on the game you're playing. In chess, for example, you'd write which piece to move and where. In games such as Diplomacy, you control entire armies, negotiate alliances with other players, and generally make like an e-mail Napoleon.

Actually, these types of games have been available in snail mail versions for years from companies such as Avalon Hill (the originators of Diplomacy, among many others). In your Net travels, you'll see references to both PBM (play-by-mail) games and PBeM (play-by-e-mail) games. In general, PBM refers to both the snail mail *and* e-mail games; when people are talking strictly about the e-mail variety, they'll use the acronym PBeM.

Play-by-e-mail games are a surprisingly huge Net sensation. I mean *thousands* of people play dozens of different games week in and week out. Everyone has his or her own reasons for playing, of course, but I think four factors in particular are responsible for the success of PBeM:

➤ PBeM games are inherently social. Other types of games are solitary affairs or, at best, are played against a computer. But computers—impassive beasts that they are—can't be taunted, so crowing after a victory is hollow, to say the least. With PBeM, though, you're always playing against (or sometimes with) other people, which just adds a whole new level of interest.

➤ All PBeM games require at least a little bit of thought (and some require a lot), and luck rarely plays a part. Yes, there's a time and a place for mindless fun, but if you're looking to exercise that muscle called the brain, PBeM games will give you quite a workout.

➤ PBeM games don't dominate your life. As I said earlier, lots of games only have turns every few days, so there's plenty of time to plan your next move. Granted, some true PBeM fanatics with addictive personalities seem to eat, sleep, and breathe whatever game they're involved in, but that kind of devotion is by no means a prerequisite. (However, if you *are* a speed freak, some games have "warp mode" versions where the turns come every few hours.)

➤ PBeM games are cheap. I don't just mean the games themselves are free, which many are. I mean that you don't need to spend a lot of time online. In almost all PBeM games, you do most of your planning and strategizing offline, so you don't run up humongous charges for connection time (like you do with some online games).

Hot Net Spots for PBeM Participants

One of the ways you can gauge the popularity of any Internet phenomenon is to see how many resources the Net devotes to it. Is there a newsgroup? Are there FTP sites? How about a World Wide Web page? As you'll see in the next few sections, PBeM games have all these resources and more, to boot.

Usenet's PBeM Newsgroups

Lots of PBeMers hang out in the Usenet newsgroup **rec.games.pbm**. You'll find people looking for games to join, hints about specific games, ads for new games, and loads of general chit-chat about the whole genre. (One recent post about the game Atlantis 2.0 had the following Subject line: "Does Abernethy suck or what?") This group is also the place to find the PBeM FAQ list. The article "rec.games.pbm Frequently Asked Questions (FAQ)" is posted to the group periodically. If you don't see it, you can use the old anonymous FTP thing to get it from **rtfm.mit.edu**. Look for the file **play-by-mail** in the following directory:

> **/pub/usenet-by-group/news.answers/games**

If Diplomacy is your PBeM drug of choice, you can schmooze with your fellow diplomats and ask questions about rules and strategies in the newsgroup **rec.games.diplomacy**. There's even a two-part FAQ called "rec.games.diplomacy FAQ," which you can also get from **rtfm.mit.edu** in the following directory:

> **/pub/usenet-by-group/rec.games.diplomacy**

In the VGA Planets game, the clashes occur in space as you and 10 other players vie for supremacy. You'll find mid-battle discussions going on in the newsgroup **alt.games.vga-planets**.

FTP Sites for PBM Info

Many play-by-mail games keep their instructions and other related files at the anonymous FTP site **pbm.com**. Look in the directory **/pub/pbm** for all the goodies.

If you can't get into that site, you can also try **ftp.erg.sri.com** in the **/pub/pbm** directory, or **ftp.funet.fi** in the **/pub/doc/games/play-by-mail** directory.

PBeM on the World Wide Web

One of the best sources for PBeM info is the World Wide Web. For starters, point your favorite Web browser to the following location:

> **http://fermi.clas.virginia.edu/~gl8f/pbm.html**

This takes you to the Play by Email (PBEM) Games Homepage, which has links to the PBM FAQ and the FTP sites. However, it also includes links to some other great PBeM info:

➤ A list of all the PBM games (e-mail, snail mail, free, and commercial), including descriptions of each game.

➤ The Play by Email (PBEM) Magazine Homepage (see the following figure). This online magazine features all kinds of articles dealing with specific games, PBeM culture, and more.

➤ Web pages that are devoted to individual games (such as Diplomacy, Atlantis, and Nomic).

All in all, the Play by Mail (PBM) Games Homepage is a real mother lode for beginning PBeM types.

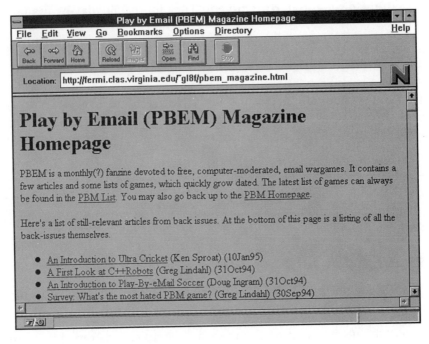

The Play by Email (PBEM) Magazine Homepage has some interesting articles on PBeM games and culture.

Richard's Play-by-E-Mail (PBeM) Server

Dedicated PBeMer Richard Rognlie has set up a computer that lets people play a bunch of different strategy games via e-mail. Strategy games (or *abstract* games, as they're sometimes called) are played on "boards" where players take turns moving pieces around. Most of the games seem to be derivatives of either chess or Go.

Before you can play any games on this server, you need to sign up. You do this by sending an e-mail message to **pbmserver@netcom.com** with the following command in the Subject line:

    signup userid password

Here, *userid* is the name you want to use to identify yourself in each game, and *password* is the password you'll be using to make your moves.

To get more info about this server, send an e-mail message to **pbmserver@netcom.com** with only the word **help** the Subject line.

In most of the strategy games, you get the results of your move back in a few minutes, so the turns can come fast and furious. To make life easier for yourself, pick a password that's easy to type and easy to remember.

PBeM in the Online Services

If you're a subscriber with either CompuServe or America Online, here's how to get to some PBeM forums:

➤ In CompuServe, type **go pbmgames** and press **Enter**.

➤ In America Online, pull down the Go To menu, select **Keyword**, type **pbm** in the dialog box, and then select **OK**.

A Look at Some PBeM Games

Of course, talking about PBeM is a poor substitute for actually playing the games themselves. However, since so many of the games require a real commitment (weeks or months in many cases), you'll need to do a bit of research before diving in. The Web's Play by Mail (PBM) Games Homepage is a good place to start, and the FTP sites mentioned earlier should give you all the info you need. To get you started, though, I'll spend the rest of the chapter looking at a few of the most popular PBeM games.

Abalone

Abalone is a strategy game for two to six players. It's contested on a six-sided board where each player controls a collection of "marbles." You push the marbles around the board (you can move up to three at a time, as long as they're connected linearly) and the object is to push your opponent's marbles off the board. It's been described as a "boardgame version of sumo wrestling," which seems about right.

This game is handled by Richard Rognlie's PBeM server. To get instructions for playing Abalone, send a message to **pbmserv@netcom.com** with **help abalone** in the Subject line.

You can also get more Abalone info at the following Web site:

http://www.daimi.aau.dk/~tusk/pbmserv/abalone/index.html

Atlantis 2.0

Atlantis 2.0 is a medieval fantasy game where any number of players can battle it out for supremacy. Each player controls a "faction" consisting of one or more workers, warriors, or magicians, and some cash. The Atlantis world is divided into regions where each faction can purchase goods, services, weapons, raw materials, or whatever. Each player moves through the regions, building up his faction by selling products the faction's workers have created, or by using its warriors to pillage hapless neighbors. Atlantis is insanely detailed (for example, you can "teach" your workers new skills) and most games last for months.

You can get the complete rules for Atlantis 2.0 by anonymous FTPing to **ftp.rahul.net** and downloading the file **rules.v2** from the directory **/pub/atlantis**.

The Atlantis Home Page on the World Wide Web is jam-packed with useful Atlantis tidbits. Here's how to get there:

http://www.cs.utexas.edu/atlantis/

Chess

Looking for a human chess opponent of similar abilities, but there's no one else in sight? Then why not try chess via e-mail? All you have to do is send a message to **franz@hemsoft.ping.dk** and include the following in the message body:

```
your_name your_address your_level
```

Here, *your_name* is your full name, *your_address* is the e-mail address you want to use for the games, and *your_level* is either **novice**, **intermediate**, or **expert**.

Diplomacy

Diplomacy is based on the original Avalon Hill board game and is the granddaddy of all play-by-mail games. Diplomacy players (there can be up to seven in each game) perform geopolitical machinations from the pre-World War I era, where each person controls a European power (Austria, England, France, Germany, Italy, Russia, or Turkey). Players move armies and fleets around for battle and try to arrange strategic alliances (through diplomatic channels, of course) with other players. Watch your back, though!

To get instructions for Diplomacy, send an e-mail message with just the word **help** in the body to one of the following addresses:

> **judge@morrolan.eff.org**
> **judge@cs.umanitoba.ca**
> **judge@nmt.edu**
> **judge@owl.und.ac.za**

Tons of Diplomacy bits and bites are available at the following URL:

> **http://www.hmc.edu/~irilyth/diplomacy/index.html**

Galaxy

Galaxy is a "space opera" game where each player controls a race of extraterrestrials. Each player "furthers his race" by traveling to, and colonizing, other planets. Once settled on the new world, you can expand your technology base and so create bigger, faster, and scarier ships. If there are no unsettled planets around, then the real fun begins as the ETs duke it out for celestial bragging rights. Most games have one or two turns a week, and last for about 50 to 80 turns.

To get the complete rules for Galaxy as well as some other useful files, anonymous FTP to **pbm.com**, and look in the directory **/pub/pbm/galaxy**. There's also a nice Web page called The Galaxy PBeM Game Home Page (see the next figure) at the following site:

> **http://www.abekrd.co.uk/Galaxy/**

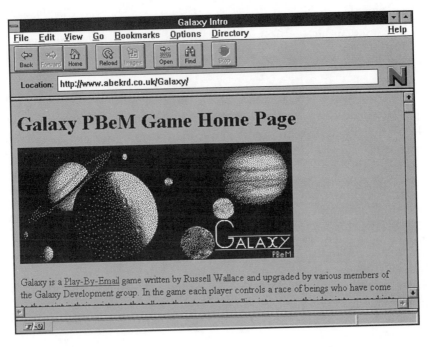

Head to this Web page for lots of juicy Galaxy morsels.

Hex

Hex is another strategy game available on Richard Rognlie's PBeM server. In this case, the board is an 11-by-11 rhombus where two players take turns adding "stones" to the board. The first player tries to place her stones so they form an unbroken, vertical chain. Meanwhile, the second player tries to position his stones so they form an unbroken, horizontal chain. And, of course, each player also tries to thwart the other's chain-building, so lots of fun is had by all.

To find out more about playing Hex, send a message to **pbmserv@netcom.com** with **help hex.faq** in the Subject line. Once you know how the game works, you can get instructions for playing Hex on the server by sending a missive to **pbmserv@netcom.com** with the Subject line **help hex**.

Both of these Hex documents and a Hex game archive can be had at the following Web site:

http://www.daimi.aau.dk/~tusk/pbmserv/hex/index.html

Nomic

Imagine a game whose rules state that the object of the game is to change the game's rules! Sounds pretty weird, I know, but that's exactly how you play *Nomic*. You start with an initial set of rules, and then each player (there can be any number) takes a turn, where a "turn" is defined as a proposal for a rule change or an entirely new rule. The other players vote on the rule change and, if the vote is unanimous, the change is adopted into the game. In theory, the rules can change so much that you end up playing a completely different game!

If you're interested, you can get the initial rules by anonymous FTP from **ftp.cse.unsw.edu.au** in the directory **/pub/doc/nomic**. Look for the file **rules.txt**. Also, the file **FAQ** contains a list of Frequently Asked Questions for Nomic, which also tells you about games that are ongoing. (One game began in June 1993 and, as I write this in February of 1995, is still going strong!)

Web-lovers should also check out Michael's Nomic Page at the following URL:

http://www.cl.cam.ac.uk/users/mn200/games/nomic/

Trax

Trax is a strategy game that'll really get your neurons firing. (It isn't called "the game for those who love a challenge" for nothing!) You and your opponent choose up sides (black or white) and take turns placing "tiles" on the game board. Each tile has sections of white or black track on it, and the idea is to place your tiles so the track forms either a closed loop or a continuous path from one end of the board to another. It's a fiendish and addictive game.

You play Trax from Richard Rognlie's PBeM server. To get game instructions, history, and strategy tips, send a message to **pmbserv@netcom.com** with **help trax.faq** in the Subject line. To learn how to play *Trax* on the server, fire off a note to **pbmserv@netcom.com** with just **help trax** as the subject.

World Wide Web surfers can get all kinds of fun Trax stuff (even a digital Trax magazine!) at the following Web locale:

http://www.daimi.aau.dk/~tusk/pbmserv/trax/trax.index.html

The Least You Need to Know

This chapter introduced you to the wild world of play-by-e-mail games. If you're looking for blood and guts, stick to Doom and Street Fighter, but if brains and guile are more your style, PBeM is a great way to kill some time. Here's a recap of some of this chapter's top stories:

➤ With play-by-e-mail, the games progress by a series of turns sent in by each player as e-mail messages. With each move, the game is updated and the players plan their new strategies.

➤ PBeM is a true Net success story because the games are inherently social, they favor skill over luck, they don't require massive amounts of time, and they keep your connection costs to a minimum.

➤ If you're on Usenet, check out the **rec.games.pbm** newsgroup for lots of play-by-mail tips and for announcements of new games.

➤ To get game rules and other files, anonymous FTP to **pbm.com** and head for the directory **/pub/pbm**. You can also try the World Wide Web at **http://fermi.clas.virginia.edu/~gl8f/pbm.html**.

➤ If strategy games are more to your liking, the place to be is the PBeM server at **pbmserv@netcom.com**.

HEY, COOL.

Chapter 24

More Mail Chauvinism: Miscellaneous E-Mail Coolness

In This Chapter

➤ Using e-mail to access the World Wide Web

➤ Getting Gopher goodies via e-mail

➤ E-mail servers for definitions, acronyms, jargon, and more

➤ A smorgasbord of e-mail tidbits, from the weather to the White House

Our look at surfing the Net via e-mail has turned out to be a real feast for e-mail gourmets: mailing lists, FTP, archie, Usenet, faxing, play-by-e-mail games. Truly an e-meal fit for a King (or Queen). I hope you've saved some room for coffee and dessert, however, because that's what I'll be serving up in this chapter. You'll be sinking your teeth into tasty e-mail morsels such as the World Wide Web and Gopher, dictionary, acronym, and jargon servers, White House addresses, and lots, lots, more. Belly up!

E-Mail Web Weaving

Everywhere you go these days, it's World Wide Web this and World Wide Web that. Sheesh, you'd think the Web and the Net were synonymous the way some folks carry on. It's understandable, though, because the Web really is where the heavy Net action is happening these days. If, until now, you haven't given a flying fig about the Web because you lacked one of those highfalutin browsing programs, you'll be happy to know your wait in the World Wide Web wilderness is over. Why? Because now you can get Web pages delivered right to your mailbox! No guff.

To try it out, send an e-mail message to **listproc@www0.cern.ch**, leave the Subject line blank, and include **send** *URL* in the message body. Here, *URL* is the Web location of the page you want (URL stands for Uniform Resource Locator). For example, the URL for the White House Web page is **http://www.whitehouse.gov/**. To get this page, your message body would look like:

> **send http://www.whitehouse.gov/**

When the message is done, let 'er rip and in a few minutes you'll receive the text of the Web page you specified (minus, of course, all those fancy graphics that infest most Web pages these days). The page will also include a list of the URLs that are referenced within the page, just in case you want to get them, too.

Rather than going through the hassle of sending a separate **send** command to get every URL referenced in a particular Web page, you can get them all sent to you in one fell swoop by using the **deep** *URL* command.

Gopher It with E-Mail

The World Wide Web may get everyone's vote as the sexiest Internet service, but I've still got a soft spot in my Net heart for the Gopher system. Maybe it's the homely name, or maybe it's the menu-driven, so-easy-even-a-dope-like-me-can-figure-it-out interface, but I truly enjoy tunneling through Gopherspace. And fast? Hah! Let's just say that in the time it takes for all those obese Web graphics to come trickling through your modem, you could've burrowed your way through a dozen Gopher menus and downloaded a morning's worth of reading.

Gopher, as you may know, deals mostly with text files, so you'd think there'd be a natural e-mail connection in there somewhere. As a matter of fact, there is: it's called *GopherMail* and it's covered in the next few sections.

The Net's GopherMail Servers

As you may know, the Gopher system works by displaying a menu of choices. Generally speaking, each menu item represents one of two things:

➤ Another menu, either at the same Gopher site, or at a completely different location.

➤ A document or some other file.

The idea is that you keep selecting the appropriate menu items until you get to the document or file you need. GopherMail works the same way by using a *GopherMail server* to request menus and files from just about any Gopher site in the world. Here are the addresses of the Net's GopherMail servers (for best results, pick one near you):

Address	Location
gophermail@calvin.edu	United States
gophermail@ftp.technion.ac.il	Israel
gophermail@eunet.cz	Czech Republic
gopher@earn.net	France
gopher@dsv.su.se	Sweden
gopher@nig.ac.jp	Japan
gopher@ccns.nips.ac.jp	Japan
gomail@ncc.go.jp	Japan

Getting a Gopher's Main Menu

Your first order of business is to get the main menu of the Gopher site you want to work with. You do this by sending a message to one of the GopherMail servers with the name of the Gopher site in the Subject line and the word **help** in the message body.

For example, let's say you're traveling to Indianapolis tomorrow and would like to know what the weather's like. You want to use the University of Illinois Weather Machine Gopher, which is located at **wx.atmos.uiuc.edu**, so you'd send the following message:

To: gophermail@calvin.edu
Subject: wx.atmos.uiuc.edu

help

The reply you'll receive will show the various items on the Gopher's main menu. Items that point to other menus will have a backslash (/) at the end.

Burrowing Down

To move to a different menu, run your e-mail software's **Reply** command and place an **X** beside the menu item, as shown here:

```
   1.  :The UofI Weather Machine
   2.  Canada/
   3.  Caribbean/
<lots of other stuff>
  12. Satellite Discussion/
  13. Severe/
X 14. States/
  15. docsave/
etc.
```

When you're ready, ship back the entire message to the GopherMail server, which will then return the items for the menu you selected. Keep repeating this until you get to the document you want. Again, place an **X** beside the document, send back the message, and the GopherMail server will send you the file.

If you select a Veronica search item (to search Gopher sites for files or directories), enter the keywords for your search in the Subject line of your reply.

An Easier Method

The GopherMail servers are pretty speedy, but it quickly becomes a pain-in-the-you-know-what to go through the whole send-and-reply rigmarole for Gopher sites you use often. This is especially true for sites that require you to tunnel through several menus to get where you want to go. For example, to get the Indianapolis weather, you have to get the Gopher's main menu, get the **States** menu, get the **Indiana** menu, and then get the forecast; that's a total of *four* messages, in all.

Who the heck has the time, inclination, or patience to go through *that* every time? Instead, once you've gone through a particular menu maze once, there's an easier way to reach your final destination each subsequent time. Whenever you get a reply from the GopherMail server, look below the menu items and you'll see a bunch of entries that look something like this:

```
Name=Indiana
Numb=14
Type=1
Port=70
Path=1/States/Indiana
Host=wx.atmos.uiuc.edu
```

This is actually the technical info that GopherMail uses to identify each of the menu items. The above example is from the University of Illinois Weather Machine Gopher, and it represents the **Indiana** item in the **States** menu. So, in the future, you can head directly to the **Indiana** menu by inserting this info into the body of a message and sending it to the GopherMail server. (Technically, you don't need to send the first two lines: **Name** and **Numb**.)

You can get Gopher documents this way, too. For example, to get the document "Metro Area Zone Fcst (Indianapolis)," from the **Indiana** menu, you'd send the following to the GopherMail server:

> Unfortunately, this shortcut doesn't work with the **gophermail@calvin.edu** server. The GopherMail server at **gomail@ncc.go.jp** is quite fast, though, so I'd recommend using that one.

Type=0
Port=70
Path=0/States/Indiana/Metro Area Zone Fcst (Indianapolis)
Host=wx.atmos.uiuc.edu

Using GopherMail to Read Usenet News

You can take advantage of the GopherMail shortcut we looked at in the previous section to read articles posted to Usenet newsgroups. The University of Manchester has a Gopher (**info.mcc.ac.uk**) that serves as a simple newsreader. To get a menu of article Subject lines for a particular newsgroup, enter the following in the body of a message and send it to your favorite GopherMail server:

Type=1
Port=4320
Path=nntp ls *group_name*
Host=info.mcc.ac.uk

Here, ***group_name*** is the name of the newsgroup.

Server City, Here We Come

A *server*, as I've said before, is just a computer that sends out whatever info you request (it "serves" the information to you). Most of the things we've seen in Part 3—FTPmail, archie, GopherMail—are run by servers of one kind or another. In fact, since the only thing most e-mail programs can do on their own is compose messages (and maybe a few other maintenance chores), the entire Internet e-mail system relies on various servers.

As a result, a real cottage industry has sprung up to create servers that supply e-mail types like you and me with all sorts of interesting, useful, and entertaining info. The next few sections give you the lowdown on a few of my fave rave e-mail servers.

The Amazing InfoMania Infobot!

A company called InfoMania has put together a great "information-by-mail" server. This server has over *two dozen* commands that can supply you with dictionary definitions, acronym expansions, almanac data, the weather, and more. If you are, like me, easily entertained, then this baby will keep you going for hours.

To see how it works, let's try looking up the word *egregious* in the InfoMania dictionary (it's a Webster's, actually). Address a message to **infobot@infomania.com**. In the Subject line, type **webster egregious**, leave the message body blank, and then launch it. A few minutes later, you'll receive a reply like the following:

```
webster: trying server at webster.lcs.mit.edu...connected

egre.gious \i-'gre—j*s\ aj [L egregius, fr. e- + greg-, grex herd - more
    at GREGARIOUS archaic  1: DISTINGUISHED  2: conspicuously bad : FLAGRANT
    - egre.gious.ly av
```

Not bad for e-mail! But there's more to the InfoMania server than that. Lots more. Here's a summary of a few interesting commands (to get the full list, send a message to **infobot@infomania.com** with just the word **help** in the Subject line):

Subject Line	What It Does
acronym *initials*	Searches for the acronym given by *initials* and returns its expansion. For example, **acronym kiss** returns "Keep it simple, stupid."
almanac	Returns a mixed bag of stuff relevant to the current day: facts, figures, sports schedules, the moon phase, and so on.

Subject Line	What It Does
area *string*	If *string* is a telephone area code, the **area** command returns the appropriate city or state. If *string* is a city or state, **area** returns the telephone area code.
findcd *string*	Searches a list of compact disks for *string*, where *string* is either a CD title or an artist. You'll also get an ad for The Record Place BBS.
geek	Returns "The Code of the Geeks," which classifies geekdom according to clothes, hair style, and the number of pocket protector pens a person lugs around.
jargon *word*	Looks up *word* in the Hacker's Jargon File and returns the definition. For example, if you get a message where someone mentions the phrase *bogon flux*, send **jargon bogon flux** to InfoMania and you'll get the following reply:

```
:bogon flux: /boh'gon fluhks/ n. A measure of a supposed field of
   (bogosity) emitted by a speaker, measured by a (bogometer);
   as a speaker starts to wander into increasing bogosity a listener
   might say "Warning, warning, bogon flux is rising". See
   (quantun bogodynamics).
```

	The words in parentheses (such as *bogosity*, in the example) represent other words in the Jargon File.
topten	Returns the latest Top Ten list from The Late Show with David Letterman.

If you'd like to get David Letterman's Top Ten list sent to you automatically every day, start up a new message, address it to **listserv@clark.net**, and then type **subscribe topten** *your user name* in the body (where *your name* is your full name).

weather *code*	Returns the weather for the state or city given by *code*. To learn more about this service, send the command **weather help**.

The WordSmith Wordserver

One of my favorite Net resources is the WordSmith "wordserver" run by Anu Garg at Case Western Reserve University. A *wordserver*? Yeah. It has all kinds of word-related features, such as a dictionary, a thesaurus, and word puzzles. A must for logophiles everywhere.

To try any of the features, address a dispatch to **wsmith@wordsmith.org** and type one of the following commands in the Subject line (leave the body blank):

Subject Line	What It Does
acronym *initials*	Returns the expansion of the acronym given by *initials*.
anagram *phrase*	Returns the anagram of *phrase*. (An anagram is a word or phrase formed by reordering the letters of another word or phrase. For example, you can reorder the word "Disraeli" to get "I lead, sir.")
define *word*	Returns the definition of **word**.
rhyme-n-reason today	Returns a word puzzle.
subscribe *your user name*	Subscribes you to the A.Word.A.Day mailing list, which sends out a word definition and a snappy quotation every day.
synonym *word*	Returns the synonyms for **word**.

Quotes from the Almanac Information Server

To get a random quote from a famous (or semi-famous) personage, send a message to **almanac@oes.orst.edu** with a blank Subject line and just **send quote** in the message body. A few seconds later, you'll receive a reply like this:

```
## Regarding your request:
   send quote


"With features like these, who needs bugs?"
              - Henry Spencer
```

Actually, the real purpose of the Almanac Information Server is to send out files, journals, newsletters, articles, and other info. To find out more, send a dispatch to **almanac@oes.orst.edu** with **send help** in the message body.

Movies by Mail

Cinemaniacs in the crowd will get a real charge out of the Movie Database Mail Server (MDMS). This service is your link to a HUGE pile of info on just about every movie ever made. You can search for, say, a particular movie and MDMS will send back everything it knows: the director, the cast, the writers, the cinematographer, you name it. You can also do searches for individual directors, actors, even costume designers for crying out loud, and the MDMS will send back a complete filmography for that person. It's a true film buff's paradise.

To figure out how the whole thing works, crank out a new message, address it to **movie@ibmpcug.co.uk**, leave the subject blank, and type **help** in the message body.

Postcards from the Net: More Mail Mania

To bring our e-surfing to a rousing finish, this section takes a quick look at a few more e-mail connections. There's no real theme here; just a random sampling of (hopefully) interesting and useful things you can use to exercise your e-mail franchise.

Democracy in Action: E-Mailing Your Congressman

Got a beef you want to bring to the attention of your congressperson? Want to get your voice heard above the rabble of lobbyists and special interest groups that normally have the ear of your House representative? Then send a note to **congress@hr.house.gov** (no subject and no body) and the Constituent Electronic Mail System will send you back a list of all the congressional e-mail addresses.

If the White House is the target of your tirade, you can e-mail the President (**president@whitehouse.gov**) or the Vice President (**vice.president@whitehouse.gov**).

If you're *really* into the democracy thing, the White House has all kinds of documents and files available for downloading. To find out how it works, send a missive to **publications@whitehouse.gov**, leave the Subject empty, and just put **help** in the message body.

An E-Mail Service for Stock Quotes

QuoteCom is an electronic stock quotes service that will send you the most recent quotes for specified stock or index. Although you normally have to pay to set up a "portfolio" with QuoteCom, the company graciously allows small-time investors to grab up to five quotes per day at no charge. To get the full QuoteCom scoop, send a message to **services@quote.com** with just **help** in the Subject line.

Electronic Journals and 'Zines

A 'zine, in case you don't know, is a small fanzine or magazine, usually put out by a single, dedicated soul. Most of these publications are, of course, available via e-mail, so there's as much reading material as you can stand.

Here are some Net resources you can use to find out more about electronic journals and magazines:

➤ If you're interested in journals related to the Internet, your best bet is to get a copy of "The Internet Press" by Kevin Savetz. It contains descriptions of Net-related journals and their e-mail addresses. To get "The Internet Press," send e-mail to **ipress-request@northcoast.com**, enter **archive** in the Subject line, and **send ipress** in the message body.

➤ For a complete list of the 200+ 'zines that are available, grab the "Zines on the Internet" article. It's available in five parts (with file names **part1** through **part5**) via anonymous FTP from **rtfm.mit.edu**. You'll find them in the following directory:

    /pub/usenet-by-group/news.answers/writing/zines

➤ To keep up with the latest goings-on in the 'zine world, be sure to keep at least one eye peeled on the Usenet newsgroup **alt.zines**. For electronic magazines with a slightly more mainstream bent, check out the group **rec.mag**.

This Just In: Strange (but True) News Stories

Randy Cassingham publishes a weekly list of wacky stories culled from the world's newswires. No, we're not talking baby-born-with-the-head-of-a-goat tabloid stuff. These are all true stories that range from the mildly humorous to the downright bizarre. (A disproportionate number of which come from Britain, for some reason.)

To get in on the fun, send a note to **listserv@netcom.com**, leave the Subject line blank, and type **subscribe this-just-in** in the message body. Before long, you'll receive a reply that gives you some introductory info and your first issue.

Finding That Special Netizen

If you're looking for love on the Net, you've probably found out that slogging through the **alt.personals.*** groups isn't the most fun way to find that certain someone. Most of the ads are either too geeky, too scary, or too far away. If you'd prefer the filter of a dating service, but want to preserve the convenience of the Net, there's a new e-mail service you can try. To get info, send a message to **iso@cobi.gsfc.nasa.gov** with just the word **help** in the message body. Good luck!

Speak Like a Geek: The Complete Archive

AAMOF   As a matter of fact.

access provider   See *service provider*.

address   Where you send your e-mail messages. Internet addresses (e.g., **paulmcf@hookup.net**) consist of a "who" part (the user name; e.g., **paulmcf**), followed by an @ sign, followed by the "where" part that includes the *domain name* (e.g., **hookup**) and either an *organization type* (e.g., **net**) or a *geographical domain*.

administrative address   See *subscription address*.

AFAIK   As far as I know.

anonymous FTP   An *FTP* session where you login using "anonymous" as your user ID, and you enter your e-mail address as the password. 99 and 44/100ths of all your FTP sessions will use anonymous FTP.

anonymous remailer   A service that strips out the e-mail address and other identifying elements of a message and then sends the message to its intended recipient.

archie   A service that searches a database of *FTP* sites for a file.

asbestos long johns   What Net types put on (metaphorically speaking, of course) before writing material they expect will get *flamed*. Other popular flame-retardant garments are **asbestos overcoats** and **asbestos underwear**.

attachment   A file that's linked to an e-mail message and hitches a ride to the recipient when the message is sent.

backbone   A high-*bandied* telephone trunk line used to connect networks together. In the U.S., the Internet backbone is called NSFNet (where NSF is the National Science Foundation). The Canadian Internet backbone is CA*net.

bandied   A measure of how much stuff can be stuffed through a transmission medium, such as a phone line or network cable. There's only so much bandied to go around at any given time, so you'll see lots of *Net* paranoia about "wasting bandied." Bandied is measured in *baud* or *bits per second*.

baud   This is a measure of how much bandied a transmission medium has. Its technical definition is "level transitions per second," but nobody knows what that means. Most people prefer to use *bits per second* to describe bandied because it's easier to understand.

Bcc   See *blind courtesy copy*.

bit   The fundamental unit of computer information (it's a portmanteau of the words "binary" and "digit"). It takes eight bits to describe a single character.

bit-spit   Any form of digital correspondence.

bits per second (bps)   Another, more common, measure of bandied. Since it takes eight bits to describe a single character, a transmission medium with a bandied of, say, 8 bps would send data at the pathetically slow rate of one character per second. Bandied is more normally measured in kilobits per second (Kbps—thousands of bits per second). So, for example, a 14.4 Kbps modem can handle 14,400 bits per second. In the high end, bandied is measured in megabits per second (Mbps—millions of bits per second).

blind courtesy copy (bcc)   A copy of an e-mail message that gets sent to a recipient without the knowledge of either the main recipient (the e-mail *address* in the To line) or the secondary recipients (the e-mail addresses in the *Cc* line).

bounce message   An error message returned by an e-mail system if a message can't be delivered (if, say, the address is wrong).

bps   See *bits per second*.

BRB   Be right back.

BTW   By the way.

burble   Similar to a *flame*, except that the burbler is considered to be dumb, incompetent, or ignorant. "Some clueless wonder sent me a burble yesterday. I'm going to flame that *luser* good."

byte-bonding   When computer users discuss things that nearby noncomputer users don't understand. See also *geeking out*.

Cc   Part of an e-mail message *header* that shows the secondary recipients of the message. "Cc" stands for courtesy copy. See also *blind courtesy copy*.

.com   An *organization type* that tells you an e-mail *address* is located in the *domain* of a commercial business.

cracker   A programmer who breaks into computer systems either to trash them or just for the sheer thrill of doing it (and, of course, to brag about it later). A *hacker* who has succumbed to the dark side of The Force.

CU   See you (as in, "See you later"). Good-bye for now.

cyberpunk   A person who is an outsider in the real world and an insider in the technological world. They often use technology to maintain and justify their existence "on the Edge." A *cyberspace* punk.

cyberspace   The place you "go to" when you reach out beyond your own computer (usually via modem) and interact with information or people on other computer systems.

cybersurfer   A person who *surfs cyberspace.*

cybrarian   A person who does full-time research or information retrieval on the *Internet.*

digest   A *mailing list* mailing that combines two or more messages into a single dispatch.

DIIK   Damned if I know.

distribution address   See *posting address.*

domain name   The part of your e-mail *address* to the right of the @ sign. The domain name identifies a particular site on the *Internet.*

.edu   An *organization type* that tells you an e-mail *address* is located in the *domain* of an educational institution.

emoticon   See *smiley.*

encode   To translate a nontext file into a text format suitable for sending through the Internet e-mail system.

encryption   To use sophisticated mathematical formulas combined with a particular key value to scramble an e-mail message. Only people in possession of the key value can unscramble the message. See also *Pretty Good Privacy.*

F2F   Face-to-face.

FAQ   The aficionado's short form for a *Frequently Asked Questions list.* The correct pronunciation is "fack."

FAWOMPT   Frequently argued waste of my precious time. Often used to describe *holy wars.*

FAWOMFT   Frequently argued waste of my foolish time (bowdlerized version; substitute your own favorite f-word).

flamage   The content of a flame. This word seems to be a portmanteau of the words "flame" and "verbiage."

flame   An emotionally charged *article* that contains vitriolic, rabid arguments combined with vicious, personal ridicule.

flame bait   Provocative material in an *article* that will likely elicit *flames* in response.

flame war   An ongoing dispute characterized by repeated reply *flames*, and people complaining about the flaming. Flame wars usually degenerate into boring, juvenile name-calling and mindless arguments of the "Did not!," "Did too!" variety. In the end, it's all just low signal, high noise (see *signal-to-noise ratio*), and a major waste of both *bandied* and time.

flamer   A person who *flames* regularly.

FOAF   Friend of a friend. Used to imply that information was obtained third-hand, or worse.

foo, bar, and **foobar**   These words are used as placeholders in descriptions and instructions. For example, someone might say "To change to the */foo* directory on a UNIX system, use the command *cd /foo.*" Here, *"foo"* acts as a generic placeholder for a directory name. If two placeholders are needed, then both "foo" and "bar" are used, like so: "To FTP two files named *foo* and *bar*, use the *mget* command: *mget foo bar.*" Foobar is often used as a single placeholder. It's derived from the military acronym FUBAR (bowdlerized version: Fouled Up Beyond All Recognition).

forward   To pass along a received message to another e-mail address.

FOTCL   Falling off the chair laughing.

Frequently Asked Questions list   A list of questions that, over the history of a newsgroup, have come up most often. If you're just starting a newsgroup, it's proper *netiquette* to read the group's *FAQ* list before posting any articles.

FTF   Face-to-face.

FTP   File Transfer Protocol. This is the usual method for retrieving a file from another Internet computer and copying it to your own. Note that it's okay to use FTP as both a noun (a method for transferring files) and a verb ("Hey bozo, before posting to this group you should FTP the FAQ file and give it a good look"). See also *anonymous FTP*.

FTPmail server   A computer that lets you do *FTP* via e-mail. You send in a bunch of FTP commands to the server and it (eventually) sends back the results (usually a directory listing or a file).

FYA   For your amusement.

FYI For your information.

geek—Someone who knows a lot about computers and very little about anything else. See also *nerd*.

geeking out When *geeks* who are *byte-bonding* start playing with a computer during a non-computer-related social event.

geographical domain Part of an e-mail *address* that specifies the country where the address resides. Examples include **au** (Australia), **ca** (Canada), and **uk** (the United Kingdom).

going postal *Net* euphemism for being totally stressed out and on the verge of losing it entirely.

Gopher A system that displays *Internet* documents and services as menu options. You just select a menu choice and the Gopher will either display a document or transfer you to a different gopher system. Gophers get their name from the mascot of the University of Minnesota, where the first Gopher was born.

GopherMail server A computer that sends Gopher menus and files through the e-mail system.

.gov An *organization type* that tells you an e-mail *address* is located in the *domain* of the government.

hacker Someone who enjoys exploring the nuts and bolts of computer systems (both from the hardware side and, more often, from the software side), stretching these systems to their limits and beyond, and programming for the sheer pleasure of it. Not to be confused with *cracker*.

HHOK Ha ha only kidding.

HHOJ Ha ha only joking.

HHOS Ha ha only serious. (Used with ironic jokes and satire that contain some truth.)

holy war A never-ending, unchanging (and *very* boring for the rest of us) argument where the opinions of combatants on both sides of the issue never budge an inch. Common holy war topics include religion, abortion, and which operating system is the best.

IAE In any event.

IANAL I am not a lawyer.

IMCO In my considered opinion.

IMHO In my humble opinion. (Although, in practice, opinions prefaced by IMHO are rarely humble. See *IMNSHO*.)

IMO   In my opinion.

IMNSHO   In my not so humble opinion. (This more accurately reflects most of the opinions one sees on the Internet.)

Internaut   An *Internet* traveler; a *cyberspace surfer*.

Internet   A world-wide collection of interconnected *networks*. A breeding ground for *geeks*, *nerds*, *hackers*, and *crackers*.

IOW   In other words.

IWBNI   It would be nice if.

IYFEG   Insert your favorite ethnic group. Used in off-color and offensive jokes and stories to avoid insulting any particular ethnic group, race, religion, or sex.

jargonaut   A person who deliberately creates and disseminates *Internet* jargon; someone interested in *Net* jargon.

Kbps   Kilobits per second (thousands of *bits per second*).

KIS   The Knowbot Information Service. This is a *white pages directory* that uses a *knowbot* to seek out information about Net people by querying various e-mail databases.

KISS   Keep it simple, stupid.

knowbot   An independent, automated program that seeks out information on other computer systems and sends back reports on its progress. (The name is a portmanteau of the phrase *knowledge robot*.)

list address   See *posting address*.

list server   A program that automates *mailing list* administrivia, such as subscription requests. The two most common list servers are Listserv and Majordomo.

listserv   A common synonym for a *mailing list*.

LOL   Laughing out loud.

luser   A portmanteau of "loser" and "user." Someone who doesn't have the faintest idea what they're doing and, more importantly, refuses to do anything about it.

mail bombing   To send numerous (and, usually, long) e-mail messages to a person's e-mail address (this is also called **e-mail terrorism**).

mail server   The computer at your *service provider* that directs e-mail messages to and from your computer. Also, a computer that sends files to your e-mail address.

mailbox   The file where your incoming messages are stored. Some e-mail software lets you divide your mailbox into different "folders" (such as one for business mail, one for personal mail, and so on).

mailing list   A system that sends out regular e-mail messages related to a specific topic. To get the messages, you need to *subscribe* to the list by sending an e-mail message to the list's *subscription address*.

Mbps   Megabits per second (millions of *bits per second*).

MEGO   My eyes glaze over.

.mil   An *organization type* that tells you an e-mail *address* is located in a military *domain*.

moderated mailing list   A *mailing list* where all messages are filtered through the critical eye of a *moderator*. Moderated mailing lists typically have a high *signal-to-noise ratio*.

moderator   Overworked, underpaid (read: volunteer), *mailing list* administrator who reads all submissions to a particular list and selects only the best (or most relevant) for distribution.

MORF   Male or female?

MOTAS   Member of the appropriate sex.

MOTOS   Member of the opposite sex.

MOTSS   Member of the same sex.

mouse potato   The computer equivalent of a couch potato.

multimediocrities—CD-ROM discs that are jam-packed with second-rate pictures, sounds, and programs.

nerd—A *geek* totally lacking in personal hygiene and social skills.

.net   An *organization type* that tells you an e-mail *address* is located in the *domain* of a networking company.

Net   The hip short form for the *Internet*.

net.   A prefix used by *Internet* types who spend *way* too much time online. These people like to add "net." in front of just about anything even remotely connected to the Internet. For example, a newcomer to the Net becomes a *net.newcomer*; an online session becomes a *net.session*. That kind of thing. However, there are a few "net." constructions that have achieved mainstream status: net.police (self-appointed *netiquette* watchdogs who flame offenders), net.gods and net.deities (Internet old-timers who've achieved celebrity status), and net.characters (irritating Usenetters who post articles designed only to attract attention to themselves).

netiquette   An informal set of rules and guidelines designed to smooth e-mail interactions. Netiquette breaches often result in the offender being *flamed*.

network   A collection of two or more computers (usually dozens or hundreds) connected via specialized cables so they can share resources such as files and printers. The *Internet* is, in its most prosaic guise, a worldwide collection of networks.

newbie   A person who is (or acts like he is) new to the *Internet*. Since this term is almost always used insultingly, most *Net* neophytes try to behave as non-newbie-like as possible. The best way to avoid this label is to bone up on *netiquette*.

NRN   No response necessary.

nymrod   A person who insists on converting every multiword computer term into an acronym.

OIC   Oh, I see.

organization type   Part of an e-mail *address* that specifies the *domain's* type of business. For example, **com** is a commercial business, **edu** is an educational institution, and **net** is a networking organization.

OS   Operating system.

OTOH   On the other hand.

OTT   Over the top.

PGP   See *Pretty Good Privacy*.

PMJI   Pardon my jumping in.

Point-to-Point Protocol   A method of *Internet* access that allows your computer to talk sensibly with your *service provider's* system via modem. See also *Serial Line INternet Protocol*.

POP   See *Post Office Protocol*.

PONA   Person of no account. Used disparagingly to describe someone who isn't part of the *Internet* set (i.e., someone who doesn't have an Internet account).

Post Office Protocol   A set of standards that allows mail servers (the computers that handle e-mail at your access provider) to act as a sort of post office. POP lets the server store your messages until such time as you log in and retrieve them.

posting address   The e-mail *address* you use to *post* messages to a *mailing list*.

postmaster   The overworked, underpaid person in an e-mail system who has the responsibility of making sure the system runs smoothly, and troubleshooting problems when it doesn't.

PPP   See *Point-to-Point Protocol*.

Pretty Good Privacy   An *encryption* program that uses a combination of public keys and private keys to ensure that a message can only be read by the recipient, and to authenticate the sender of the message.

rave   A particularly irritating type of *flame* in which the writer rambles on *ad nauseum*, even after a *flame war* has ended. Also used to describe messages that evangelize or proselytize.

regional backbone   A *backbone* that connects *networks* within a relatively small geographic area. In the U.S., regional backbones cover individual states or, sometimes, several adjoining states.

ROTF   Rolling on the floor.

ROTFL   Rolling on the floor laughing.

ROTFLOL   Rolling on the floor laughing out loud.

RSN   Real soon now (read: never).

RTFF   Read the fugacious *FAQ*. (Insert your own f-word.) See also *RTFM*.

RTFM   Read the fabulous manual. (Another bowdlerized version; as usual, insert your own f-word.) This is an admonition to users (usually *newbies*) that they should try to answer a question themselves before asking a Net veteran. This may seem harsh, but self-reliance is a fundamental characteristic of *Internet* life. Most Net types have figured out things for themselves, and they expect everyone else to do the same. This means reading hardware and software manuals, and checking out newsgroup *FAQ* lists. (By the way, this is what the "rtfm" means in **rtfm.mit.edu**: the *FTP* archive of Usenet FAQs.)

Serial Line Internet Protocol   A method of *Internet* access that enables your computer to dial up a *service provider* and exchange info reliably. See also *Point-to-Point Protocol*.

server   A computer that sends out stuff. Check out *FTPmail server* or *GopherMail server* for examples.

service provider   A business that sells Internet connections to individuals and small companies. See also *access provider*.

sig   Short for *signature*.

signal-to-noise ratio   This electronics term is used ironically to compare the amount of good, useful info ("signal") in a *mailing list* or newsgroup, with the amount of bad, useless dreck ("noise"). The best lists have a high signal-to-noise ratio, while lists that have lots of *flame wars* and *spamming* rate low on the signal-to-noise ratio totem pole.

signature   Text added to the bottom of a message to give the reader more information about yourself. Signatures longer than four or five lines are considered wasteful.

Simple Mail Transport Protocol   The Internet standard that governs how electronic mail messages are sent from site to site.

SLIP   See *Serial Line Internet Protocol*.

smiley   A combination of symbols designed to indicate the true intent or emotional state of the author. Smileys are fine in moderation, but overusing them not only indicates that your writing isn't as clear as it could be, but it also brands you as a *newbie*.

SMTP   See *Simple Mail Transport Protocol*.

snail mail   The somewhat derisive term that e-mail fans use to describe regular paper mail sent through the post office.

SO   Significant other.

spam   Irrelevant prattle that has nothing whatsoever to do with the current topic under discussion. Aimless drivel noticeably lacking in any kind of point or cohesion.

subscribe   To get on the distribution list for a *mailing list*. See also *subscription address* and *unsubscribe*.

subscription address   The e-mail *address* you use for *subscribing* and *unsubscribing* to a *mailing list*. Whatever you do, don't send subscription requests to the list's *posting address*.

surf   To travel through *cyberspace*.

telnet   A program that lets you log in to another computer on the *Internet* and use its resources as though they existed on your machine. The most common use for Telnet is to use software (such as an e-mail program) on another computer.

TFS   Thanks for sharing.

TIA   Thanks in advance.

TIC   Tongue in cheek.

TPTB   The powers that be.

TTFN   Ta-ta for now.

TTYL   Talk to you later.

unsubscribe   To remove your name from a *mailing list's* distribution list.

Usenet   A system that distributes a collection of newsgroups throughout the *Internet*.

Web   See *World Wide Web*.

white pages directory An Internet service that lets you search a database for a person's name or e-mail address. The most common white pages directories are *Whois, Knowbot,* and *Gopher* phone books.

Whois A *white pages directory* that lets you search for names in databases that reside in different organizations.

World Wide Web A system of documents containing text, graphics, and other multimedia goodies. Each Web document serves two purposes: it contains information that is useful in and of itself, and it contains specially marked words or phrases that serve as "links" to other Web documents. If you select the link, the Web loads the other document automatically.

WWW See *World Wide Web.*

YABA Yet another bloody acronym.

YMMV Your mileage may vary. This acronym means the advice, info, or instructions just given may not work for you exactly as described.

YOYOW You own your own words. This refers to the copyright you have over your private e-mail compositions.

Index

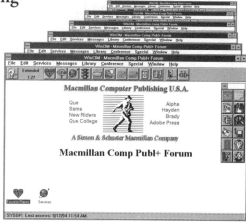

PLUG YOURSELF INTO...

THE MACMILLAN INFORMATION SUPERLIBRARY™

Free information and vast computer resources from the world's leading computer book publisher—online!

FIND THE BOOKS THAT ARE RIGHT FOR YOU!

A complete online catalog, plus sample chapters and tables of contents give you an in-depth look at *all* of our books, including hard-to-find titles. It's the best way to find the books you need!

- **STAY INFORMED** with the latest computer industry news through our online newsletter, press releases, and customized Information SuperLibrary Reports.

- **GET FAST ANSWERS** to your questions about MCP books and software.

- **VISIT** our online bookstore for the latest information and editions!

- **COMMUNICATE** with our expert authors through e-mail and conferences.

- **DOWNLOAD SOFTWARE** from the immense MCP library:
    - Source code and files from MCP books
    - The best shareware, freeware, and demos

- **DISCOVER HOT SPOTS** on other parts of the Internet.

- **WIN BOOKS** in ongoing contests and giveaways!

TO PLUG INTO MCP: ➤   **WORLD WIDE WEB: http://www.mcp.com**

GOPHER: gopher.mcp.com

FTP: ftp.mcp.com